CARIBBEAN CONSTITUTIONAL REFORM
Rethinking the West Indian Polity

To Winston Griffith
with sincere thanks

Randy McIntosh

June 13, 2003

Medgar Evers College
Brooklyn, New York.

CARIBBEAN CONSTITUTIONAL REFORM

Rethinking the West Indian Polity

SIMEON C.R. McINTOSH

The Caribbean Law
PUBLISHING COMPANY LTD

Kingston

First published in Jamaica 2002 by
The Caribbean Law Publishing Company
11 Cunningham Avenue
Box 686, Kingston 6

ISBN 976-8167-27-0 hardback
ISBN 976-8167-28-9 paperback
A catalogue of this book is available from the National Library of Jamaica.

Cover and Book Design ProDesign Limited
Printed in the United States of America

For my brother

James McCauley McIntosh

'... a verray, parfait gentil knyght'

Contents

Preface

This is a work in constitutional theory. It is therefore not an attempt at a historical or descriptive account of West Indian Independence Constitutions, the existing constitutions of the Commonwealth Caribbean. However, as a way of giving a proper introduction to the work, it was absolutely essential that a brief historical narrative of the constitutional development of the West Indies, leading up to political independence, be constructed. But given that I am not a professional historian and therefore not having the expertise nor the opportunity to attempt a study of primary sources, I have had to rely heavily on the work of historians and others in constructing an historical narrative of the constitutional development of the Commonwealth Caribbean. For this, I am truly grateful, and I hope I have shown my gratitude and indebtedness in the extensive footnoting of their work.

In the main body of the work, particularly in the first chapter, some of the central issues in constitutional reform are explored; issues that, in the main, are matters of constitutional fundamentals for the Commonwealth Caribbean: for example, the question of the 'patriation' of the *West Indian Independence Constitution* and of our continuing relationship with the British Sovereign. In addition, in the final chapter, the issue of the establishment of a regional supreme court and the abolition of appeals to the British Privy Council is addressed. These issues are, in my opinion, the most critical and defining issues in constitutional reform, for they go to the heart of a postcolonial Commonwealth Caribbean political identity. For given the juridical origin of West Indian Independence Constitutions as enactments of the British Imperial

Parliament and our supposed 'retention' of the monarchy and the Privy Council, it can hardly be said that we are substantially removed from the colonial moment.

These issues are intimately linked, for the story of the origin of the *West Indian Independence Constitution* underscores the fact that our constitutions were not the products of our own deliberate collective efforts; and the supposition that we have retained the Crown, plus the absence of a formal declaration of republic in constitutions which are essentially republican, rather indulges the assumption that we are constitutional monarchies and that we remain subjects of the Crown. Thus we continue to pledge allegiance to the British Sovereign, Queen Elizabeth II, her heirs and successors. Patriation should therefore remove, once and for all, this stigma of imperial enactedness from our constitutions, in addition to the Crown itself, which is the foundation and ultimate instance of imperial rule. In a word, then, patriation becomes the defining act whereby we affect to make our constitutions our own, and thereby begin the completion of an unfinished nationalist project of constructing an authentic postcolonial Commonwealth Caribbean identity.

My thesis, then, is that constitutional reform must, above all else, result in a redefining of postcolonial Commonwealth Caribbean identity. In order to achieve this, constitutional reform must necessarily engage the Commonwealth Caribbean citizenry in a communal or national conversation on the true nature of our constitutions and the form of politics that they inform. In a word, constitutional reform must be a collective rethinking of the *West Indian polity*.

But constitutional reform must also take account of the central role that constitutional adjudication might play, through the agency of textual exegesis, in the construction of a postcolonial Commonwealth Caribbean identity. For the authoritative reading or interpretation of a constitutional text is the discursive practice whereby meaning is given to the text that constitutes a people's political identity. On this view, then, the reserve of interpretive authority over Commonwealth Caribbean Constitutions in the British Privy Council not only constitutes a negation of our sovereignty, it leaves to a foreign institution a constituent role in defining Commonwealth Caribbean political identity. To my view, therefore, constitutional reform would be incomplete if the issue of establishing a Caribbean Court of final appeal and of abolishing appeals to the Privy Council were to remain unresolved. For this question of abolishing appeals to the Privy Council and of establishing a regional supreme court (to be titled the Caribbean Court of Justice) is intimately linked to the issue of 'patriating the constitution' and of redefining our relationship with the British Sovereign. They are all together conjoined at the heart of the nationalist project of completing our political independence and constructing an authentic post-independence identity.

This work is the result of a rather extensive development and rewriting of two principal essays previously published in The Caribbean Law Review: *Constitutional Reform and the Quest for a West Indian Hermeneutics* (1997); and *West Indian Constitutional Discourse: A Poetics of Reconstruction* (1993). I wish to express my gratitude to the Editorial Board of the Caribbean Law Review for permission to republish portions of these essays.

The writing of this book has been inspired by the intellectual and moral support of two of our region's best and our brightest: Professor the Hon. Rex Nettleford, Vice-Chancellor of the University of the West Indies, and the dean of West Indian letters, Mr. George Lamming. I am eternally grateful to them. And then there is my friend and colleague Richard Kay, the George and Helen England Professor of Law at the University of Connecticut School of Law, who has been involved in my work ever since our first meeting at a legal and political philosophy seminar back in the summer of 1978. This present work has not escaped his scrutiny.

Among my colleagues at the University of the West Indies I say many thanks to Lloyd Best, Woodville Marshall, George Belle, Rupert Lewis, Brian Meekes, Winston Anderson, and Kim Small. On a point of personal privilege, however, I reserve a special mention of the assistance I have received from my colleague Stephen Vasciannie. Through his insightful critique, Stephen has forced me beyond my limits and has helped a rather dense colleague understand the issues more deeply and more clearly. I also wish to thank Dr. Richard Cheltenham, QC for sharing and discussing his very important work on the Barbados Constitution with me; Nicole Sylvester for helping me rethink certain portions of the last chapter on the Caribbean Court of Justice; Ralph Jemmott for reading the introductory chapter; and Amanda Byer for the tremendous assistance she rendered in the preparation of the bibliography and in reading and correcting the final proofs.

Next, I wish to thank the Law Library staff for their assistance during the research and writing of this book. I also wish to thank Mr. Carlisle Best, Reference Librarian at the University Library at Cave Hill, for performing some remarkable searches for me. I consider his assistance beyond the call of duty. Thanks are also due to Valda Maynard and Marcia Bradshaw for their assistance in typing earlier drafts of this book, and to Pat Worrell for her excellent work in preparing the final draft which was submitted to the publishers.

Finally, I wish to express my deep appreciation to Roy McCree, Research Fellow, Sir Arthur Lewis Institute for Social and Economic Studies, St. Augustine, Trinidad, for his outstanding work in editing the entire manuscript. I also wish to express my sincere gratitude to Professor Wayne Hunte, Deputy Principal and Coordinator of Graduate Studies and Research at Cave Hill, for the very generous financial support and his overall encouragement.

Introduction

Making Our Constitutions Our Own

On the occasion of the 350th anniversary of the Barbados Parliament, the then Governor-General, the late Sir Hugh Springer, remarked that 'Our Constitution came from Britain but a dozen generations of Barbadians have made it their own.'[1] These words, in fact, tell the story of the historical relationship of the entire Commonwealth Caribbean with Britain, the imperial power, and more specifically, of the process of constitutional founding and of the method of acquiring our Independence Constitutions and the substance of their provisions. So although Sir Hugh Springer's words may hardly do justice to the profundity of the historian's enterprise of crafting the social memory of our *people*, they are nonetheless the most compelling part – the 'core' – of any possible narrative construction of our political identity. As Professor Norma Thompson remarks: 'The stories that succeed most compellingly in accounting for the "facts" of a people's past become the core of that people's political community.'[2]

West Indian Independence Constitutions, which are, for all intents and purposes, written versions of the constitutional arrangements that evolved in the United Kingdom over many centuries, have had their formal juridical origins in statutes of the British Imperial Parliament, and trace their historical beginnings back to July 1627, when the King of England granted letters patent to

James, first Earl of Carlisle, 'over the whole of the Caribee Islands, from 10° to 20° north latitude; a wide range which made express mention of Grenada, St. Vincent, St. Lucia, Barbados, Dominica, Guadeloupe, Montserrat, Antigua, Nevis, and St. Christopher, as well as smaller islands.'[3] Thus was born, according to Professor Lloyd Best, 'the political system of the West Indies', which was marked by a series of developmental changes through the centuries to the granting of political independence from the 1960s to the 1980s.[4] These developmental changes can be said to have begun in earnest with the emancipation of the slaves in the West Indian colonies in 1834; an event which Professor Rex Nettleford describes as 'the greatest watershed event in the history of this part of the Caribbean which millions have come to call "home."'[5] By this he means to say that the Abolition of Slavery Law on August 1, 1834, by which Caribbean society would have been emancipated from the 'debilitating transgressions of slavery', had 'made possible the emergence of an entire set of rules governing conditions of work and industrial relations, and safeguarding future society against the viler consequences of the wanton exploitation of labour which had persisted for two centuries before.'[6] We are then, the *creatures* of *that* Law; not merely in some abstract sense of being the subjects of law's empire, but rather in some more organic sense of relatedness, in that the abolition of slavery would have constituted the critical starting point, or at least set the stage, for the development of a new trend in colonial government in the West India colonies, which, over a century later, culminated in political dependence and the full restoration of civil status to all the inhabitants of this Archipelago. For, with the abolition of slavery, and the granting of civil status to those persons who lacked it prior to emancipation, the question of how these colonies were henceforth to be governed became a central concern of British colonial policy. Thus, for Professor Nettleford, the Emancipation Statute must be accorded canonic status as the foundation document of modern Commonwealth Caribbean constitutionalism.

The historian D.J. Murray reminds us that in the late eighteenth and early nineteenth centuries, it was the current opinion that the West India colonies formed the heart of the British Empire. Among the colonies, they were the most prized. 'Their commercial worth and the contribution they made to the maintenance of British power is said to have led George III to regard the West India colonies as a jewel in his Crown.'[7] In the opinion of many who counted in British politics, the West India colonies constituted the hub of Britain's trading system. Clearly, Britain's fortunes were tied to the success of its West India colonies.[8]

In the early nineteenth century, however, though these colonies were still regarded of major importance in Europe, they were less and less regarded as an invaluable part of Britain's trading system. The Golden Age of the West Indies was fast coming to an end.[9] They remained important largely because they continued to be slave colonies. This, in consequence, made them the most time-consuming and troublesome part of the Empire with which the British Government and Parliament had to deal in the first third of the nineteenth century.[10]

By that time, the institutions and procedures of colonial government would already have been established in these West India colonies, which had been acquired by Great Britain between the early part of the seventeenth century and the beginning of the nineteenth, by settlement, conquest and exchange. The form of colonial government found in the old West India colonies conformed broadly to the same pattern: it was the 'old representative system' under which the power of initiative in colonial government, in everything that related to internal affairs, was left mainly with the colonists. This afforded the colonists the opportunity to fashion their government as they saw fit, and in their interest. This policy, by and large, dictated the outline and form of government in colonies conquered from other European powers during the Revolutionary and Napoleonic Wars.[11] Trinidad and Barbados would have been the outstanding exceptions.

But, alas, this was government of the slave society in the West Indies by white colonists. From the standpoint of the slaves, given the horrid conditions under which they were forced to exist, such a system of government was hardly beneficent or liberal. Indeed, it would have been the evil practices of slavery in the West India colonies that had fueled the campaign for the amelioration of conditions of the slaves and, ultimately, for their full emancipation and for reform of colonial administration. Due to the pressure of the Anti-Slavery movement, and led by dissatisfaction arising from the ineffectiveness of the government in the colonies, Britain 'explicitly and intentionally remodelled first that in the conquered colonies, introducing Crown Colony government, and then began a reconstruction of that in the old West India Colonies.'[12]

With the emancipation of the slaves, however, the main stimulus for action was removed. British politics was no longer the major stimulus for action in the colonies. Crown Colony government remained in the conquered colonies but, for all intents and purposes, the institutions of colonial government in the West India colonies, developed in the seventeenth and eighteenth centuries, were claimed to be modelled on that of England, such that the Jamaican planter Bryan Edwards would describe the government existing in these islands 'as nearly conforming to that of the Mother Country'. Each colonial constitution had its own Governor, its Legislative Council and Legislative Assembly, just as England had its King, Lords and Commons.[13] The prevailing assumption would have been that, for the government of the colonies, English laws and institutions were the best in the world.[14] Murray writes that 'in Jamaica and the Lesser Antilles – Barbados, the Leewards Group, Grenada, St. Vincent and

Dominica – a Governor and appointed Council performed legislative, executive and judicial duties; as a third division of the legislature there was an elected Assembly; while there were Courts in theory modelled on those of Westminster, for the execution of justice.'[15] He notes that the greatest development in the machinery of government would have taken place in Jamaica but in all these islands development was comparable, and the more extensive powers of government in Jamaica matched the greater demands placed on government in the largest of the colonies.[16] In all the colonies, then, the machinery of government which existed at the end of the eighteenth century enabled the colonists to control to a considerable extent their own government. Colonists in the old West India colonies largely ruled themselves.[17]

But with the emancipation of the slaves, Colonial Office opinion was divided as to the most suitable form of government for the colonies. For some, a fundamental alteration in the system of government was inevitable since, as a practical matter, representative government was unsuitable for colonies where slaves had recently been freed.[18] It was thought that the form of government developed in the conquered colonies was more suitable for primarily black colonies; indeed, it was the development of this form of government which allowed for a separation in the Empire between white and black colonies and for the progress of the former to responsible government and dominion status.[19] The alternative view, however, is that it was the government in the Crown Colonies, and not that in the old colonies, which was called into question with the emancipation of the slaves. For, notwithstanding that there would have remained a number of problems regarding the form and working of the representative system in the old colonies, it was felt that, in the final analysis, the ultimate goal should have been to secure representative institutions for all West India colonies, along with an independent Judicature.[20]

But progress towards this goal was by no means swift. In fact, the influence of Henry Taylor's views on Colonial Office policy resulted in constitutional retrogression rather than progress, in some instances.[21] Taylor had advanced the view that in a society where property and knowledge were not widely diffused and the mass of society not yet fit to exercise the vote, elected assemblies would inevitably lead to government by an irresponsible oligarchy of either black or white. On the strength of such arguments, representative government was not extended to Trinidad or British Guiana. As H.A. Will writes, 'the final triumph of Taylor's views was reflected in the constitutional retrogression from representative to crown colony government which took place in Jamaica and other British West Indian Colonies during the 1860s and 1870s.'[22]

By the late nineteenth century, however, agitation for constitutional reform within the West Indian colonies would have been influenced to an important degree by the course of events and currents of thought in Britain and elsewhere in the Empire.[23] Will writes that 'Jamaicans advocating change drew encouragement from the climate of opinion in England, and from constitutional reform and unrest elsewhere in the Empire.'[24] But constitutional and political development in the Commonwealth Caribbean was to take place within a constitutional framework established or adopted by the British government and which could only be changed by its policy decisions.[25] In the event, the framework for constitutional development that was to emerge was that of a transition to semi-representative and representative government, and eventually semi-responsible and responsible government.[26]

Colin Hughes writes that constitutional reform in the British colonies has been based on the familiar British notion that 'the only form of self-government worthy of the name [was] government through ministers responsible to an elected legislature'.[27] He further notes that this goal was responsible government and that

The major territories of the British Caribbean [had] reached that penultimate stage of development, the crucial one where for the first time power and responsibility are wedded in the persons of Ministers who have power over policy and administration, and are responsible to legislatures elected on the basis of universal adult suffrage, although certain subjects of state may be reserved for official Ministers. The struggle to reach this level lasted more than two decades, from the Wood Report of 1922 which restored elected representation to those territories of the eastern Caribbean which had lost it during the 19th century, to the Jamaica Constitution of 1944, under which semi-responsible government was first achieved.[28]

It is notorious that the social and economic conditions of the colonies at this time were tragic, and local negro leaders blamed imperialism in general and Crown Colony government in particular for their political frustration and their economic and social distress.[29] Disturbances and riots swept the West Indies, including Barbados, in 1935-38. Coupled with this, popular mass movements led by such figures as Bustamante of Jamaica or Uriah Butler of Trinidad would have heightened the pressure for constitutional reform. This was given due notice by the Moyne Commission of 1938, which reported that

> rightly or wrongly, a substantial body of public opinion in the West Indies is convinced that far-reaching measures of social reconstruction depend, both for their initiation and their effective administration, upon greater participation of the people in the business of government.[30]

The Report rejected out of hand the notion of complete self-government for the colonies, and rather advised that in order to meet the just aspirations of the people, they should have the right to a greater share in government and that the colonial Legislative Councils should be made truly representative. It approved the inclusion of elected members in the Executive Councils, and recommended that qualifications of both electors and representatives should be reduced and universal suffrage should become the recognized goal of policy. But above all, it was the considered opinion of the Commission that the future well-being of the West Indies lay in federation.[31] In this regard, it is instructive to note that a Labour Congress of the West Indies and British Guiana had recommended to the Moyne Commission that there be a federation, a wholly elected legislature based on adult suffrage, a Governor who would have the powers comparable to a constitutional monarch, nationalization of the sugar industry, state ownership of public utilities, and economic and social reforms compatible with the achievement of a welfare state.[32]

The outbreak of the Second World War is said to have marked a turning point in the history of all British colonial dependencies. 'Until then the advance of non-self-governing territories of the British Commonwealth to a status resembling that of the self-governing dominions had never been seriously considered as practical politics except in two instances. Only in India and Ceylon did constitutional reform, by the inter-war period, come to be recognized as part of a process of transition to independent status, thus involving a radical change in the structure of the Commonwealth.'[33] But in the British West Indies, as late as 1939, a special commission (the Moyne Commission) appointed to investigate disturbances throughout the islands in fact reaffirmed the traditional assumptions underlying British conceptions of permanent metropolitan responsibility for the control of the dependent part of the Commonwealth.[34] 'The principles of Crown Colony government were still unequivocally upheld.[35] The desideratum, in the judgment of the Commission, was not the transformation of representative into responsible government or, in other words, an advance from colonial to dominion status.'[36] In essence, the Commission held that 'the formulation and execution of policy should remain an exclusive imperial responsibility even if combined with enlarged opportunities for more direct and comprehensive criticism of the measures of which the imperial government is to remain the arbiter.'[37]

The outbreak of the Second World War, however, occasioned a fundamental change in British colonial policy. Certainly, by that time, the West Indian colonies had ceased to be of any economic benefit to Britain. In addition, colonialism was now seen to be inconsistent with the principles Britain was to defend in the War, and decolonisation was thus emerging as the 'new' international law imperative. Thus, in the political sphere, British policy was declared to be the advancement of colonial dependencies to self-government within the British Commonwealth. Henceforward, constitutional reform reflected a process of transition from colonial subordination to colonial autonomy. As E.W. Evans puts it,

> In the Caribbean area Jamaica was selected for the first experiment in a transitional constitution under the new dispensation. In 1944 Jamaica was provided with a new constitution in which, apart from changes in the character of the legislature as a representative body, responsibility for the formulation of public policy became largely a colonial responsibility for the first time. It was laid down that the policy-making body, to be known as the Executive Committee, should consist of ten members of whom as many as five were to be elected by, and thus by implication responsible to, the colonial legislature; of the remainder three were to be officials holding office under the Crown and two unofficial members nomi-

nated by the Governor from amongst the members of the legislature.[38]

This arrangement can be described as representing an embryonic ministerial system capable of expansion by stages.[39] 'In the new constitution the legislature was remodelled. The lower house became an entirely elected body on the basis of universal adult suffrage, with an upper house consisting of three *ex officio,* not more than two official and not less than ten unofficial members appointed by the Crown ... The upper house had no final power of veto, but only delaying powers.'[40]

In the structure of the legislature, no less than in its ministerial system in embryo, the Jamaica Constitution of 1944 represented a substantial instalment of responsible government.[41] Further changes were to follow in 1953

> when the Executive Committee was reconstituted so as to consist of eight ministers from among the members of the lower house of the legislature; *viz.*: a Chief Minister appointed by the Governor with the approval of the lower house and seven other ministers appointed on the recommendation of the Chief Minister, ... and entrusted with the management of all public departments except for the reservation of official authority of responsibility for defence, external affairs, and the public service.[42]

Similar constitutional changes on the model of the Jamaica Constitution of 1944 subsequently followed in British Guiana, Trinidad and Tobago, Barbados, and in the Windward and Leeward Islands. It bears emphasis, however, that current opinion in the late 1940s and 1950s held that political independence for the British West Indian colonies was only feasible through federation. It was therefore with the breakup of the 1958

Federation in 1962 that the idea of self-government for the islands on an individual basis became a genuine possibility.

Lawful Devolution
Jamaica

The two decades following the Second World War witnessed the progressive liquidation of the European colonial empires - in Asia, Africa, and the Caribbean - in some cases voluntarily, and with perhaps a certain sense of relief of being able to shed a military or economic burden, and in other cases reluctantly and most tardily. The process of decolonisation usually involved, in stages, the progressive devolution of qualified home rule, then self-government, and finally independence.[43] This, in essence, describes the process of 'lawful devolution of sovereignty' by which Britain granted independence to countries like India, Pakistan and Ceylon between 1947 to 1948, and ultimately to its colonies in the West Indies, starting with Jamaica and Trinidad and Tobago in 1962, and ending with St. Kitts and Nevis in 1983. This process, in its totality, often involved the constitutional transition of a colony through stages of semi-representative and representative government, and eventually semi-responsible government, culminating in full independence with the formal enactment of the independence constitution by Her Britannic Majesty in Council.

This process, it bears repeating, was established or adopted by Britain for treating with its colonies. Therefore, it is notorious, as Edward McWhinney observes, that

> the new post-colonial constitutions were invariably highly derivative, and tended to borrow very heavily from the constitutional institutions and developed practices of the

"parent" European colonial power involved. Since the approach to self-government and independence on the part of the colonial territory concerned was usually conditioned upon the development, within that territory, of a democratic system of government as evidence of its capacity finally to govern itself, free from the benevolent paternalism of the erstwhile colonial power, it is perhaps not surprising that the emerging new, post-colonial, indigenous local political élite should find it good practical politics to copy the constitutional models of the colonial power, and that the influence of the old colonial office legal draftsmen should often be pervasive.[44]

He further states that

In instances of decolonization, where a parent, imperial government finally resolves to devolve political-legal authority to an indigenous, local, colonial community, the imperial government – normally in control of the constitutional rules of the game from the beginning – may prefer an orderly, 'arranged' state succession from its own government to a new local government created, ad hoc, for the purpose. The transfer of constitutional power thus becomes an elitist, oligarchic exercise, with the constitutional charter of the newly created state often being one prepared in advance by the imperial government's own colonial office functionaries.[45]

McWhinney notes that 'when there has been adequate time, the British Empire practice was, as far as possible, to try to co-ordinate the imperial initiative in favour of constitutional devolution with some form of local constituent activity in the colonial territory concerned and on the part of the local people on some more or less genuinely representative basis.'[46] This was indeed the case in respect of that older and narrower European segment of the empire – Canada, Australia, and even the Union of South Africa – and the process was also successfully applied in the case of decolonisation and devolution of constitutional self-government and independence on the Indian subcontinent, where a local representative constituent assembly functioned from the beginning to work out the general principles as well as the detailed institutions of the new constitutional system or systems.[47]

This measured process of constitutional devolution was not, however, affordable to the rest of the empire – to Africa and to the Caribbean. By the late 1950s, decolonisation had become a 'new' international law imperative which the United Nations and the emerging Third World sought to impose on often unwilling or uncooperative parent imperial states or governments.[48] In the circumstances, the actual transfer of power was often ungracious and hurried, 'with the consequence that the post-independence constitutional systems ... were often improvised or makeshift arrangements, with a predominantly European "colonial office" personality reflected in [the] constitutional institutions ...'[49] In other words, the post-decolonisation 'succession states' of the late 1950s, 1960s and 1970s did not really have the time to develop, in comparative leisure and on their own proper constitutional initiative, their own genuinely local source of sovereignty in place of the 'received', imperial *Grundnorm* at the time of independence; in a word, their own 'locally developed constitutional institutions and practices more nearly reflecting the local, indigenous society and its aspirations.'[50] In sum, then, in the era of rapid decolonisation, British Empire constitutional systems were, with the notable exception of the Indian subcontinent, normally devolved from above from the parent authority. They thus tended to have an elitist, and certainly non-popular, root of political and legal sovereignty.[51]

Certainly, in the Commonwealth Caribbean, there was no

active popular participation in constitutional drafting through a representative, elected constituent assembly and later ratification by a referendum. Rather, the process of constitutional founding, allowing for differences in matters of detail in respect of each particular island, was one in which local political leaders journeyed to London to enter into negotiations with colonial office functionaries over the terms of our constitutional arrangements. Thus, it is fair to say, notwithstanding the risk of over generalisation, that the process of establishing the *West Indian Independence Constitution*, to mark the founding of a 'new' independent sovereignty, was, as described by McWhinney, an 'elitist, oligarchic exercise.' Constitutional founding in Jamaica, for example, the largest of the (British) West Indian islands, and the first to gain political independence, was quite representative of the process which obtained in the rest of the Commonwealth Caribbean, and did not involve the mass of the people as such, but was essentially an elitist policy of negotiating with the Colonial Office.

This last point however should not be overstated, for, as Professor Woodville Marshall advises, the *'uprisings'* throughout the West Indies in the late 1930s, coupled with the rise of mass political parties in the 1940s, would have allowed for some measure of popular participation in the constitutional development of the West Indies. In other words, constitutional reform would have resulted in large measure from popular pressure. As a general premise, therefore, it must be conceded that the West Indian 'uprisings' in the late 1930s, in response to the abuses of colonialism, would have sparked the quest in earnest for constitutional reform, for a more democratic constitutional order through which all sections of society would allegedly benefit, and for the development of the appropriate instruments of self-government.[52] In Jamaica, for example, the new Constitution in 1944 was largely the result of specific Jamaican agitation begun in 1938 and of a consequent change in colonial policy. This change in colonial policy witnessed the need for rationalisation of the administration of the West Indies. 'In the post-war Colonial Office, Jamaica and the other British Caribbean territories were seen as viable autonomous constitutional entities only in Federal formation. Official thought held that a colony had to be able to attain a certain level of economic development, probably beyond the capacity of any single territory, in order to qualify for self-government.'[53] Federation thus became a policy of the Colonial Office.

The years following the inauguration of the 1944 Constitution saw much agitation for further constitutional change, largely due to the perceived inadequacies of the new Constitution. As Professor Trevor Munroe puts it, 'within two years of its inauguration disillusionment with the Constitution had begun to set in. Dissatisfaction over the constitutional arrangement propelled the need for further constitutional reform, specifically for self-government.'[54]

This agitation for constitutional reform culminated in the inauguration of a new Constitution in 1953. The new Constitution was welcomed but it fell well short of guaranteeing self-government to the colony. The changes that it provided for were largely administrative, with the Crown still retaining some measure of control. Full internal self-government was to come in August 1959 with the inauguration of yet a new Constitution.[55]

But as noted earlier, constitutional advancement toward self-government was linked to the idea of a Federation of the British Caribbean territories – at least as far as imperial policy was concerned. There was a clear Imperial determination to bring about a union between Jamaica and several units of the British Caribbean territories. The Jamaican Legislature, as did the Legislatures of the various territories, acquiesced in this Imperial policy and in 1958, the Federation of the West Indies was established.[56]

It bears emphasis, however, that, following the struggles of the late 1930s, political agitation for constitutional advancement was largely an 'affair' of the political leaders or élite and the Imperial Government. The mass of the people were virtually excluded from the details of constitution-making; notwithstanding that it was their eruption on the political scene that would have set the stage for the political leaders to pursue changes in constitutional form. As Ann Spackman has written, 'although the post-war period saw important constitutional changes taking place, including the formation and dissolution of the Federation, and the achievement of formal independence or associated statehood, there was no real involvement of the mass of the people in this process, despite the fact that it was their eruption in the 1930's which, if it did not start this movement, certainly speeded it along its way.'[57] And Professor Trevor Munroe adds:

With regard to local constitutional advance, its discrete tutelage served as an additional guarantee of the strict observance of Westminster constitutional practice. With regard to Federation, the immediate impact of the Imperial determination to bring about the union had the consequence of making unnecessary the cultivation of popular awareness on the issue ... It was therefore no accident that the Jamaican Legislature committed the colony to West Indian Federation without any attention to the formation of popular opinion on the question ... In no election before 1958 was Federation an issue; hence it remained outside the main medium of mass opinion – formation — the political meeting. But the fact that there was considerable agreement among the legislative groups was sufficient to commit the island to a Federal union, even before the legislators had persuaded themselves, much

less the population, of the desirability of self-government.[58]

The Federal Constitution was, therefore, largely the work of the
Imperial Power. The Federation package came direct from
Whitehall. Even the West Indian political elite, to say nothing of
the West Indian electorate, were subjugated to a secondary role
in the Federalizing process. Thus, when in Jamaica serious dis-
content emerged over the Federation, thereby resulting in a referendum, it is instructive that this referendum was largely caused
by conflict among political leaders, and was not the expression of
popular dissatisfaction.[59]

The point to be made here is that even in the case of Jamaica
which held a referendum immediately prior to political independence, there is no compelling evidence that the referendum
was indeed a reflection of wide citizen-engagement in the process
of constitutional founding. For although mass participation
ensued as a result of the disagreement among Jamaican political
leaders over the Federation, it is not evident that the electorate
did much more than decide on September 19, 1961 that Jamaica
should withdraw from the Federation, with the possibility that
they would be seeking political independence from Britain on
their own.[60] As J.B. Kelly puts it, 'until 19th September, 1961,
Jamaica had given no thought to the outline of an independence
constitution.'[61]

Again, it can hardly be gainsaid that constitutional founding in
Jamaica – like the rest of the Commonwealth Caribbean – was
virtually the exclusive province of the political leaders and the
Parliament of Jamaica. As Professor Trevor Munroe observes,
within two weeks of the referendum, a Jamaica mission was in
London and an official release declared that 'Her Majesty's
Government will receive a delegation from the Parliament of
Jamaica in January or February 1962 to consider proposals' for a

Jamaican Independence Constitution.[62] Professor Munroe further notes that by the third week in October, both of the Jamaican Houses of Parliament had appointed Committees 'to prepare proposals for a Constitution for Jamaica to take effect on Independence.'[63]

The first of the Joint Meetings of these two Committees was held at Gordon House in Kingston on October 31, 1961. The idea was to have a draft constitution ready by early January 1962 in order to use it as a basis for discussions with the Colonial Office regarding independence. Therefore, at this first meeting, this Drafting Committee, (representing both main political parties and both branches of the legislature), began in earnest to consider the outline of an independence constitution. With virtually no input from the public, the first draft of the Constitution was produced on January 18, 1962, approximately four months after the referendum.[64]

The absolute priority on completing a constitutional document in short order resulted in the fundamental law being drafted by a few men in secret conclave, which was eventually presented to Parliament and passed as the basic law of the land. Basic decisions regarding whether Jamaica should be a 'Constitutional Monarchy', whether it should retain an appointed Upper House, and whether the Privy Council should remain the final appellate court for Jamaica were taken by the Drafting Committee to the exclusion of any public debate whatsoever.[65]

To put it more bluntly, the 'Jamaican Constitution was almost entirely the creation of the leading legislators and the influences to which they were most susceptible.'[66] As J.B. Kelly puts it, 'the Jamaican Constitution was drafted by representatives (either elected or nominated) from a legislature which was two and a half years old at the time drafting began. Drafting was done by a group which included five (i.e. approximately 30%) non-elected members from the Legislative Council.'[67] It is therefore not surprising that in all essentials of form and substance, the Jamaican Constitution reflected the dominant influence of the Westminster tradition. Indeed, as then Premier Manley was to remark, 'We did not attempt to embark upon any original or novel exercise for constitution building.'[68] The method of acquiring the new Constitution and the substance of its provisions would bear this out.

In summary, Jamaica's need to draft a new constitution for independence was one of haste following the September 19, 1961 referendum on the question of Jamaica's continued participation in the West Indies Federation. On that date a majority of the Jamaican electorate had voted to take their island out of the West Indies Federation of which it had been a member since 1958. Following the referendum, Jamaica's two main political parties – (the People's National Party of then Premier N.W. Manley and the Jamaica Labour Party Opposition) – had closed ranks in remarkable unanimity on the question of independence from Britain at the earliest feasible opportunity. The idea was to have a draft constitution by early January 1962 in order to use it as a basis for discussions with the Colonial Office regarding independence. This inevitably led to a rather hasty drafting procedure in which a Drafting Committee (representing both main political parties and both branches of the legislature) produced a Draft Constitution by January 18, 1962, just barely four months after the referendum of September 19, 1961, when, for the first time, Jamaicans would have had to give serious thought to the outline of an independence constitution. Needless to say, four months would hardly have been sufficient time for the people to have formed an intelligent opinion as to the form and content of an independence constitution. In consequence, a Draft Constitution was produced without meaningful consultation of the people. In the final analysis, a Draft Constitution was precipitately produced in Committee, was hardly debated in public, was taken to London where important alterations were agreed on, and ultimately ratified by a legislature not elected with a specific mandate to draft and ratify an Independence Constitution. From the standpoint of democratic legitimacy, this procedure as described hardly measures up to the standard of constitutional legitimation required for a democratic constitution.[68a]

Thus, the Jamaican Independence Constitution, like its sister Constitutions throughout the region, reflected 'the normal tendency of the successor political class to copy the political culture of the Imperial Power.'[69] This is in the very nature of the colonial experience where the colonial society is penetrated at all levels of decision making, even in areas beyond its economic and political life.[70] And it bears out the truth of Edward McWhinney's observation that the new post-colonial constitutions were invariably highly derivative, and tended to borrow very heavily from the constitutional institutions and developed practices of the 'parent' European colonial power involved.[71] This was a basic feature of the development of post-colonial constitutionalism, which was a natural sequel to the progressive liquidation of the European colonial empires in Asia, Africa, and the Caribbean.[72] Given that the approach to self-government and independence on the part of the colonial territory concerned was usually conditional upon the development, within that territory, of a democratic system of government as evidence of its capacity finally to govern itself, free from the benevolent paternalism of the erstwhile colonial power, it is perhaps not surprising that the emerging new, postcolonial, indigenous local political élite should find it good practical politics to copy the constitutional models of the colonial power, and that the influence of the old colonial office legal draftsmen should often be pervasive.[73]

Trinidad and Tobago

This process of constitution-making, sketched above, was common to the entire Commonwealth Caribbean. The draft of the Jamaican Constitution, which was produced in January 1962, was taken to London, where significant alterations were made, and subsequently ratified by the Jamaica Parliament on February 27, 1962. The Constitution, however, came into force, 'in strict law,' by Imperial legislation - the Jamaica Independence Act 1962. This process, allowing for minor differences in details, was replicated throughout the region in the 1960s,1970s, and 1980s.

Trinidad and Tobago, however, might well prove to have been the exception. In the twin-island colony, the populace would have been engaged in the process of constitution-making to a degree quite unlike the rest of the Caribbean, including Jamaica. This might well have been due in large measure to the entry of Dr Eric Williams into active politics of the country in the mid 1950s. It is hardly contestable that, upon his return to Trinidad, following his studies at Oxford University and a brief stint as a professor at Howard University in the United States, Dr Williams had established himself as arguably the most dominant figure in the politics of Trinidad and Tobago and the leading advocate for constitutional change, leading ultimately to political independence. Williams' public lectures on politics and constitutional reform at the 'University of Woodford Square' in Port-of-Spain and throughout the country, in the mid-to-latter 1950s, had introduced a level of civic education to Trinidad and Tobago quite unmatched in any of the islands, including Jamaica. In addition, he was primarily responsible for establishing the first really organized political party with a coherent programme in Trinidad and Tobago, which he led to victory in the general elections of 1956.[74] In essence, then, with the establishment of the People's National Movement (PNM), Williams had successfully

introduced party politics to Trinidad and Tobago. As Dr Ann
Spackman puts it:

> The germ of the P.N.M. is to be found in the lectures
> given by Dr. Williams throughout the colony in 1955,
> and the real beginnings of the P.N.M. can be seen in July
> of that year, when Dr. Williams lectured on constitu-
> tional reform and presented a Memorial embodying these
> reforms to his audience, to be signed by them. The
> Memorial was eventually signed by about 15,000 people
> and an *ad hoc* committee was formed in order to direct
> activities. This led to the Inaugural Conference of the
> People's National Movement on Sunday, January 15,
> 1956, at which a statement of fundamental principles was
> adopted called the People's Charter.[75]

Quite interestingly, Ann Spackman, in her essay on constitutional development in Trinidad and Tobago, takes the year 1956
to be the watershed year in the constitutional development of
Trinidad and Tobago since, prior to that date, the constitutional
changes which took place were largely concerned with increasing
the representative nature of the Legislative Council.[76] However,
in and after 1956, Trinidad and Tobago moved rapidly towards
fully responsible government until, in 1962, the country became
independent.

Following its success in the 1956 elections, the PNM pressed
for constitutional change based largely on the Memorial for constitutional change it had drafted. From then on, the Constitution
was amended quite considerably until the Colony was granted full
internal self-government in 1961.[77] These amendments generally
followed the pattern of additional grants towards full responsible
Cabinet government. For example, in 1957, the Government had
advocated amendments to the Constitution 'which would recognise the conventions of Cabinet Government', in that the

Governor would call upon the leader of the majority party in the Legislative Council to form the government, or the man most likely to command a majority, and that the Governor should select and remove Ministers from office and distribute portfolios on the advice of the Chief Minister. The Government also recommended that the Chief Minister be styled the Premier; the Executive Council, the Cabinet; the Colonial Secretary, the Chief Secretary; that the Premier should preside at Cabinet meetings and not the Governor; and that the Chief Secretary and Attorney-General should remain in the Cabinet but with no vote.[78] Further suggestions for reform were to come in June 1958, which were primarily concerned with the executive power. It was suggested, among other things, that the number of Cabinet Ministers be increased to nine, including a Minister of Home Affairs who would be responsible for police, security and immigration, and limitations were put on the Governor's powers of reservation and Her Majesty's powers of disallowance.[79]

These suggested reforms were however joined together with further recommendations and together they were brought into force in June 1959 by Order-in-Council. These reforms of 1959 constituted the last stage of constitutional development before the formal adoption of internal self-government in 1961.[80] This was to come with the Trinidad and Tobago (Constitution) Order-in-Council, 1961. According to Dr Spackman, this Order did little more than recognise the full conventions of Cabinet government which had been effectively in force since the PNM gained power in 1956. She writes: 'Theoretically, prior to 1961, the Governor could have rejected the advice given to him by the Premier and other Ministers. In practice he had acted far more like a constitutional monarch than a colonial governor.'[81] This was institutionalised, however, with the 1961 Order-in-Council which stated that the Governor, in performing most of his functions, could only act on the advice of the Cabinet or of any

Minister acting with full Cabinet authority.[82] Of course, the Governor retained, among others, the critical powers of appointment of the Premier; the revocation of this appointment; and the dissolution of Parliament.

Towards the end of 1961, following the collapse of the West Indies Federation upon Jamaica's decision to withdraw therefrom in September of that year, the PNM Government under Dr Eric Williams decided to concentrate its efforts on attaining full independence. By April 1962, in reply to a despatch from the Governor, the Secretary of State for the Colonies agreed that Trinidad and Tobago should become independent as early as practicable in 1962. He proposed that an independence conference be held in London towards the end of May to agree on a constitution and the date for independence.[83]

In the meantime, however, in February 1962, the Government published a Draft Independence Constitution for public comment. Individual citizens and public and private organizations were invited to submit memoranda. Those responding to the invitation were invited to a three-day conference at Queen's Hall, April 25 to April 27, to discuss the Draft Constitution.[84] The press was excluded from this conference, popularly known as the Queen's Hall Conference, but the proceedings were later broadcast and published uncensored.[85] Following the Conference, the Government made certain amendments to its draft which was then presented to a Joint Select Committee of Parliament. On May 11, 1962, the Report of the Joint Select Committee to consider Proposals for an Independence Constitution for Trinidad and Tobago was laid before the House of Representatives and adopted.[86] It was this draft that the Trinidad and Tobago delegation took to London for the Independence Conference on May 28, 1962. Trinidad and Tobago became independent on August 31, 1962.

But the Government's handling of the independence issue and

its method of consulting the people on the Independence Constitution had provoked severe criticisms. 'Organizations and individuals vociferously condemned the Government's "indecent haste" in putting the Independence Constitution on the political agenda with only six weeks allotted for comment, especially since nothing had yet been done to consult the people on the unitary-state proposition.'[87] Moreover, the original draft constitution which was presented for debate by delegates at the Queen's Hall Conference was not a bipartisan document.[88] Further criticisms of the draft concerned the sections on civil liberties, the provisions for entrenchment, the composition of the Senate, the appointive power of the prime minister, and the machinery for the conduct of elections.[89]

But the Government responded that the original draft embodied the elected government's thoughts on the desirable form of constitution for Trinidad and Tobago, and was intended to be the basis for discussion in the Queen's Hall Conference, to which all individuals and organizations, including the political parties, were invited. Therefore, since it was the amended draft resulting from the Queen's Hall Conference, and not the Government's original draft which went to the Joint Select Committee, of which the Parliamentary Opposition was a part, it therefore could not be claimed that they were excluded from any vital stage in the national debate on the constitution.[90]

Still, it was felt by some delegates and the main opposition parties that, by limiting discussion at the Queen's Hall Conference to the government's draft, no really fundamental questions with regard to the constitution could be put: whether, for example, Trinidad and Tobago should be a Republic as opposed to a constitutional monarchy within the Commonwealth.[91] Ironically, there was probably greater consensus of opinion about remaining a monarchy within the Commonwealth, with a responsible form of parliamentary government, than on any other issue.[92] Only a minority at the Conference openly expressed any preference for a republican constitution.[93] Be that as it may, in the round, very few changes were made in 1962 except those which could be anticipated in the change-over from a colonial to an independent regime. The basic structure of the Constitution remained that which had been laid down by the 1961 Order-in-Council. The more substantive areas of change, as was earlier intimated, concerned the sections on civil liberties, the provisions for entrenchment, the composition of the Senate, citizenship, and the authority of the political executive, particularly the Prime Minister.[94] On this last issue, according to Professor Selwyn Ryan, the question about the relationship between the Governor-General and the Prime Minister posed a fundamental question about the basic ideological foundations of the constitution.[95]

But notwithstanding the criticisms levelled at the Government, it is quite remarkable that a process of constitutional founding of that sort had been undertaken in the Commonwealth Caribbean on the eve of political independence. The Premier had boasted that the process was an honest and sincere attempt to achieve a democratic consensus on a matter of national concern. No other country (in the West Indies), he thought, had adopted the course that Trinidad and Tobago had decided upon in soliciting public reaction to constitutional proposals. As Professor Selwyn Ryan puts it, 'the constitutional conference held at Queen's Hall on April 25 to 27 1962 was perhaps one of the finest democratic exercises that Trinidad had yet witnessed. Quite accidentally, the government had hit upon a method of obtaining popular participation in the constitution-making process.'[96] And, as Dr Williams himself has stated:

> The presence of some 200 citizens from all walks of life, including representatives of religious, economic, labour, civic, professional and political organizations as well as

governmental agencies, constitutes a landmark in the history of our Territory. Today's meeting represents the closest approximation we have yet achieved towards the national community ... All of you added together, with your collective views however divergent or contradictory, constitute a citizens' assembly the like of which has seldom been seen in the world ... You are all here this morning ... the nation in conference, an educated democracy in deliberations, a Government seeking advice from its citizens.[97]

Still, all was not well. On the question of the exclusion of the press, among other things, the Opposition had walked out of the Queen's Hall Conference, never to return. So although they would have participated in the work of the Joint Select Committee and in the debate in Parliament on the Draft Independence Constitution, the Government and Opposition forces did not go to the London Conference with a united front. To repeat, this lack of agreement between the Government PNM and the Opposition Democratic Labour Party, prior to their departure to London, was in large measure ascribed to the procedure the PNM had chosen to adopt in framing the constitution. As Dr Capildeo, leader of the DLP had argued:

Wider measure of agreement would have been achieved if an attempt had been made to secure our co-operation from the outset. ... The Government, however, chose to ignore us and proceeded to prepare a draft on its own, so that when the joint select committee was belatedly appointed, the Government members of the committee had already closed their minds, and in committee they were not disposed to discuss issues but were determined to defend a draft to which they appeared to be irrevocably committed. The joint select committee was, therefore, prejudiced from the beginning.[98]

At the Marlborough House Conference on May 29, 1962, Dr Capildeo stated the DLP claims for an independent judiciary; for provisions effectively guaranteeing the rights and freedoms which ought to exist in a democratic society; a democratically constituted Parliament; a procedure for the amendment of the Constitution which effectively protects the citizenry from the arbitrary exercise of the power to amend; and the various service commissions so constituted as to ensure that they function effectively and impartially.[99]

But proceedings at the Conference were hardly harmonious; Dr Williams and Dr Capildeo had locked horns. On the question of entrenchment the DLP demanded a three-quarter majority in both Houses, and an entrenched right of appeal to the Privy Council on all issues relating to the interpretation of the Constitution.[100] Dr Capildeo declared himself as having no faith in the integrity of Dr Williams, and accused him of 'tearing up' the federal constitution and the old Trinidad Constitution and there would be nothing to stop him from 'tearing up' the new constitution and making Trinidad and Tobago a republic, as Nkrumah had done in Ghana.[101] He also complained that at present, 'one section of the community was armed against the other'; therefore, for him, it was critical that the police force and the national guard be more representative of the ethnic make-up of the country.[102]

In due course, however, in an effort to avoid the collapse of the Conference, Dr Williams and the PNM delegation made certain concessions which he hoped would meet some of the objections of the DLP.[103] In the event, the Conference was saved, and the British officials, for their part, were quite pleased about the outcome of the deliberations. Trinidadians were equally pleased that the Conference had been brought to a happy conclusion.[104] It was decided that Trinidad and Tobago should become independent on August 31, 1962; and, further, that an independent Trinidad and Tobago would continue in allegiance to Her Majesty the Queen as Queen of Trinidad and Tobago.

Barbados

Perhaps no country in the Commonwealth Caribbean more strongly bears out the truth of Sir Hugh Springer's words than Barbados. It was an 'ancient British colony' of over 300 years old at the time of independence.[105] From 1625, when it was claimed for, and subsequently settled in 1627, in the name of King James 1 of England, to 1966, when it became an independent sovereign State, Barbados, unlike the neighbouring islands, had never known another imperial master. According to Dr Richard Cheltenham, this unbroken attachment to a single metropolitan power has bequeathed to Barbados a set of values and a political style essentially British.[106] In this regard, Barbados provides a rather interesting case study of the process of decolonisation. It is not that Barbados' case is radically different from that of the other British West Indian colonies; rather, it is to emphasize the point that Barbados presents a classic example of the incremental, evolutionary process toward constitutional self-government that was reminiscent of the Canadian experience, say, a century earlier.[107]

Today, Barbados is the most stable parliamentary democracy in the Commonwealth Caribbean. It boasts the longest tradition of parliamentary government of the Westminster model. Unlike neighbouring dependencies, Barbados has never experienced Crown Colony government, the colonial constitution originating in the early days of British overseas settlement in the seventeenth century having survived through the centuries. Under this constitution Barbados has enjoyed a considerable measure of self-government through the existence of a legislative body dating back as far as 1639.[108] As Dr Cheltenham states,

> In the history of the Commonwealth, no former British territory has moved into independence with a longer tradition of Parliamentary Government than Barbados. No country had endured a longer period of tutelage. In recent years, of all the British colonies to achieve independence, Jamaica alone possessed a representative assembly going back, though not without interruption, to 1664. Important countries like Ceylon, Ghana, Nigeria, Cyprus and Malta, and even Trinidad and Tobago, enjoyed responsible Government only a few years immediately preceding their attainment of independence.[109]

But in spite of Barbados' celebrated tutelage in British parliamentarism – or maybe because of it – the 'founding' of the Barbados Independence Constitution remained very much an *affair* of the local political élite and the officials of the Colonial Office in the United Kingdom. That is to say, the process of *constitutional founding* was not one in which it can truthfully be said that the people were engaged in a discursive, deliberative, collective *conversation* as to the foundational terms of their political order. In this regard, as was common to the entire Commonwealth Caribbean, the Independence Constitution was not the product of collective, democratic *authorship*; so that even though there were general elections in November 1966, prior to independence, this could hardly be said to have been adequate public expression on the terms of the Constitution, given that by then these would already have been settled at the London Conference earlier in the year.[110]

It bears reminding that the idea of political independence for a country the small size of Barbados was never on the cards –

except of course in federation with the other British West Indian territories. And even then, in 1962, following the break-up of the West Indian Federation, the idea of political independence for Barbados was considered only to be feasible in federation with the rest of the Eastern Caribbean islands (the Windwards and the Leewards). So it was not until 1965, when negotiations towards that federation broke down, that the idea of political independence was seriously considered.[111]

By that time, small states like Cyprus, Malta, Jamaica and Trinidad and Tobago had already achieved political independence. What is more, Barbados had by then 'matured as an outstanding legacy of British colonial rule. Its economy was growing both in strength and diversity. There was no longer a total reliance on sugar. This state of affairs would certainly have boosted the confidence of the local political élite.'[112] What is more, there had been constitutional changes in 1964, which represented the most advanced state short of independence a colony could possibly have achieved. It was therefore natural that the country would have proceeded to independence on the tacit assumption that the constitutional arrangements then in operation, and to which she had become accustomed, would be retained on independence.[113]

Following the break-down of negotiations in 1965 on the question of federation with the Eastern Caribbean islands, the Barbados Government issued a White Paper announcing Barbados' intention to seek political independence on its own.[114] The procedure adopted in formulating the Independence Constitution was as follows:

> In or around March 1966, the Government published a Draft Constitution and invited public comments thereon. The plan was to follow this up with a debate in the House of Assembly to approve the Draft Constitution, following which the Constitutional Talks in London were to be

held. This procedure, however, met with fierce resistance from the Opposition Parties, who, in the end, boycotted the debate. They are said to have objected to the procedure adopted because, they claimed, the constitution had not been drafted in consultation with them. They also feared that, in a debate, the Government would use its majority to defeat all the opposition's proposals for amendments. The result, they insisted, would be to stamp the constitution with a "spurious authority" and limit their impact at the London Talks. And, finally, they were opposed to the arrangements with respect to the size of the delegations allowed them at the London Conference.[115]

Comments on the Draft Constitution were submitted by certain organisations, most notably the Chamber of Commerce, the Bar Association and the Junior Chamber of Commerce. Among other things, the Chamber of Commerce recommended that elections be held before independence, that arrangements for a common court of appeal be made with other Caribbean countries, that a referendum procedure be inserted for amending entrenched clauses, and for deciding on proposals for a union with some other territory.[116]

At the London Conference there was bitter wrangling between the Government party and the Opposition delegation. The disagreements centered, among other things, on the composition of the Senate. It was felt that the composition of the Senate should be such that a Government, regardless of the size of its majority in the House, should not be able to secure an amendment to an entrenched provision of the Constitution without at least some support from the Opposition. The Government, however, rejected such proposals on the premise that to accommodate them would mean giving the Opposition Senators an influence on important issues out of proportion to the strength of the Opposition in the House of Assembly.[117]

These few details would suffice to underscore the salient point that the Independence Constitution that came out of the London Conference was hardly a *consensus document*, but was moreso the Government's *document*.[118] But in any event, as earlier noted, it was hardly to be expected that the constitutional arrangements at the time would have been deviated from. As was the case with other British territories adopting a written constitution at independence, a Bill of Rights was appended to the Barbados Constitution. Another very significant addition was the 'Supremacy Clause', declaring the Constitution to be the supreme law of Barbados, and that any law inconsistent with the Constitution is void to the extent of the inconsistency.[119] This provision, according to Dr Cheltenham, makes the Constitution a body of fundamental law; a provision which no Barbadian constitutional instrument in the past could claim.[120] In all other respects, however, the Barbados Independence Constitution remains very much a legacy of British constitutionalism: a parliamentary, constitutional democracy with the British Monarch as the head of state, thus assuming its 'monarchical status.'[121]

If the story of the founding of the Jamaican, the Trinidad and Tobago, and the Barbados Independence Constitutions is indeed representative of the process that obtained throughout the region, then at least two essential points are underscored: that political independence in the Commonwealth Caribbean was not a revolutionary repudiation of our colonial past and, equally important, that the people were not the 'authors' of that which they have *accepted* as their 'Fundamental Law'. The virtual absence of the people from the political independence process meant that Commonwealth Caribbean constitutional founding fell far short of the democratic ideal – which, to paraphrase Professor Frank Michelman, is the idea that a country's people see themselves, 'in some nonfictively attributable sense', as the authors of the laws that constitute their polity; 'the laws, that is, that fix the country's "constitutional essentials" – charter its popular-governmental and representative-governmental institutions and offices, define and limit their respective powers and jurisdictions, and thereby express a certain political conception [of themselves].'[122] Such authorship, according to Professor Seyla Benhabib, requires that a country's processes for fundamental lawmaking be so designed and conducted that outcomes will be continually apprehensible as products of 'collective deliberation conducted rationally and fairly among free and equal individuals.'[123]

Commonwealth Caribbeans are heirs to a constitutional tradition that derived in large part from English constitutional theory and practice. Until independence, Commonwealth Caribbeans were British subjects living under a constitutional monarchy. With independence, however, and unlike the Americans, Commonwealth Caribbeans did not reject the British constitution and affirm their own constitutional tradition. Rather, in the fundamental design of their political institutions, their 'retention' of the Privy Council and their continuing allegiance to the Crown, West Indians implicitly attest to a 'constitutional faith' in that English constitutional tradition. The words of the Wooding Constitution Commission are instructive

> The Constitution under which Trinidad and Tobago achieved independence in 1962 was in all its essentials a written version of the constitutional arrangements evolved in the United Kingdom over many centuries.[124]

But could the process of constitutional founding in the Commonwealth Caribbean have been fundamentally different? Could it have taken a more 'revolutionary' path, say, resulting in a repudiation of the Westminster-style constitution and much of its attendant practices? And could it have engaged the populace in a more open communal conversation as to the kind of constitution they should wish for?

Stephen Vasciannie suggests hardly not; strong political and intellectual forces – the education and social formation of West Indian nationalists and political élite – would have militated in favour of the Westminster system and against any 'revolutionary' change.[125] Moreover, the decision of the British Government, at a constitutional conference in London in June 1961, to grant political independence to some of its Caribbean territories comprising the Federation, would certainly have meant independence within the constitutional framework established by Britain over the years for granting independence to its colonies. But particularly in the case of the British West Indies, the rapid pace at which independence came, following the break-up of the Federation, meant there was hardly much time for any careful rethinking of the received constitutional forms and institutional arrangements. For, unlike the case of that older and narrower European segment of the empire, Canada, Australia, and even the Union of South Africa and, subsequently, in the case of decolonisation and devolution of constitutional self-government and independence on the Indian subcontinent (when there was adequate time, and where the imperial initiative in favour of constitutional devolution was co-ordinated with some form of local constituent activity in the colonial territory, such as a representative constituent assembly able to work out the general principles as well as the detailed institutions of the new constitutional system), in the case of the West Indies, the imperial initiative might well have been occasioned by an urgent need to be rid of the burdensome West Indian territories.[126] Time was therefore of the essence.

In any event, as Stephen Vasciannie observes, in the case of Jamaica, following the results of the Federal Referendum in 1961, the constitutional process became a matter of identifying the shortest, and least controversial, route to independence. In addition, the British tradition of imperial tutelage would have required a colonial allegiance to the institutional requirements of constitutional government, which meant adopting the Westminster-style constitution and its Australian-Canadian-Indian export versions.[127] Certainly, political leaders like Norman Manley would have been well aware that one sure way to prove to the British that the West Indian colonies were indeed ready for independence was to express a desire for the unbroken continuity of the Westminster-style constitution and its attendant practices – in particular, our continuing allegiance to the Crown. In the circumstances, therefore, political leaders would not have encouraged any debate but that which showed a clear preference for the Westminster-style constitution. An early comment from Manley in 1952 would seem to bear this out:

> One thing we have learned from history in all this colonial development, is the greatest desirability of complete unity on the part of those in the colony who are making the demand.
>
> It is the natural tendency of colonial powers to doubt the ability of the governed to rule themselves. That must be so, otherwise they would not dare to continue to rule. If a man did not believe in his superiority to govern, he could not do so. Colonial powers must find reasons to justify slow progress. And they are not to be quarrelled with for that because it is based on the historical process.[128]

So notwithstanding that constitutional change and development in the Commonwealth Caribbean would have resulted in part from the political uprisings of the late 1930s, say, it still remains the case that the colonial imperial process – the experience of being colonized – would have planted in the West Indian consciousness a negative perception of *self* and would have encouraged a longing to be like the colonial master. As our eminent *man of letters*, Mr. George Lamming, puts it,

> [Colonialism] was not a physical cruelty. Indeed, the colonial experience of my generation was almost wholly without violence. No torture, no concentration camp, no mysterious disappearance of hostile natives, no army encamped with orders to kill. The Caribbean endured a different kind of subjugation. It was the terror of the mind, a daily exercise in self-mutilation ... This was the breeding ground for every uncertainty of self.[129]

There is no question, then, that our political imagination has been shaped by the historical experience of British colonialism. Therefore, the kind of constitutional discourse that would have attended the quest for political independence would have limited itself to reinforcing the belief that we were indeed ready for independence and, above all, that independence did not mean any radical departure from the 'pre-existing colonial constitution'; that is to say, it did not mean the founding of a new constitution. In essence, then, the desire for political independence would not have indulged any serious reflection on an alternative constitutional frame, such as the US presidential model, say, which, in any event, would have required a 'critical mass of intellectual exchange and awareness among non-governmental sectors of the society.'[130]

A constitution is a document of political founding or refounding.[131] It is an architectonic plan for the founding and ordering of a political society, commonly understood in modern terms as the 'State'. It defines the arrangement of those essential powers, *viz.*, the executive, the legislative, and the judicial, that mark the sovereignty of the State and its authority over the countless other institutions of social life – familial, economic, cultural, and the like. In a broader, more fundamental sense, the term 'constitution' comprehends virtually the whole of what is sometimes called the 'form of life' of a human community, describing what that life should be like, and ordering the institutional design for achieving that life in a given society. In a word, the constitution is a plan for a way of life.[132] And this entails an enunciation of those values that would support a certain conception of the good life, and also a certain conception of justice, and an elaboration of those institutions by means of which this way of life is to be achieved;[133] the range of activities on which these institutions will bear and who, as full citizens, those holding full political rights, will share in the operation of those institutions.[134]

Constitutional founding, the giving of form to collective life or the organisation of a political community in which all its members are, in theory at least, implicated in a common life, is certainly one of the most fundamental of human endeavours. Indeed, it is reckoned to be the most notable action of which political man is capable. It is deemed to be superior to other types of political acts because it aims to shape the lives of citizens by designing the structure or 'dwelling' which they and their posterity will inhabit.[135] It is an act addressed to a fundamental and universal human problem: the problem of defining some of the most fundamental relationships in which members of society are to stand to one another and to their State.[136] A constitution affects to define how human beings are to live with one another in society; more specifically, the 'political' ways in which people may live together; politics here taken as being fundamentally concerned with the proper life of man in the polity. Constitutional law is, therefore, very much the study of human collective life. It addresses the problem of the way in which certain fundamental claims and needs of human beings are treated in the society in which they live; indeed, it addresses the very fundamental questions of who are to be included as members of the political community, and the kinds of rights, liberties, and responsibilities that are thereby entailed.[137] Thus, the constitution's reach, in a conceptual and practical sense, into the lives of the citizens can be extraordinary. As Professor Peter J. Steinberger puts it

> Wherever humans live together there is likely to be some ultimate practice, in terms of which particular forms of social life are, according to the fashion, either actively regulated or generously allowed to operate without overt interference, and where the decision actively to regulate or not is itself subject to review and revision. This practice – however formulated and instituted – is the practice of politics conceived in the broadest possible terms and, as such, is the defining characteristic of political society. It follows, then, that all our ways of living together are, at least in theory, subject to the claims and judgments of politics – [to which the constitution is central].[138]

So if it is indeed the case that the constitution, in the broader sense, speaks to the conditions of the common life, then, in theory at least, all our ways of living together are subject to constitutional injunctions. In other words, the constitution speaks to our moral and political life, since it concerns not only the structure of power and, therefore, the ways in which the government may treat the citizens, but also the ways in which individuals may treat each other in society. Thus, the constitution must be conceived as defining both a moral and a political community, since it can be, at one and the same time, both an instrument of political order and an expression of a people's moral aspirations for political life. It is, ideally, a collective, public expression of the essential political commitments of a people; of the kind of people they are and wish enduringly to be. This expresses two critical senses of the word 'constitution'. As Professor Hanna Pitkin reminds us, the use of the word 'constitution' may refer to 'a characteristic way of life, the national character of a people, a product of their particular history and social conditions.'[139] This is the sense of Aristotle's *politeia*, which refers not to fundamental law or locus of sovereignty but to the distinctive shared way of life of a *polis*, its mode of social and political articulation as a community.[140]

The second use of the word 'constitution' points to the act of constituting, that is, of founding, framing, shaping something anew. In this sense, *our constitution* is 'an aspect of the human capacity to act, to innovate, to break the causal chain of process and launch something unprecedented.'[141] This underscores an elemental truth: that 'constitutions are *made*, not found; ... that they are human creations, products of convention, choice, the specific history of a particular people, and (almost always) a political struggle in which some win and some lose.'[142]

These two senses of constitution – as fundamental character or way of life and as the activity of constituting – conjoin in the political and legal sense of 'constitution'. On this view, the political constitution of a people is an act of collective self-definition and self-interpretation; an act by which a people constitute themselves *as a people*. As Professor Donald Lutz puts it, 'At some point, if a political system is to endure, a people must constitute themselves *as a people* by achieving a shared psychological state in which they recognize themselves as engaged in a common enterprise and as bound together by widely held values, interests, and goals.'[143] Constitutional founding is therefore a process of collective self-definition; and constitutional reform, as an essential aspect of the continuation of that process – of rethinking and reshaping our constitution through our collective activity – is equally an act of self-definition and self-interpretation. From this perspective, and in view of the foregoing story of our constitutional *origin*, the project of constitutional reform in the Commonwealth Caribbean assumes a very urgent and profound mission: above all else, the task of constitutional reform must engage our human capacity for collective and deliberate creative action in rethinking and reshaping the polity; in a word, to make our constitutions *our* own.

The distinctive challenge for constitutional reform today is therefore the redefinition of Commonwealth Caribbean political identity. For whether or not we are mindful of the fact, *West Indian Independence Constitutions* provide us with images of ourselves and representations of our political identity. They demonstrate the importance of authorship in the construction of political identity,[144] as evidenced by our willingness to surrender to their inscriptions of the *West Indian constitutional self*. The question, then, for us, is whether, on a critical and comprehensive understanding of the *origin* and nature of our constitutional texts, of the constitutional *world* they have brought into being and of the images they provide us of ourselves, we would wish to reaffirm, rather than *remake*, as it is within our human capacity to do, the foundational terms of our political order and the inscriptions of the collective *constitutional self* provided in our Fundamental Laws.[145]

To repeat, then, constitutional reform becomes an act of critical self-understanding because, in this enterprise, we recur to our *plan* for public life in the hope of grasping who we authentically are, or aspire to be, even beyond the current state of our constitutional realization and the imaginings of our founders.[146] Constitutional reform therefore becomes an interpretive enterprise that seeks to understand and explain the connections between the written texts and the political order they have signalled into existence; our collective identity and the form of our politics. In a word, it becomes a project of active, affirmative theorising, radical in the sense of getting at the root of things; beginning at the starting point of critical consciousness of what we really are, and of knowing 'ourselves' as a product of the historical process to date.[147]

The central claim of this Introduction has been that our post-colonial constitutions were drafted from above as part of an oligarchic, elitist exercise, and this helps to explain precisely why we still do not yet perceive our Independence Constitutions as 'our own'; why we do not yet fully recognize the collective *self* as the *author* of the political community; why we do not yet have a sense of having constituted ourselves a sovereign people in some positive act of communal self-constitution.[148] A possible corrective to this situation is given in the terms of reference regarding the 'patriation' of the *Independence Constitution* and a re-examination of our continuing relationship with the British Crown and, possibly, the establishment of a Caribbean court of final appeal and the abolition of appeals to the British Privy Council.[149]

Patriation of the *Constitution* is taken here to imply some local event (or series of events) that may be taken as a measure of constitutional autochthony; meaning that the *Constitution* may now be seen to derive its validity and authority from the local events, rather than from an Act of the British Imperial Parliament.[150] The patriation term of reference is therefore all important because it is the starting point in any possible replication of the *ideal* of constitutional founding: the idea of a people grounding their political community and establishing their own political identity in some positive act of fundamental law-making. The issue of patriation must therefore be fully addressed in the first chapter on constitutional reform.

But patriation is closely linked to the terms of reference regarding the continuing presence of the British Crown in the Commonwealth Caribbean constitutional order, and the abolition of appeals to the Privy Council and the establishment of a Caribbean court of final appeal. It can hardly be gainsaid the defining impact of the British Monarchy and its Judicial Committee on conceptions of the West Indian constitutional *self*. On the assumption that we have retained the monarchy, we continue to define ourselves as 'subjects' of the British Crown. Hence our continuing pledge of fealty. And the Judicial Committee's continuing location at the top of the Commonwealth Caribbean judicial hierarchy virtually ensures that our constitutional practices and judicial habits of mind would carry a distinctly British cast.[151]

Our colonial tutelage has no doubt resulted in the historical entrenchment of certain constitutional forms and practices. The institutions of constitutional democracy that emerged from that tutelage have, for the most part, remained remarkably stable, paradoxically producing a powerful impetus to preserve and to be faithful to that which we have 'inherited'. Still, the very strong opposition, in some quarters, to either the 'removal' of the British Crown or the abolition of appeals to the Privy Council suggests a blindedness to the fact that the continuing presence of the Crown and its Judicial Committee represents a vestigial incongruity, a contradiction in the constitutional symbolism of a politically independent sovereign people.[152] This incongruity is further underscored when one considers that the *West Indian Independence Constitution* is a written constitution with an entrenched Bill of Rights; very much in contrast to the largely unwritten British constitution and the absence of constitutionally entrenched rights. This means that the domiciling of ultimate judicial power over Commonwealth Caribbean Constitutions in London would leave them too much under the dominance of British constitutionalism and their interpretation less open to cosmopolitan intellectual influences.[153] Thus, in a separate chapter offering a philosophical justification for the proposed Caribbean Court of Justice, it is shown that the establishment of our own court of final appeal constitutes an essential part of the process of *West Indian decolonisation* and could have tremendous implications for the redefining of our political identity, through a hermeneutical reading of the *West Indian constitutional text* and of the *polity* it recommends, in the more appropriate *language* of modern republican constitutionalism.

In summary, this entire work presents itself as a hermeneutical enterprise in constitutional theory – a re-conception of the *West Indian polity*, and a re-definition of *West Indian political identity*. Our political independence from Britain was only the beginning of this mission: the *starting point* in our struggle to make ourselves a free people. Achieving this goal must mean, among other things, refusing to 'inhabit', without question, an identity constructed for us by a colonial past and scripted by the texts (and institutions) that emerged from that tutelage. We can only be *free* by giving to ourselves, texts, bequests, and commitments by which we propose to live our lives over time;[154] in a word, by a re-definition of the political *Grundnorm* inherited from Britain.

This, according to Professor Jed Rubenfeld, is the *ideal* of democratic, constitutional self-government; an understanding of constitutional law initiated by American written constitutionalism.[155] That is to say, 'breaking from a two-thousand-year-old tradition, in which a democratic constitution meant a constitution establishing a democratic politics, America understood a democratic constitution to mean, in addition, a constitution *democratically* made. America made democratic *constitution-writing* part of democracy.'[156] Thus, the authority, the legitimacy, and the value of American constitutional law, in large measure depend on its claim to being law that embodies the nation's *self-given* fundamental political and legal commitments.[157] The task of constitutional reform, therefore, is to afford us the opportunity of realizing this idea of a nation living out commitments of its own authorship over time.[158]

Our written constitutions are certainly democratic in content, but as long as they continue to be perceived as the received constitutional instruments from our former colonial master, they would forever bear the taint of fundamental illegitimacy, of subjection to imposition from without.[159] As Professor Rubenfeld puts it, 'a nation that lives under a constitution imposed from without – imposed, say, by an occupying army or a colonial power now departed – might come to accept the document, to embrace its authority, perhaps even to revere it.'[160] Still, such a situation would constitute a betrayal of an ideal conception of self-government – of a people living out, over time, commitments of its own authorship.[161] In the current enterprise of constitutional reform, we invoke this ideal of democratic constitution-making, which must include the possibility of the people's *re*-authorship of their fundamental law.

But, then, even a founding moment of perfect popular will will not suffice to secure the legitimacy of the constitution once and for all. Constitutions are lived under over time and, in due course, they would come to suffer temporal dysfunction: aspects of a constitution may become unsuitable or the people may no longer recognize some of the constitutional commitments as their own.[162] Happily, democratic constitutionalism rests on the very supposition that the process of framing a constitution – *la politique politisante* – continues long after the founding moment,[163] in the judicial, political and cultural discourse through which a political community continuously reassesses and reshapes itself. Democratic constitutionalism therefore entails the continuing possibility of a democratic *re*-writing of the fundamental law.[164] Our current constitutional reform project should at least achieve that much, so that our Constitutional Charters can be said to have acquired, though only *ex post facto*, an unimpeachable popular root of sovereignty.[165]

Endnotes

1 Address to both Houses of the Barbados Parliament, (Monday June 26, 1989).
2 Norma Thompson, *Herodotus and the Origins of the Political Community: Arion's Leap* 1 (1996).
3 Frederick G. Spurdle, *Early West Indian Government: Showing the Progress of Government in Barbados, Jamaica and the Leeward Islands, 1660-1783* 7 (1963).
4 Lloyd Best, *The Trinidad and Tobago Review* 26 (November 27, 1998).

5 Rex Nettleford, 'Emancipation: The Lessons and the Legacy' (*unpublished; on file with the author*). See also A.R. Carnegie, 'The Importance of Constitutional Law in Jamaica's Development,' *West Indian Law Journal* 43 (October, 1985) (A Special Issue Commemorating the 150th Anniversary of the Abolition of Slavery).

6 *Ibid.*

7 D.J. Murray, *The West Indies and the Development of Colonial Government, 1801-1834* (1965).

8 *Ibid.*

9 C.M. MacInnes, 'Constitutional Development of the British West Indies,' in *Developments Towards Self-Government in the Caribbean* 3 (A Symposium Held Under the Auspices of the Netherlands Universities Foundation for International Cooperation at The Hague, 1954).

10 Murray, *supra* note 7, at *xi*.

11 *Ibid. xii.*

12 *Ibid.*

13 *Ibid.* 3.

14 *Ibid.* 1.

15 *Ibid.* 26.

16 *Ibid.*

17 *Ibid.* 30.

18 *Ibid.* 205.

19 *Ibid.*

20 *Ibid.* 216.

21 H.A. Will, *Constitutional Change in the British West Indies, 1880-1903* 1 (1970).

22 *Ibid.* 2.

23 *Ibid. viii.*

24 *Ibid.* 22.

25 *Ibid. vii.*

26 Colin A. Hughes, 'Power and Responsibility: A Sociological Analysis of the Political Situation in the British West Indies,' in *Developments Towards Self-Government in the Caribbean* 95, *supra* note 9.

27 *Ibid.*

28 *Ibid.*

29 MacInnes, *supra* note 9, at 18.

30 Hughes, *supra* note 26, at 100.

31 MacInnes, *supra* note 9, at 19.

32 Hughes, *supra* note 26, 100.

33 E.W. Evans, 'A Survey of the Present Constitutional Situation in the British West Indies,' in *Development Towards Self-Government in the Caribbean* 23, *supra* note 9.

34 *Ibid.*

35 *Ibid.*

36 *Ibid.* 24.

37 *Ibid.*

38 *Ibid.*

39 *Ibid.* 25.

40 *Ibid.* 26.

41 *Ibid.*
42 *Ibid.*
43 Edward McWhinney, *Constitution-making: Principles, Process, Practice* 4 (1981).
44 *Ibid.*
45 *Ibid.* 24.
46 *Ibid.*
47 *Ibid.*
48 *Ibid.* 25.
49 *Ibid.*
50 *Ibid.*
51 *Ibid.* 38.
52 I am very grateful to Professor Woodville Marshall for stressing this point to me.
53 Trevor Munroe, *The Politics of Constitutional Decolonization: Jamaica 1944-62* 33 (1983).
54 *Ibid.* 64.
55 *Ibid.* 111.
56 *Ibid.*
57 Ann Spackman, *Constitutional Development of the West Indies, 1922-1968* 37 (1975).
58 Munroe, *supra* note 53, at 121.
59 *Ibid.* 122, 127.
60 *Ibid.* 128.
61 James B. Kelly, 'The Jamaica Independence Constitution of 1962,' 3 *Caribbean Studies* 18, 36 (1963).
62 Munroe, *supra* note 53, at 138.
63 *Ibid.*
64 *Ibid.*
65 *Ibid.* 152.
66 *Ibid.* 143.
67 Kelly, *supra* note 61, at 37.
68 From the *Proceedings of the Jamaica House of Representatives*, No. 4 at 719 (1961-62); quoted in Margaret DeMerieux, *Fundamental Rights in Commonwealth Caribbean Constitutions* 1 n. 2 (1992).
68ª See Kelley, *supra* note 61.
69 McWhinney, *supra* note 43.
70 Spackman, *supra* note 57, at 27.
71 McWhinney, *supra* note 43.
72 *Ibid.*
73 *Ibid.*
74 Ann Spackman, 'Constitutional Development in Trinidad & Tobago,' 4 *Social and Economic Studies* 283, 289 (1965).
75 *Ibid.* 290.
76 *Ibid.* 283.
77 *Ibid.* 291.
78 *Ibid.*
79 *Ibid.* 292.
80 *Ibid.* 293.
81 *Ibid.* 294.

82 *Ibid.*
83 I am very grateful to The Hon. Mr. Justice Mustapha Ibrahim for this point.
84 Spackman, *supra* note 74, at 298; Selwyn Ryan, *Race and Nationalism in Trinidad and Tobago* 314 (1972).
85 Spackman, *supra* note 74, at 298.
86 *Ibid.*
87 Ryan, *supra* note 84.
88 Spackman, *supra* note 74, at 298.
89 Ryan, *supra* note 84.
90 Spackman, *supra* note 74, at 298.
91 *Ibid.* 299.
92 *Ibid.* 300.
93 Ryan, *supra* note 84, at 319.
94 *Ibid.* 314; Spackman, *supra* note 74, at 301.
95 *Ibid.* 318.
96 *Ibid.* 316.
97 Quoted in *ibid.* 317.
98 Quoted in *ibid.* 329.
99 *Ibid.* 330.
100 *Ibid.* 332.
101 *Ibid.*
102 *Ibid.*
103 *Ibid.* The concessions were:
1.   Special entrenchment of an increased number of provisions by a three-fourths majority of the members of the lower house and a two-thirds majority of the members of the upper house.
2.   An independent boundaries commission which would delineate new constituencies which would vary by no more than a margin of 20 per cent.
3.   An elections commission which would be responsible for the conduct of elections and the registration of voters. The commission was also to be responsible for ensuring the accuracy and competence of voting machines and for seeing that these were fully tested and sealed in the presence of representatives of political parties. The commission was to be completed free of any direction or control from the executive or any other authority.
4.   The widening of the right of appeal to the Privy Council in matters other than constitutional rights.
5.   Limitation to six months of the period during which a proclamation of a state of emergency could remain in force without being extended by Parliament.
6.   Strengthening of the provisions for the independence of the auditor general.
7.   Entrenching of the provision that Trinidad remain a constitutional monarchy.
8.   Entrenching of provisions relating to the independence of the judiciary from partisan political pressure.
9.   Consultation with the Leader of the Opposition on important appointments including the chairmanship of the elections and boundaries commissions, and on all the important national issues. *Ibid.* 333.

104 *Ibid.* 336.
105 See Richard L. Cheltenham, *Constitutional and Political Development in Barbados 1946-1966.* (Ph.D. Thesis, 1970. Faculty of Economics and Social Studies, University of Manchester, England). This narrative of the Barbados situation is taken mainly from Dr Cheltenham's work.
106 *Ibid. vii.*
107 Evans, *supra* note 33, at 29.
108 *Ibid.*
109 Cheltenham, *supra* note 105, at 233.
110 Again, I wish to acknowledge my indebtedness to Professor Woodville Marshall for this point.
111 Cheltenham, *supra* note 105, at *ix.*.
112 *Ibid.* 1.
113 *Ibid.* 28.
114 *Ibid.*
115 *Ibid.* 29.
116 *Ibid.*
117 *Ibid.* 30.
118 *Ibid.* 35.
119 *Ibid.*
120 *Ibid.*
121 *Ibid.*
122 Frank Michelman, 'How Can the People Ever Make the Laws? A Critique of Deliberative Democracy,' in *Deliberative Democracy: Essays on Reason and Politics* 147 (James Bohman and William Rehg eds. 1997).
123 Seyla Benhabib, 'Deliberative Rationality and Models of Constitutional Legitimacy,' 1 *Constellations* 26, 31 (1994); quoted in Frank Michelman, *Id.* at 149.
124 Report of The Constitution Commission of Trinidad and Tobago, (1974), which was chaired by the late Sir Hugh Wooding.
125 I am very grateful to Dr Vasciannie for his very thoughtful comments in a letter to me, (May 20, 2000).
126 McWhinney, *supra* note 43, at 24.
127 Vasciannie, *supra* note 125.
128 Rex Nettleford, ed., *Norman Washington Manley & the New Jamaica : Selected Speeches & Writings 1938-1968* 124-5 (1971).
129 George Lamming, 'In the Castle of My Skin : Thirty Years After,' in *Conversations with George Lamming: Essays, Addresses & Interviews 1953-1990* 49 (Richard Drayton and Andaiye eds. 1994).
130 Vasciannie, *supra* note 125.
131 Donald S. Lutz, *The Origins of American Constitutionalism* 3 (1988).
132 *Ibid.* 13.
133 *Ibid.*
134 *Ibid.* 14.
135 Sheldon Wolin, 'Max Weber : Legitimation Method, and the Politics of Theory,' in *Legitimacy and the State* 63 (William Connolly ed. 1984).
136 Frederick A. Olafson, *The Dialectic of Action* 234 (1979).
137 *Ibid.*

138 Peter J. Steinberger, *Logic and Politics : Hegel's Philosophy of Right* 190 (1988).
139 Hanna Pitkin, 'The Idea of a Constitution,' 37 *Journal of Legal Education* 167 (1987).
140 *Ibid.* 168.
141 *Ibid.*
142 *Ibid.*
143 Lutz, *supra* note 131, at 6.
144 See Anne Norton, *Reflections on Political Identity*, Chapter One (1994).
145 William F. Harris, *The Interpretable Constitution xi* (1993).
146 *Ibid.*
147 *Ibid.* 6.
148 See Peter Russell, *Constitutional Odyssey : Can Canadians be a Sovereign People?* (1993), making the point that Canadians have not yet constituted themselves a sovereign people.
149 See, for example, the Terms of Reference of the Barbados Constitution Review Commission (1997).
150 See Peter Hogg, *Constitutional Law of Canada* 53-55 (1992).
151 Alan C. Cairns, *Charter versus Federalism : The Dilemmas of Constitutional Reform* 22 (1992).
152 *Ibid.*
153 *Ibid.* 20.
154 Jed Rubenfeld, *Freedom and Time: A Theory of Constitutional Self-Government* 13 (2001).
155 *Ibid.* 12.
156 *Ibid.* 13.
157 *Ibid.*
158 *Ibid.*
159 *Ibid.*
160 *Ibid.* at 14.
161 *Ibid.*
162 See also, Richard S. Kay, 'Constitutional Chrononomy,' 13 *Ratio Juris* 30 (2000).
163 Stephen Holmes, *Passions & Constraint : On the Theory of Liberal Democracy* 161 (1997).
164 Rubenfeld, *supra* note 154, at 14.
165 McWhinney, *supra* note 43, at 38.

Chapter 1

Constitutional Reform and Caribbean Political Identity

The Question of Origin

The story of *origin* of *West Indian Independence Constitutions*, briefly sketched in the Introduction, is very much a critical aspect of the story of Commonwealth Caribbean political identity. Not only did our constitutions come from Britain, as is evident in the fundamental design of our political institutions, but we have, we believe, for the most part, remained 'constitutional monarchies', with the British monarch serving as our head of state. On the understanding that she remains our queen, we continue to pledge allegiance to her. This, in essence, is the story we continue to tell about ourselves. In other words, the story of origin of our Independence Constitutions, plus the British monarch's continuing *presence* in the Commonwealth Caribbean political order, continues to foster our central notions of collective identity. In a most critical sense, therefore, *West Indian Independence Constitutions* remain our most prominent attempt at self-definition. They are our principal political texts. And, by 'accepting' or 'adopting' them as our own, we purport to share their conceptions of the world and human nature; to adopt their categories of speech, thought and action; to accept their definition of us as to the kind of people we are and wish to be.[1]

But the critical historical truth that 'our constitutions came from Britain', that the 'originating consciousness' behind the production of our constitutional texts was not our own, should make compelling our ambition for a rational reconstruction of a coherent constitutional narrative that would give expression to a vision of ourselves as a sovereign *people*, no longer in any way subject or subordinate to British sovereignty. In this regard, the current project of constitutional reform, now underway in several countries,[2] presents the most auspicious occasion for a 'new' beginning, for the possible construction of a new 'story of origin'. This exercise in constitutional reform must therefore be the occasion for a critical reassessment of our Independence Constitutions and constitutional practices, with a view to correcting and removing, once and for all, some of the more critical errors from our constitutional jurisprudence. This would necessarily engage us in the central interpretive task of rethinking the dominant, influential role of the British constitution on our constitutional design and practices. In other words, essential questions, such as the way in which our constitutions should be re-designed in order to better secure their essential purposes in our collective life; whether the British constitution with its mixture of hereditary and republican elements, and its central, organizing principle of parliamentary sovereignty, is the appropriate model of governance, should be engaged. But, above all, constitutional reform should be the occasion for a discursive engagement of the Caribbean citizenry on some of the larger questions of constitutional democratic governance: questions, for example, concerning the very process of constitutional founding; the amendment process; issues about presidential versus parliamentary democracy; proportional representation versus single-member districts; unicameralism versus bicameralism; legislative supremacy versus judicial review and, above all, the question whether the Caribbean should establish its own final Court of Appeal. The current undertaking of constitutional reform offers an auspicious occasion for philosophical reflection on our constitutional tradition and on the possibility of redefining our political and civic identity, thus removing it from the shadow of a dominant English theoretical perspective.

This chapter attempts to address some of these issues. For convenience, some of the 'terms of reference' of the Barbados Constitution Review Commission are mainly referred to, given that they address, by and large, the salient issues which must be addressed by the region as a whole. But the question of constitutional reform must be addressed within a broader constitutional theory of founding and amendability; a sketch of that theory is here immediately expressed.

Towards a Constitutional Theory of Founding and Amendability

In a democratic society, the constitution – constitutional law – is foundational: it concerns the most basic arrangements of political power in the community and establishes the ultimate ground for the legitimate exercise of political power by some over the rest of the society. It is the defining institution of political society. On this view, the constitution is constitutive of collective life, and it is for this very reason that the democratic founding of a constitution – the giving of form to collective life – is reckoned amongst the most notable acts of which political man is capable. According to Professor Sheldon Wolin, the founding of a constitution is superior to other types of political acts because it aims to shape the lives of citizens by designing the structure or 'dwelling' which they and their posterity will inhabit.[3]

Constitutional founding is therefore a defining act of collective and political identity. The truth of this proposition has been borne out in the act of founding on the American continent over two hundred years ago. When eighteenth-century Americans established their political independence from Britain, one of their most critical concerns was to define their collective identity as a 'separate people' so that they might rightfully 'assume among the powers of the earth, the separate and equal station to which the Laws of Nature and of Nature's God entitle them.'[4] In a word, they were concerned to define themselves collectively and politically, no longer in the British image. In fine, they created their own system of meaning; a new way of thinking and speaking of themselves. The founding of a constitution is therefore both a political and a hermeneutical event. As a political event, the American Constitution, for example, represented a settlement about power on terms supposedly agreed upon by the politically significant part of the population, according to the constructed 'myth' of the founding.[5] And as a hermeneutical event, the Constitution was a document whose content created a new structure of meaning which was to be interpreted.

Constitutional reform – the amending of a democratic constitution according to its own terms – is equally a political and a hermeneutical event: it addresses the most profound issues about constitutional essentials and basic justice on a critical understanding of the political ideals and values embraced by the very idea of constitutional governance. In seeking to 'revise' the original document of collective existence, a democratic people approximates a re-enactment of the founding act begun by the constitutional framers. This necessarily entails a critical engagement with the constitutional past; with what the framers had accomplished and failed to accomplish; and with the most appropriate ends or purposes for which the text was constructed. This link between founding and reform has been drawn most beautifully by Professor William Harris of the University of Pennsylvania:

> The *constitutiveness* (of making and grounding a new political world), the *interpretability* (of generating collective meaning

that sustains a particular form of politics from within its limits), and the *amendability* (of imagining more perfect or alternative versions of this political world) are intertwined in any compelling theory of the constitutional enterprise. This essential possibility of fundamental amendment or constitutional rethinking is included in the very concept of *constitution*, whether the devices for accomplishing it are given institutional form by the constitutional document or not.[6]

Constitutional reform, therefore, within an existing paradigm of constitutional democracy, is not a revolutionary act; it does not seek a radical transformation of the character of the constitution and of the political society. Neither does it seek 'to deconstitute and reconstitute' the constitutional order, or to abandon its primary principles.[7] In other words, it does not aim to achieve anything similar to what has been accomplished in Eastern Europe, where communist constitutions have been changed into liberal democratic ones. For what has been accomplished in Eastern Europe was nothing short of a wholesale destruction of the old and the creation of the new. On this view, the legal transformations underway in Eastern Europe must be seen as constitutional revolutions rather than constitutional revisions.[8]

Rather, constitutional reform places itself in a continuity of the temporal development of the legal order. It is a process of better realizing the substantive values already present in the legal order.[9] Constitutional reform therefore aims to make changes or corrections to the constitution that experience reveals to be required by justice or the general good, in order to strengthen the political values to which the society has committed itself. For example, one idea of constitutional reform, in the sense in which the term is herein used, is to adjust basic constitutional values to changing political and social circumstances, or to incorporate into the constitution a broader and more inclusive understanding of those values, of which the constitutional text is but a specific and historically contingent articulation.[10] The three Civil War Amendments to the US Constitution are an excellent example of the latter. At the Founding there was a blatant contradiction between the idea of equality in the Declaration of Independence and the Constitution and chattel slavery of a subjugated race. These amendments were therefore necessary to bring the Constitution more in line with its original promise as enunciated in its Preamble – 'to establish justice.'[11]

Equally important is the idea of constitutional reform of basic institutions in order to remove weaknesses that come to light in subsequent constitutional practice.[12] Such changes concern the institutional design of democratic government, and may involve such questions as whether to adopt a presidential or parliamentary system; whether a unicameral or bicameral legislature would best serve the ends of democratic governance in a particular society. What is of the utmost importance is that the structure of government be changed only as experience shows it to be required by political justice or the general good, and not as prompted by the political advantage of one party or group that may at the moment have the upper hand.[13]

Ideally, the founding and amending of a democratic constitution is the constituent act of a political society exercising an intellectual and moral power, rooted in the capacities of its human members, sharing the status of equal citizenship.[14] The subject of their reason is the good of the public: what a shared political conception of justice requires of society's basic structure of institutions, and of the purposes and ends they are to serve.[15] In other words, the whole enterprise of constitutional founding and reform must take place within a framework of what each citizen regards as a political conception of justice based on values that all can reasonably be expected to endorse, and of what each is, in good faith, prepared to defend as that conception so understood.[16] This must be so, for, to paraphrase Professor John Rawls, the act of constitutional founding and reform engages questions of constitutional essentials:

(a) The fundamental principles that specify the general structure of government and the political process: the powers of the legislature, executive and the judiciary; the scope of majority rule; and

(b) The equal basic rights and liberties of citizenship that legislative majorities are to respect: such as the right to vote and to participate in politics, liberty of conscience, freedom of thought and of association, as well as the protection of the rule of law.[17]

But we must be careful not to overstate the relationship between constitutional founding and reform to the point of conflating the two. Constitution-making stands as *the singular* act of the political sovereign conceived of as that which precedes law and creates law through its word.[18] That is to say, constitution-making involves the idea of an authority and an author whose willpower is the ultimate cause of the polity.[19] In a democratic society, the empirical subject of constituent power is the people; therefore, the constitution is the institutionalization of the people's will. This, for example, is the *story* of the American founding.

But does this constituent power remain unaffected by the act of creation, determined to re-emerge manifestly, to act as the guardian of the revolution and preserve the original and undomesticated spirit of the act of founding?[20] Or is the constituent power rather consumed by the very act of creating a constitution? Are the people, for example, free to unbind themselves – to repeal the commitments which have been stipulated in the constitution?

These are serious questions which are at the heart of the current debate in Europe and in the United States. In respect of the United States, for example, Professor Akhil Reed Amar of

Yale Law School has argued quite persuasively that the US Constitution may be amended outside of Article V by direct appeal to, and ratification by, the People.[21] He holds the view that the People – or more specifically a majority of them – enjoy the fundamental, inalienable and indefeasible right to amend the Constitution in ways not expressly provided for by the Constitution. After all, the Constitution guarantees to the People – or, at least, the People have guaranteed to themselves – the *public* liberty of democratic self-governance. Therefore, the People may amend their Constitution by a simple majority of the polity. Failing this, Amar argues, the Constitution loses its most defensible claim to derive from the People.[22]

For Amar, this right of the People follows naturally from the very idea of the People as the sovereign constitution maker; and, as sovereign constitution maker, they forever retain the right to alter or abolish their form of government. As sovereign, the people are incapable of waiving or relinquishing their sovereignty. This argument is reinforced by reference to certain words from the Declaration of Independence:

> That... Governments... derive[d] their just powers from the consent of the governed. That whenever any form of government becomes destructive of [its] ends, it is the right of the People to alter or abolish it, and to institute new Government, laying its foundations on such principles and organizing its Powers in such form, as to them shall seem most likely to effect their Safety and Happiness.[23]

These words from the Declaration of Independence are a ringing endorsement of the principle of democratic self-governance: the right of the people to amend, alter, or re-constitute their Government. The story of the American founding has in fact been a studied endorsement of this principle. The Constitution has legal force because it is presumed to derive from the People. The most relevant provisions in this regard are the Preamble, the First, Ninth and Tenth Amendments. The very logic of popular sovereignty, for example, itself implies that there is an unalienable core to the First Amendment right of free speech – that minimal amount of free expression constitutive of republican self-government itself, and logically implied by the People's right to alter and abolish.[24] So, for Amar, although the Constitution would have redefined the relevant polity, that redefinition did not change the basic nature of popular sovereignty.

But assuming *arguendo* that the people do have a right to alter or abolish their government outside of the amendment procedure, is this right a *legal* and *constitutional* right? Or is it rather a supra-constitutional, extralegal, philosophical, revolutionary principle, but definitely not a *legal* and *constitutional* right?[25]

One reading of the Constitution (and the Declaration of Independence) would suggest the former; that it is a *legal* and *constitutional* right. This is the view that the revolutionary *right* to alter and abolish government, articulated in the Declaration, has in fact been *domesticated* and *legalized* in the Constitution. The Constitution is the supreme law; the people have inscribed their sovereignty in that text. Therefore, the legal rules the Constitution has specified for its own amendment are part of the supreme law. In a word, the people have bound themselves to the stated procedure.

But does amendment outside of the amendment procedure necessarily imply amendment *outside* of the Constitution? If Amar is understood correctly, the answer is 'no'. This is so because, on an alternative reading, the People have retained the *constitutional right* to change their Constitution by legal mechanisms akin to the legal mechanisms by which they ordained and established it.[26] In sum, on a hermeneutic reading of the Constitution against the background of its founding, Amar understands the Constitution to have codified and given legal protection to the principle of popular sovereignty.

If this argument is sound, then what is of critical importance is not so much the correctness of Amar's specific claim that the US Constitution may be amended outside of Article V but, rather, his more fundamental claim that, once established, a democratic constitution in turn establishes the conditions under which all other constitutional norms may be legally displaced. In a word, the constitution may not be amended outside of the constitution, for there is no place in a constitutional polity for any kind of extraconstitutional power. The essential possibility of fundamental amendment or constitutional rethinking is included in the very concept of constitution, whether the devices for accomplishing it are given institutional form by the constitutional document or not. If this is correct, then it helps to answer our query: what happens to the constituent power in the act of creation? In short, is there an important theoretical distinction between the 'Sovereign People' and the 'Constitutional People' – the people as constitution-maker and the people 'created' by the constitution?

By the former is meant the sovereign constitution-making people conceived as a preconstitutional source of the constitution. And by the latter, the 'People' of the constitutional text, whose existence is deemed to be established with the constitutional authority of the document. From an empirical standpoint, the constitutional people made by the text and the popular sovereign are the same; but we may properly speak of the popular sovereign as the potential remaker of the constitutional order, capable of reasserting its revolutionary posture, and of maintaining its capacity to rethink the constitutional order as a whole.[27]

But the reality of constitution-making is that this sovereign people's identity is codified by the text; its sovereignty a function of the constitution, created by it for its own enactment and sustenance.[28] 'This People may be the author of the text, but it is also a textually bound creature of its own constituent act. And as a Constitutional People, it is constrained to act in ways that preserve and fulfill its collective identity, the core of its character as solemnly announced now in its self-revealing text.'[29] Put differently, 'the people are now bound within sets of institutional structures that direct the exercise of power, and in consequence, resistance to it... They are bound within systems of meaning that designate the attributes and accoutrements of power and that are constitutive of their political culture.'[30] So then, this sovereign power is, henceforth, always mediated by the constitution. This leads to two related questions: the question of 'self-binding,' and the question of the scope and limits of amendability. That is to say, the problem here is one of a sovereign power binding itself, and the implications of this for any possible limits on amendability.

Constitutional Self-binding

Indeed, a democratic constitution might be viewed as a principled expression in higher law of the political ideal of a people to govern itself in a certain way. Such a constitution is conceptually construed as an 'agreement' of the people among themselves as to how they wish to live their collective life. It is therefore conceivable that in a democratically ratified constitution, a people may be understood to have constrained their own quotidian legislative actions by some broader vision of what their political life should be like. For example, constitutional governance is generally understood to be consistent with the notion of entrenched basic rights beyond repeal, even by the people themselves. And the existence of terms by which the constitutional document specifies how it may be changed exclusively by its own institutional creatures (e.g. legislatures or conventions) further underscores this critical problem of constitutional self-binding. A classic argument for constitutional self-binding was made by

James Madison at the Federal Convention in Philadelphia. Madison observed that

> A people deliberating in a temperate moment, and with the experience of other nations before them, on the plan of Govt. most likely to secure their happiness, would first be aware, that those chargd. with the public happiness, might betray their trust. An obvious precaution agst. this danger wd. be to divide the trust between different bodies of men, who might watch & check each other....It would next occur to such a people, that they themselves were liable to temporary errors, thro' want of information as to their true interest, and that men chosen for a short term, & employed but a small portion of that in public affairs, might err from the same cause.... Another reflection equally becoming a people on such an occasion, wd. be that they themselves, as well as a numerous body of Representatives, were liable to err also, from fickleness and passion. A necessary fence agst. this danger wd. be to select a portion of enlightened citizens, whose limited number, and firmness might seasonably interpose agst. impetuous counsels. It ought finally to occur to a people deliberating on a Govt. for themselves, that as different interests necessarily result from the liberty meant to be secured, the major interests might under sudden impulses be tempted to commit injustice on the minority.[31]

Jon Elster, on this question of constitutional self-binding, speaks of political constitutions as examples of imperfect rationality, that is to say, as devices of precommitment against future weakness of will; devices that bind both the current people and future generations.[32] As was intimated earlier, the hurdles against constitutional change are commonly taken to be a form of *self-binding*. But constitutions rarely bind in an absolute sense, given that it is usually possible to unbind 'oneself' by going through the required procedure – except, of course, in those cases where there are constitutional clauses that cannot be undone by the usual amendment procedure or indeed in any other way. For example, the Constitution of West Germany made it impossible to undo the federal nature of the political system.[33] However, amendment clauses are constitutional constraints on constitutional change, designed to ensure some delay between the time a proposal to change the constitution is first made and when it is finally adopted.[34]

Still, this argument would seem to go against the early-modern notion of sovereignty, which was initially coupled with the idea of the absolute ruler.[35] By sovereignty was meant 'unfettered power of legislation.'[36] Therefore, the very idea of the sovereign being bound – even by its own enactment – seems a contradiction in terms. It is therefore necessary to recast the concept of sovereignty in terms appropriate to the core meaning of constitutional democracy; that is to say, the idea that sovereignty resides in the people as a whole.

This idea of popular sovereignty is a theoretical view of who does or ought to have power in a democratic society. But there must necessarily be mechanisms whereby the people express their sovereign power, given that the complexity of the modern pluralist society makes it impossible that there could be unanimity of action. The idea of popular sovereignty is therefore variously understood to mean 50 per cent plus one, as well as a plurality, or a supermajority. And, above all, the constitutional arrangements of political authority among legislative, executive, and judicial organs may correctly be viewed as a practical and normative device by which popular sovereignty expresses its will. What is of the utmost importance here is that once the sovereign people have expressed their will in a *written* constitution, they are *bound,* for the possibility of rescinding the *agreement* does not depend on the act of a single will. It would follow, then, that the idea of constitutional self-binding makes eminent sense in a way that the individual binding himself might not, or for that matter a legislature binding itself and its successors. The people are not as free to unbind themselves – to repeal the commitments which have been stipulated in the constitution. For in a pluralist society, it is always a matter of historical contingency whether the requisite democratic agreement for undoing the constitution will be summoned.

Once the idea of constitutional self-binding is grasped, the critical question of limits on amendability may now be addressed. The point of the foregoing argument is that those who constitute themselves in writing are in fact transformed by that writing: they attempt to bind themselves and their posterity to act within its authorized commands. The question remains as to the scope of the amendment power, one of the constitution's authorized commands. That is to say, may the *people* use the amendment power to make any changes they wish, or are they rather constrained by the fundamental character of the constitution and the nature of its political project?

Professor Walter Murphy notes that the word *amend*, which comes from the Latin *emendere*, means to correct or improve. Amend does not mean 'to deconstitute and reconstitute,' to replace one system with another or abandon its primary principles.[37] And according to Carl Schmitt, whatever the formal limits of the amendment process, its procedures cannot be used, either for logical or fundamental political reasons, to amend a constitution out of existence, or to create a new one.[38] In other words, the powers constructed by the constitution are provided to preserve, fulfill, and improve the document's project of sustaining the political world it has established.[39] For textual provisions, including the amendment provision, do not purport to debilitate the power they delineate; nor do they represent verbal warrants to unmake other commitments of the document in which they are situated or to undo the conditions for its political meaningfulness.[40] So, to repeat, in the act of constitution, the people agree or 'bind' themselves to live within the substantive limits in the constitutional text, and therefore within its structures of meaning. The amending power must therefore be understood in terms of a broader understanding of the character and meaning of the constitutional order purportedly established by the text. This means that the proper scope of the amendment power is to correct, improve and strengthen the foundational terms of the political order. For it is precisely the need to maintain the nature of the constitutional order, to refine the character of its political structure and thus to prevent the overthrow of its institutions of governance, that animates amendability in the first place.[41] On this view, the question arises as to the proper limits on the amending power. In other words, are there certain terms of the constitutional order that are beyond amendment? For example, might the amending power be used to repeal the right of free speech or of the equal protection of the law? Might the amendment power be used to introduce a new substantive norm that contradicts, rather than elaborates, the existing constitution?[42]

It is submitted that such 'amendments' to a democratic constitution would be substantively *unconstitutional*, notwithstanding that they might meet the formal requirements of *legal* validity, for such 'amendments' would be in contradiction with the fundamental character of the constitutional text, even though they may conform to the document's legalistic criteria for addition.[43] So, assuming that such 'amendments' would be legally binding, they would nonetheless constitute a fundamental contradiction within the constitutional text and represent a serious challenge to its integrity and coherence of meaning. The question therefore remains as to how a supreme court would negotiate such contradictions.

In sum, then, the amending power is ultimately constrained by the fundamental character of the constitutional text and the nature of the political order it recommends. For amendment, as a process of reform, is bound by the rule of law as well as the substantive limits in the constitutional document as a whole. That is to say, constitutional changes, even to the prescribed amendment procedure itself, must take place within an understanding of the core meaning of constitutional democracy. The legal process for amending the constitution expresses a deeper value of fidelity: it honours the deepest norms of the constitution. Fundamental rights, for example, are defining elements of the fundamental nature of a democratic republican constitution; therefore, they could not possibly be substantively changed in fidelity to the constitution. In other words, an amendment to amend away fundamental rights may be treated by judges as *unconstitutional* – that is to say, as violative of the first principles of a democratic constitutional order, despite formal compliance with the amendment procedure.

Commonwealth Caribbean Constitutions

It is submitted that constitution making and constitutional reform are quintessential political acts.[44] In addition to addressing basic problems regarding models of right governance, they are attempts at forging a common self-identity rooted in a shared constitutional text. Indeed, the fundamental question of constitutional studies is that of the relation between the constitutional choices a people make and the kind of people they become.[45] Who or what they are is a contingent achievement, the product of a particular history and geography and specific constitutional arrangements and policies.[46] For 'a constitution not only constitutes a structure of power and authority; it constitutes a people in a certain way. It proposes a distinctive identity and envisions a form of politicalness for individuals in their new collective capacity.'[47] The Preamble to the US Constitution, for example, although it has no judicial standing, is a striking example of the assertion of a new collective identity replacing the one expressed in the Articles of Confederation. It specifies the political values by which the new collectivity aspires to be known.[48]

Indeed, the act of writing a nation's constitution – of constituting a nation in writing – bears the coincidence of power and semeiotics: the exercise of power and the inscription of meaning.[49] The constitution is the act that founds the nation and the sign that marks it.[50] The act of writing a constitution is an act of signification: an expression and annunciation of collective identity. Thus, in the act of constitution, a democratic people agree to bind themselves to live within institutional structures that direct the exercise of political power, and within systems of meaning that are constitutive of their political culture.

Collective identity, which is largely defined by the constitution, is not merely an inheritance. Rather, it is, in large measure, created by and perpetuated through a public discourse which consists of the vocabulary, ideologies, symbols, images, memories, and myths that have come to form the ways a people think and talk about their political life.[51] Cognisance of this puts in high relief the fact that *West Indian Independence Constitutions* are enactments of the British Imperial Parliament. This, joined with the common understanding that the 'Crown' remains a potent symbol of Commonwealth Caribbean constitutional identity, and with the presence of the British Privy Council at the apex of our legal system, gives substance to the claim that our constitutional discourse and political identity reflect and are shaped by a cluster of values, intellectual orientations and practices that carry a distinctly British cast. The current undertaking of constitutional review and reform must therefore proceed on a comprehensive and critical understanding of our constitutional world;

on a rethinking of the basic presuppositions of our founding and constitutional practices, in order to determine whether we may wish to reaffirm and/or to remake the foundational terms of our political order; in short, whether the Commonwealth Caribbean political order can be sustained on its own affirmative account. In fine, the supreme challenge is whether this opportunity should be seized for constitutional reform to reconstruct Commonwealth Caribbean political identity under the nurturance of amended constitutional arrangements.

With political independence, we became the holders of constituent power and, as the holders of constituent power, we are in a position to exercise our will to redefine our 'constitutional self' in our own image; to 'create a political world *ex nihilo*.'[52] Of course, as Professor Michel Rosenfeld of the Benjamin Cardozo Law School observes, in the realm of human affairs, there is ultimately no such thing as creation *ex nihilo*.

> Not even the radical rupture of violent revolution makes for complete differentiation between prerevolutionary and postrevolutionary political orders. In many cases, prerevolutionary traditions are not completely eradicated, but transformed and selectively incorporated into the new order fashioned by the constitutional subject.[53]

Still, the point is made: if the making and amending of a constitution is a constituent act, then, in the current endeavour we are faced with the question of choice – whether we would use the amendment process to effectuate a thorough overhaul of our constitutions, thus truly giving to ourselves a '*new*' constitutional '*image*', or whether we would merely engraft a few changes onto the core structure, thereby leaving our constitutional identity virtually unchanged. An example of a truly profound change would be an amendment of the very process by which the constitutions are to be amended. In the Commonwealth Caribbean we have largely accepted or voluntarily acquiesced in the terms of our Independence Constitutions, and are subject to the weight of their prescriptions, notwithstanding our rather nebulous and tangential relation (as a people) to their creation. We may therefore wish to use this opportunity for constitutional reform to ensure that, henceforth, our constitutions are conceived as acts of our constituent will.

The point may be better appreciated if the issue of constitutional founding in the Commonwealth Caribbean were placed in high relief against the process of constitutional founding on the American continent back in 1787. The constitutional enterprise on the American continent represented the deliberative founding of a polity in words. At a most sublime level, it carries the biblical image of Yahweh creating the universe by speaking words, thereby giving form to inchoate matters. The story of the Constitution's origin is told *as if* the whole people were the Constitution's author.[54] Note that the Preamble speaks specifically of the collective origin and scope of the Constitution in designating its author as 'We the people'. 'The precise historical veracity of this story of the whole people constituting themselves into a polity may well be open to qualification, but disproof would not invalidate it.'[55] Indeed, at the time of the American founding, the 'people' who in fact exercised constituent power, the authors and ratifiers of the Constitution, were a group of propertied white men, who were in no way representative of all those who would be subjected to their constitutional prescriptions.[56] Still, the ritual story over time of the people constituting themselves gives credence to a view of the Constitution as 'the authoritative language of the American people.'[57] Thus, 'the constitutional "People of the United States" is an exemplar of constitutive self-referentiality.'[58] As Chief Justice Jay puts it in *Chisholm v. Georgia*,

The people, in their collective and national capacity, established the present Constitution. It is remarkable that in establishing it, the people exercised their own rights, and their own proper sovereignty, and conscious of the plenitude of it, they declared with becoming dignity, "We the People of the United States", "do ordain and establish this Constitution."[59]

The logic of the above argument extends equally to amending or changing the Constitution. That the Constitution derives its authority from the people as a whole admits of their fundamental right to 'alter or abolish the established Constitution, whenever they find it inconsistent with their happiness.'[60] Thus,

> Until the people have, by some solemn and authoritative act, annulled or changed the established form, it is binding upon themselves collectively, as well as individually; and no presumption, or even knowledge, of their sentiments, can warrant their representatives in a departure from it, prior to such an act.[61]

The theory of the origin of the American Constitution places the people in the *constitutive* position, as *pourvoir constituant*, where they must *remake* the political world. In a word, the American polity is a manifestation of collective speech.[62]

On the American continent, various towns had objected, in principle, to the idea that either a legislature could properly draft or could approve a constitution meant to be supreme over that very legislature. It was rather on the strength of this skepticism that the 'first true constitutional convention in Western history, a body of representatives elected for the exclusive purpose of framing a constitution, met in Cambridge, Massachusetts on September 1, 1779.'[63] Its draft constitution was to go into effect only when independently ratified by the towns.[64] The founding of the American

Constitution would later follow this procedure; so that the federal constitution was neither drafted nor ratified by legislatures – 'continuous governmental institutions of incumbents with an incidental and secondary commission to pass on the national charter.'[65] This procedure of constitutional founding serves to reinforce the claim that 'The people are the only legitimate fountain of power, and it is from them that the constitutional charter, under which the several branches of government hold their power, is derived.'[66] And, of course, these derived powers have no authority to rewrite the commission under which they function.[67] As Madison remarked, 'the important distinction so well understood in America between a constitution established by the people and unalterable by the government, and a law established by the government, seems to have been little understood and less observed in any other country.'[68] Thus, constitutional amendment by a simple or special parliamentary majority is inconsistent with the kind of constitutionalism of which Madison and Hamilton had conceived.

The story of the American founding then, is in essence that of a shared belief in the 'fiction' that the government is of, by, and for the people; that what really happened in 1787 was that the Founding Fathers invented the idea of the American people and used it to impose a government on the actual, living subjects of the new nation. The American founding in fact entailed a reassessment of the British Constitution, with its central principle of parliamentary sovereignty, as a leading exemplar of constitutional government. This doctrine of parliamentary sovereignty had the consequence of endowing Parliament not simply with a part of the powers of government, but with the people's inherent power to begin, change, and end governments.[69] It is true that some degree of plausibility derived from the election of the House of Commons (at that time) by what passed for a popular vote. That is to say, parliamentary elections were the act by which the people supposedly endowed Parliament with their sovereign power.

In Britain, this theory of parliamentary sovereignty as it evolved left no room to the people for any higher expression of their will. On the American continent, there was therefore the need to establish a set of fundamental laws or 'fundamental constitutions' that would embody the will of the people in some enduring way, superior to the changing needs and ambitions of the persons who might be designated to conduct the day-to-day operations of government.[70] This, as Professor Edmund Morgan of Yale University puts it, required a scheme of government that gave a separate and superior institutional voice to the people, to protect them as subjects from themselves as governors.[71] In other words, a scheme of government within which to locate the people's rights as subjects and at the same time recognize their sovereignty. This was effected by the use of the elected convention that would express enduring popular will in fundamental constitutions superior to government.[72] Of course, this idea was fictional, for it ascribed to one set of elected representatives meeting in convention a more popular character, and consequently a greater authority, than every subsequent set of representatives meeting as a legislature.[73]

The problem for the Americans was how to overcome the characterization or perception of the Constitution as legislative enactment – a creature of Parliament – rather than the constituent act of the people constituting a separate and superior authority to that of Parliament. The American revolutionary and constitutional project was therefore to show that a more legitimate form of constitutionalism than that of the British was indeed practicable. Accordingly, they defined their task as that of constructing a new kind of republican government that could learn from the excesses of the classical republics without accepting the anti-republican premises of the British Constitution with its hereditary classes (the monarchy and the House of Lords).[74]

The American model of constitutional founding gave the people at large a more direct part in the process of establishing or altering the fundamental law. 'To entrust this task to a legislature which performed the work of day-to-day governance would not satisfy the American demand for a fundamental law binding on the legislature itself.'[75] And, as was earlier intimated, this argument extends to ratification as well. At all cost, it was necessary to avoid ratification by the state legislatures, for that procedure, it was reasoned, would have put the law of the Constitution on the same legal footing as other laws of those bodies.[76] 'A state which had ratified by an act of its legislature could therefore by a similar instrument legally override provisions of the constitution or laws made under its authority, or indeed revoke its original assent and withdraw from the Union.'[77]

The American founding therefore underscored the original inalienable power of a people to determine their own political institutions. This power to make and remake the constitutional framework, whether exercised as the unlimited power of the people or as the amending power, was not the agent of normal, day-to-day governance.[78] This could otherwise be explained in terms of Ackerman's conception of the dualist nature of the Constitution.[79] The philosophical core of Ackerman's claim is based on the eighteenth century American theory of popular sovereignty, according to which valid constitutions and constitutional revisions are acts of the sovereign people outside of all duly-constituted legislatures.[80]

From the foregoing, it is obvious that the American constitutional founding was not intended to imitate or reenact English parliamentary traditions and politics. In fact, the Constitution defied English precedent by denying its basic premise regarding the source of legitimate power.[81]

> The generation that framed the American form of government meant it to be, not only in mechanism but in theory, a contradiction to opinions commonly accepted in Europe.

The men who made the Constitution intended to make by its means an issue with antiquity; they had a clear conception of the issue itself, and of their own purposes in raising it. These purposes were perhaps chimerical; the hopes then felt were almost certainly delusive. Yet persons who grant the probable failure of the scheme, and expect the recurrence of the great problems in government which were thought to be solved, cannot but look with satisfaction at the history of the Federal Constitution as the most convincing and most interesting experiment ever made in the laboratory of political science, even if it demonstrates the impossibility of success through its means.

The great object of terror and suspicion to the people of the thirteen provinces was *power*; not merely power in the hands of a president or of a prince, of one assembly or several, or many citizens or of few, but of power in the abstract, wherever it existed and under whatever name it was known. "There is and must be", said Blackstone, "in all forms of government, however they began or by what right soever they exist, a supreme, irresistible, absolute, uncontrolled authority, in which the *jura summi imperii*, or the rights of sovereignty, reside", and Parliament is the place "where that absolute despotic power which must in all governments reside somewhere is entrusted by the Constitution of the British kingdoms." Supreme, irresistible authority must exist somewhere in every government – was the European belief; and England solved her problem by entrusting it to a representative assembly to be used according to the best judgment of the nation. America, on the other hand, asserted that the principle was not true; that no such supreme power need exist in a government; that in the American government none such should be allowed to exist, because absolute power in any form was inconsistent with freedom, and that the new government should start from the idea that the public liberties depend upon denying uncontrolled authority in the political system in its parts or its whole.[82]

Note, for example, that sovereignty, in the sense of the ultimate authority in the state was, according to English jurisprudence, vested in parliament, while in American jurisprudence, it was in the American people in their constituent capacity. Thus, whereas in English jurisprudence there is no man-made law vesting sovereignty in parliament, given that parliament is itself the ultimate author of such law; in American jurisprudence, to the contrary, the idea of a government bound by the (man-made) law of a constitution was made a living reality. In consequence, British jurisprudence has ascribed to parliament, rather than to the people, a peculiar prominence in the making and unmaking of the fundamental law. In British jurisprudence, government could be self-limiting in accordance with its inner mechanisms, but it could not be limited or conditioned by a superior man-made law setting out the organs and procedures of government and the purposes, such as the protection of individual rights and the promotion of the public interest, which the government was to serve.[83]

The contrast drawn between the British and American models of constitution making and reform teaches an instructive lesson for the current enterprise of Commonwealth Caribbean constitutional reform. It bears emphasis that the making of West Indian Independence Constitutions stands in sharp contrast to that of the American Constitution. The Independence Constitutions are Orders-in-Council of the British Imperial Parliament. They are in fact amended versions of the colonial constitutions, with Bills of Rights engrafted onto them. This meant an empirical constitutional continuity, which provided for an easy transition from colony to independent state. This continuity implied no important changes between the colonial and Independence Constitutions. The parliamentary system remained virtually the same, and the constitutions, for the most part, are said to have remained monarchical.

It is submitted that the nurturance in the tradition of British constitutional theory and practice has rather encouraged some form of parliamentary sovereignty rather than democratic constitutionalism in constitutional creation and revision. *West Indian Independence Constitutions* have, in the main, reserved to parliament the extraordinary power to conclude and amend the fundamental law. In other words, the British model of parliamentary constitution making and revision remains very much an entrenched idea of Commonwealth Caribbean constitutional practice, in opposition to the American idea of constitution making power – *pouvoir constituant* – which would exclude legislative and executive powers from the constitutional convention. Therefore, the marked distinction that American theory draws between constitution making and revision, on the one hand, and normal legislative politics, on the other, does not hold for the West Indies.

The Amending Power

A constitution is in its very essence amendable. This characteristic arises from the central logic by which it becomes a *constitution*.[84] Thus a constitution, conceived of as the fundamental institutional authority in a democratic society for collective decision making in pursuit of the common good under a condition of popular sovereignty, in fact rests on an assumption about human fallibility. And human fallibility implies the need for some method of altering or revising the constitution after experience has revealed its flaws and unintended consequences. 'Originally, therefore, the [idea of the] amendment process was predicated not only on the need to adapt to changing circumstances but also on the need to compensate for the limits of human understanding and virtue.'[85] A written constitution deliberately establishing a public order for life generally specifies how it may be changed exclusively by its institutional creatures, and tends to limit the sovereign power of the people as putative constitution maker.[86] The amending power, like all other powers organized in a constitution, is a delegated, and hence a limited power. As the political philosopher Carl Schmitt has observed, whatever the formal limits of the amendment process, its procedures cannot be used, either for logical or fundamental political reasons, to amend a constitution out of existence, or to create a new one.[87] In a word, the amendment power within the constitutional document may not be used to transform the very foundational terms of the constitutional world. Thus, even, as in the case of the United States, where the people are conceived of as the 'author' of the text, they are, in consequence, a textually bounded creature of their own constituent act and, as a constitutional people, they are constrained to act within the terms of the document in order to preserve and fulfill their collective identity. As Justice Byron White of the US Supreme Court has written: 'The sovereignty of the people is itself subject to those limitations which have been duly adopted and remain unrepealed.'[88]

The essential possibility of fundamental amendment or constitutional rethinking, is included in the very concept of constitution and the occasion of such an exercise may be driven by certain factors, such as the fact that the normative views of the citizens may change; their factual beliefs about institutional means to political ends may be modified as they learn more about the effects of the system; or changes in external factors such as technology or international relations may force a rethinking about constitutional matters.[89] The question therefore arises as to the legitimate scope of the amending power or what is legitimately entailed by the concept of amendability. In other words, if constitutional amendment according to the terms of the document is change generated from the *inside*, that is, change bound by the rules of the constitutional enterprise, as Professor William Harris puts it, then, can the amendment power be used to transform the constitutional order into a new one, thus inferentially constructing a new story of origin? How far, in other words, can one get outside of the existing constitutional order – that is, at what point can it be said that the political 'linguistics' of the current constitutional system that we have are no longer being used?[90] For Barbados and Jamaica and the rest of the Commonwealth Caribbean, the crucial question is, whether we would still be within the bounds of legitimate amendment if we were to aspire to a rewriting of the constitutional text, making such fundamental changes such as introducing a new amendment and ratification scheme adequate to the text's nature as a constitution and not a legislative document. In other words, can the people of Barbados exercise their sovereign authority to amend the Constitution outside of Parliament, thus superseding Parliament as the pivotal agency in the amending process?

Indeed, questions of amendability may throw light back on themes such as the theory of constitution writing, the nature of 'constitutionalism' as preoccupied with the setting of limits, the constraints on constitutional interpretation, and the status of ritualistic stories of origin about the source of the Constitution's authority – whether in a sovereign people or in a supreme parliament.[91] A careful distinction must therefore be drawn between amending a constitution and changing a constitution in the sense of putting a new and different constitution in place of the old. As George Ticknor Curtis perceptively observes, the existence and operation of a prescribed method of changing particular features of a government marks the line between amendment and revolution, and render resort to the latter, for the purpose of amelioration or reform, save in extreme cases of oppression, unnecessary. Thus, the process of amendment, according to prescribed form, preserves the continuity of the existing system of government, and changes only such of its fundamental rules as require revision, without the destruction of any public or private rights that may have become vested under the former rule.[92] So 'even were the whole people, by unanimous action, to effect organic changes in modes forbidden by the existing organic law, it would be an act of revolution.'[93] Therefore, the sense in which the term 'amendment' is herein used is to suggest additions to, or deletions from, the text of the constitution consistent with its spirit or tenor and according to its letter. And a change of the constitution, means the creation of an entirely new text that rests on a new or different – dominant – political theory or ideology. In other words, a revision or rewriting of the constitution in order to make more evident its fundamental promises and intentionality would be a legitimate amendment and would not constitute a change of the constitution.

The problem may be otherwise explained in terms of the difference between a constitution and a statute, that is, the difference between 'a rule which exists in its own right (constituted by assumptions of its own bindingness) and a rule which exists because it is valid under a higher rule (where the assumptions of bindingness are of the bindingness of that higher rule).'[94] Only a constitution (the historically first constitution) or rule of recognition exists in its own right and not by virtue of its validity under a higher rule of recognition. Anything therefore validly enacted under this ultimate rule of recognition will be called a statute.[95] If, then, the amendment provision of an historically first constitution is used to amend the constitution, the constitution resulting from the amendment is a statute. Treating the resulting amendment as a statute helps to preserve the distinction between a rule which exists in its own right and a rule which exists because it is validly enacted.

But could the amendment provision be used to amend itself? On the above reasoning, the amended amendment provision is a statute. But does the old provision continue to exist as the source of validity of the statute? There is obvious confusion here in treating the resulting amendment as a statute, since the latter actually becomes part of the constitution. This has led some scholars to conclude that 'a rule of recognition cannot ever justify its own amendment because any amendment which it justifies (validates) must by definition be a statute, something, conceptually separate, not something part of itself.'[96] The Scandinavian jurist, Alf Ross, for example, argues that 'the rules of the Constitution governing the special procedure for amending the Constitution are rules which establish a constituent authority distinct from the legislative.'[97] Ross was speaking specifically in reference to article V of the United States Constitution:

> According to art. V any amendment of the Constitution requires the ratification by three-fourths of the states. If by this majority it is decided that in the future a ratification by four-fifths of the states shall be required, the new rule of amendment cannot be regarded as derived from the old one. If that were the case it would be possible to amend the new basic norm in the same procedure in which it had been created, that is, by a majority of three-fourths, and the present amendment rule would continue to be the highest norm of the system.[98]

Thus, for Ross, art. V cannot be legally amended. 'Any amendment of art. V of the Constitution which in fact is carried out is an alegal act, and not the creation of law by way of a procedure that has been instituted.'[99] By this Professor Ross is understood to be saying that an amendment to art. V must logically hold a different status to that of any other constitutional amendment. That is to say, an amendment to art. V would radically change the Constitution in a way another would not.

Ross's challenges can be met by keeping the conceptual distinction between a constitution (the ultimate rule of recognition) and a statute. On the logic of this distinction any new amend-ment (even an amendment of the amending provision) is valid on the authority of the constitution – which is itself valid in its own right. Thus, even though an amendment is different from ordi-nary legislation in that it becomes part of the constitution whereas the latter does not, still, there is pre-existing (legal) authority for determining what can validly become part of the constitution. Therefore, we may confront the paradox of self-amendment by noting that, by an act of pre-commitment, a dem-ocratic people – the constituent power – may determine that their power to amend the constitution may be written into the text and transferred to the legislature, say, upon the adoption of the con-stitution. In other words, the people may determine that, upon the adoption of the constitution, any amendment thereto accord-ing to the procedures stipulated in the constitution would become part of the law of the constitution.

The foregoing discussion is particularly relevant to the instant question of constitutional reform in the Commonwealth Caribbean, given parliament's role as the pivotal agency in the amending process. We may wish to rethink this, thus instituting a greater role for the people in the amending process. It must be remembered that amending a constitution is part of the funda-mental and ongoing task of constitutional creation. Therefore, it is of the very essence of the constitutional enterprise that a govern-ment (either a legislature or a combination of governmental agents) cannot constitute, since political creatures cannot plausibly define the terms of their creation, nor plausibly construct a warrant for their own existence, character, and power.[100]

The issue of parliament as the exclusive amending agency in Commonwealth Caribbean Constitutions must therefore be seri-ously addressed. This speaks to a broader issue of the 'supremacy of the constitution versus the supremacy of parliament,' which remains a viable issue in West Indian constitutional discourse given the plenitency of parliament's power with respect to the founding and altering of the fundamental law. Under Commonwealth Caribbean constitutions, generally, this power to 'alter or amend the constitution' has been left wholly with parliament. This power is in fact included among the powers of parliament 'to make laws for the order and good governance of society.' Section 49 of the Barbados Constitution, for example, states that, 'subject to the provisions of this section, Parliament may, by an Act of Parliament passed by both Houses, alter this Constitution.'[101]

This is a legacy of British constitutional practice, whose central premise is the sovereignty of parliament – sovereignty in the sense of the ultimate authority in the state; the 'unfettered power of legislation.' Thus, it has been said that, in Britain, there could be no man-made law vesting sovereignty in parliament, since parliament is the ultimate author of such law.[102] So, as Professor Richard Kay of the University of Connecticut has observed, English judges have responded to challenges to the validity of Acts of Parliament not by citing some legal authority for the rule of parliamentary supremacy, but by putting it forward as an axiom of the legal system:[103]

> What the statute itself enacts cannot be unlawful, because what the statute says is itself the law, and the highest form of law that is known to this country. It is the law which prevails over every other form of law, and it is not for the court to say that a parliamentary enactment, the highest law in this country, is illegal.[104]

'This language faithfully reflects the doctrine of parliamentary supremacy which has been, for more than two hundred years, dogma in British law.'[105] Of course, the idea of parliamentary sovereignty rests on a fundamental logical error. For, in modern political theory, it is commonly understood that it is the state as a single, irreducible whole that is sovereign; and this sovereignty may *actively* manifest itself in one or another of its members. Thus, to say that parliament is sovereign over against the rest of the state, including the constitution itself, is to ignore the state's fundamental unity.[106]

Still, the substantive vision underlying the practice of constitutional amendment under Westminster model constitutions is a vision of parliamentary, rather than popular, sovereignty. This is necessarily so because the process by which the British imperial government devolved sovereignty upon the former colonies in the Commonwealth Caribbean engaged the elected representatives to the virtual exclusion of the people at large. It were as though parliament – or at least some of the representatives – had garnered the power to constitute the fundamental law and, by extension, had reserved to itself the fundamental 'right' to amend and alter it. As Mr. Justice Diplock has put it – quite diplomatically: 'Constitutions of the Westminster model, of which the Constitution of the Republic of Trinidad and Tobago is an example, provide for their future alteration by the people acting through their representatives in the Parliament of the state.'[107] This might afford one plausible explanation as to the way the English principle of parliamentary sovereignty was imported into post-independence West Indian constitutional law and practice.

But if the matter of constitutional revision and reform is to be taken seriously, we must accord due regard to one of the central principles of democratic constitutionalism: that constitution making and revision occupy a different democratic 'plane' to normal legislative politics.[108] And for this, the American rejection of parliamentary constitution making and revision remains the best starting point.[109] It is notorious that constitutional founding on the American continent roundly rejected the notion of parliamentary sovereignty 'as a bare assertion of factionalized self-aggrandizing power masquerading as an elevated impartiality in the balanced assessment of evolving historical practice for the greater good of all.'[110] In consequence, the American Constitution enjoys a special eminence above all other law; and the elaborate process for its amendment is not simply to protect the citizenry from the tyranny of changing factions within the society, but is rather a deeper expression of a constitutional faith that the Constitution, as the constituent act of a sovereign people, must be amended in a manner designed to approximate the same sort of collective exercise of deliberative reflection on an enduring constitutional design.

It is therefore regrettable that, in our blind 'faith' in the English constitutional tradition, we have ignored the instructive lessons of the American founding. By making the power to amend the constitution virtually the exclusive province of the legislature, we have, maybe quite unwittingly, in fact reinforced the claim of parliamentary sovereignty as a viable principle of Commonwealth Caribbean constitutional law and practice. As James Madison perceptively observed, whenever legislatures retain the power of constitutional revision, they are in a position to establish themselves as oligarchical replacements of the power they claim to represent.[111] For,

> Evidently, when questions of changing the operations or institutional relationships of the legislature are the themes of constitutional revision, the legislature should not be the body with power to judge the issue on its own behalf. Even more importantly, if constitutionalism is to be a limit on the operation of the legislative branch of government, it is unwise to allow the same legislature the power to alter the relevant limits according to its own design.[112]

Emphasizing special legislative majorities for altering the constitution does not change anything in principle. It only serves to link the avoidance of ill effects to contingent electoral outcomes.[113]

Thus, in the final analysis, putting constituent power in the hands of legislatures may either lead to frivolous use of constitutional revision, which produces patchwork constitutions, or to increased constitutional inflexibility in order to counteract potential constitutional chaos.[114]

But Commonwealth Caribbean constitutions are written texts; and this fact of writtenness must carry important consequences for giving effect to the principles of democratic constitutionalism. Thus, notwithstanding the peculiar way by which Commonwealth Caribbean constitutions were drawn, conceptually, they are not the creatures of any parliament; and, more specifically, the local parliaments are the creatures of the Independence Constitutions. The parliaments derive all authority – including the very power to amend – from the constitutions. For, in a constitutional democracy, amending bodies like parliament are not sovereign, given that they derive their authority internally from the constitutional scheme, which attributes its authorization to a full and sufficient sovereign outside itself.[115] And this plenary constitution-making sovereignty cannot be delegated to any set of agents in the world it has created. Therefore, to say that parliament (as an amending body) is sovereign is to assume a relocation of the sovereignty on which a democratic constitution is established, moving it to an agency created within the constitution and derivative from it.[116]

Therefore, on the logic of the claim that constitutional revision is part of an ongoing process of constitution making in a democratic society, it would be a fundamental contradiction in terms for the legislature, say, a political creature, to define the terms of its own creation. To this extent, a purely parliamentary procedure for constitutional review would seem quite undemocratic. On this view, in the practical amending process, where the *machinery* of government purports to act as the *agent* of the people in its sovereign capacity, we are well advised to keep in mind the necessary distinction between the power to legislate embodied in an elected representative assembly, on the one hand; and on the other hand, what today would be called the constituent power – that is, the power to begin, end, or alter the government of which that assembly is a part.[117] For the existence of terms by which a constitutional document specifies how it may be changed exclusively by its own institutional creatures, such as the legislature, may tend to limit and debilitate the sovereign power of the people as putative constitution maker, whose authorizing of the text depends on its ability to will it to be other than it is.[118]

It therefore behoves us to rethink quite carefully the enormous powers of parliament – (or rather, the powers of a prime minister *through* parliament?) – under Commonwealth Caribbean Westminster model constitutions. For the vesting of the full-scale amending power in parliament may have (and has had) the consequence of subjecting the integrity of the constitution itself to the virtually unrestrained will of those who hold power in trust for the sovereign people. In very recent times, the almost callous 'tinkering' with the Trinidad and Tobago Constitution by the then People's National Movement (PNM) government in its attempt to have the Speaker of the House removed from office, should serve to underscore the point. The idea here is not to remove parliament completely from any involvement in the amendment process; rather, it is to make parliament a partner with the electorate in the amending of the Fundamental Law. Put simply, the amending power in a constitutional democracy must assume the existence of a sovereign people authorizing the constitutional settlement and capable of reshaping it.[119]

In light of the foregoing arguments, Barbados, for example, may consider amending the very amendment provision of its Constitution; the overriding reason being to have the amendment process approximate the same sort of collective exercise of deliberative reflection ideally required for the creation of the original document in a democratic polity. This is, at bottom, the problem of 'precommitment and the paradox of democracy' which necessarily attends the question of constitution making in a democratic society. As Professor Jon Elster of the University of Chicago explains it, we may consider political constitutions as examples of imperfect rationality, that is, as devices of pre-commitment against future weakness of will. 'To the extent that constitutions are considered as devices that bind later generations, we may inquire into the optimal tightness of the bounds as well as the optimal difficulty of untying them.'[120]

The idea is to posit a constitution in a democratic society as a 'higher law' that cannot (or ought not) be changed through normal lawmaking procedures in a popularly elected assembly. In other words, exceptional legal entrenchment that exempts constitutional rules from the majoritarian controls that govern ordinary legislation, is designed to discourage frivolous attempts to amend or revise the constitution every time a political crisis arises. In short, to ensure some delay between the time a proposal to change the constitution is first made and when it is finally adopted.[121]

Now, it is commonly asserted that constitutional constraints on constitutional change constitute a form of 'self-binding'. But a constitution usually binds more than the 'founding generation'; it is almost invariably intended to last beyond the current generation.[122] This therefore means that the principle of pre-commitment goes against the grain of the 'fundamental principle of republican government' as 'the right of the people to alter or abolish the established Constitution whenever they find it inconsistent with their happiness.'[123] Still, pre-commitment is deemed to be morally defensible when it reinforces the prohibition against collective self-destruction, or cabins the right of the majority to abolish or alter their government to the detriment of certain fundaments of constitutional democracy, such as the right to vote, freedom of assembly, and the right of the citizens to criticize the government. In other words, the proper conceptualization of a constitution as 'higher law' imports the idea of withdrawing certain subjects from the vicissitudes of political controversy, and placing them beyond the reach of majorities.[124] As the philosopher John Rawls notes, a democratic constitution is a principled expression in higher law of the political ideal of a people to govern itself in a certain way; and in this constitution with a bill of rights, the citizen body fixes once and for all certain constitutional essentials, for example, the equal basic political rights and liberties, and freedom of speech and association, as well as the rights and liberties guaranteeing the security and independence of citizens, such as freedom of movement and the protections of the rule of law.[125]

It bears reminding, however, that a democratic constitution not only limits power and prevents tyranny, it also constructs power and guides it toward socially desirable ends. On this view, it is necessary to avoid against dangerous rigidities. A democratic constitution should therefore not be immutable *en bloc*. It should allow for the human capacity for self-correction. We therefore need an optimal balance between stability and rigidity. The constitution must not be too easily changed, nor must it be impossible to modify. 'In a given space of time the constitution may be destroyed by lack of change just as much as by too many changes.'[126]

Patriating the West Indian Independence Constitution

It is submitted that the British parliamentary procedures by which Commonwealth Caribbean states had gained political independence have, among other things, tended to encourage a form of parliamentary sovereignty rather than democratic constitutionalism in the new political *order*. West Indian Independence Constitutions have, in the main, reserved to parliament the extraordinary power to conclude, amend and revise the fundamental law. The truth of this is evidenced in the call for the patriation of the *West Indian Independence Constitution*. Quite recently, Prime Minister Patterson of Jamaica, in speaking to a bill tabled in Parliament for instituting a Republic of Jamaica and to abolish the Oath of Allegiance to the Queen, reflected on the fact that the Constitution of Jamaica is anchored on an Order-in-Council of Her Majesty and is not a creature of Jamaica's Parliament.[127] In a word, he wishes to have 'our basic law established as an Act of the sovereign Jamaican legislature'. Similarly, by its 'Terms of Reference', the Barbados Constitution Review Commission has been charged 'to advise and make recommendations concerning the patriation of the Constitution so as to ensure that it draws its authority and validity from an Act of the Parliament of Barbados; [rather than from an Act of the Parliament in the United Kingdom].'[128] In essence, we would now seek to accomplish what Trinidad and Tobago had effectively done back in 1976.

This call for the patriation of the *Independence Constitution* in fact puts in sharp relief the story of constitutional origin. It underscores the fact that the *Constitution* was not the creation of the sovereign will of the people; that they were not *le pouvoir constituant*. In other words, the *Constitution's* status as supreme law was not established by an autochthonous legal process, one that rested on West Indian will alone. Rather, to re-echo the words of the late Sir Hugh Springer: 'Our *Constitution* came from Britain, but a dozen generations of [West Indians] have made it their own.'[129]

Consider Barbados, for example. The question of the patriation of the Barbados Constitution must be addressed in its proper context. Barbados became an independent sovereign state in 1966 through a procedure of lawful devolution of sovereignty devised by the imperial power (Britain), to which it was formerly politically subordinate. With political independence, however, a national legal order was officially established in the territory that formerly had not been the 'sphere of validity of a constitution and a national legal order based on it.'[130] True, the Barbados Independence Constitution was an Order-in-Council of the British Imperial Parliament; however, once the process of devolution of sovereignty upon the territory was complete, the act became irrevocable, and the Independence Constitution became the charter or the highest norm of the 'new' legal order, whose validity is now presupposed. On this view, the Independence Constitution no more derives legal validity from the Act of the Imperial Parliament than if it were extracted by force. In other words, from the standpoint of British law, any legislation granting independence to a colony would be valid law; but such legislation does not remain the highest norm for the 'new' national legal order. All it means is that Britain has removed itself – which it certainly has the power to do – as the ultimate authority for the territory in question; and that power has now been assumed by the people of the territory – assuming a new democratic political order.

Professor Hart's descriptive account of what is entailed in a devise of lawful devolution is particularly compelling. He speaks of the 'new' legal system emerging from the womb of the 'old' – and sometimes by 'Caesarian' operation.[131] However, at a minimum, the most profound consequence of political independence to a colony is the 'rupture' in the continuity of British sovereignty over that colony. He writes:

> The converse of the situation [of revolution] ... is to be seen in the fascinating moments of transition during which a new legal system emerges from the womb of an old one – sometimes only after a Caesarian operation. The recent history of the Commonwealth is an admirable field of study of this aspect of the embryology

of legal systems. The schematic, simplified outline of this development is as follows. At the beginning of a period we may have a colony with a local legislature, judiciary, and executive. This constitutional structure has been set up by a statute of the United Kingdom Parliament, which retains full legal competence to legislate for the colony; this includes power to amend or repeal both the local laws and any of its own statutes, including those referring to the constitution of the colony. At this stage the legal system of the colony is plainly a subordinate part of a wider system characterized by the ultimate rule of recognition that what the Queen in Parliament enacts is law for *inter alia* the colony. At the end of the period of development we find that the ultimate rule of recognition has shifted, for the legal competence of the Westminster Parliament to legislate for the former colony is no longer recognized in its courts. It is still true that much of the constitutional structure of the former colony is to be found in the original statute of the Westminster Parliament: but this is now only an historical fact, for it no longer owes its contemporary legal status in the territory to the authority of the Westminster Parliament. The legal system in the former colony has now a 'local root' in that the rule of recognition specifying the ultimate criteria of legal validity no longer refers to enactments of a legislature of another territory. The new rule rests simply on the fact that it is accepted and used as such a rule in the judicial and other official operations of a local system whose rules are generally obeyed. Hence, though the composition, mode of enactment, and structure of the local legislature may still be that prescribed in the original constitution, its enactments are valid now not because they are the exercise of powers granted by a valid statute of the Westminster Parliament. They are valid because, under the rule of recognition locally accepted, enactment by the local legislature is an ultimate criterion of validity.[132]

Professor Hart further observes that such a change from colony to independent state may be achieved in at least two principal ways: the parent legislature may finally renounce legislative power over the former colony or the break may be achieved by violence. 'In either case we have at the end of this development two independent legal systems. This is a factual statement and not the less factual because it is one concerning the existence of legal systems.'[133]

Further light may be thrown on the question of the patriation of the Constitution by drawing an analogy to the patriation of Canada's Constitution. Canada's Constitution, originally known as the British North America Act, 1867, was a formal enactment of the British Parliament. It has never been a Canadian Act. This Act, however, created the Dominion of Canada. In 1931 the Statute of Westminster determined to dissolve the formal legal subordination of the self-governing dominions – Australia, Canada, Eire, New Zealand, and South Africa – to the imperial Parliament. But Canada 'was not yet prepared to take its Constitution into its own hands.'[134] At Canada's request, the British government retained formal legal authority over Canada's Constitution. For example, Canada still had to go to Britain for formal amendment of its Constitution. When, therefore, in 1982, Canada decided to take custody of its highest law, the Constitution was finally patriated from Britain.

As Professor Peter Hogg writes in his text:

The Canada Act 1982 and its Schedule B, the Constitution Act, 1982, were enacted by the United Kingdom Parliament on March 29, 1982, when they received the royal assent. The Canada Act 1982 came into force as Canadian law immediately. The Constitution Act, 1982, by virtue of s. 58, did not come into force until "a day to be fixed by proclamation". That proclamation was issued by the Queen, who came to Canada for the purpose, at a ceremony in Ottawa on April 17, 1982; and the proclamation fixed April 17, 1982 as the day upon which the Constitution Act, 1982 was to come into force.[135]

Professor Hogg continues, however, that

At first blush, it does not seem plausible to regard the enactment of the Canada Act 1982 and the Constitution Act, 1982 as a patriation of the Canadian Constitution. Their enactment added two more imperial statutes to the series that existed before. Since 1982, more, not less, of Canada's Constitution is to be found in the statute book of the United Kingdom. Nor have any formal steps been taken to give the Canada Act 1982 or the Constitution Act, 1982, or any of the other constitutional instruments enacted in the United Kingdom, some form of Canadian imprimatur. It is true that the two 1982 statutes were requested by a joint resolution of the two Houses of the Canadian Parliament; but that has been true of every statute enacted for Canada by the United Kingdom Parliament since 1895, and so it cannot be regarded as a new development, let alone as a patriation ... The enactment of the 1982 statutes has not been followed by ratification, either by Canadian legislative bodies or by popular referendum. If the Constitution has been patriated – brought home to Canada – that event has obviously not occurred in the physical world. It must have occurred in a metaphysical world stocked with the ideas of constitutional lawyers.[136]

It means, then, that the 'patriation' of the Canadian Constitution did not effect any measure of constitutional autochthony; meaning, that the Constitution cannot be said to derive its authority solely from events within Canada. Unlike the United States of America, whose Constitution is autochthonous, and whose 'revolution had broken the chain of legal authority which in the colonial period had linked the American assemblies to the imperial Parliament, ... in Canada no such revolution (or break in legal continuity) occurred – and certainly not in 1982. The legal force of the Canada Act 1982 and the Constitution Act, 1982, like other United Kingdom statutes extending to Canada, depends upon the power over Canada of the United Kingdom Parliament. These instruments have an external rather than a local root.'[137]

But patriation of the Constitution *must* mean at least 'the effective termination of the authority over Canada of the United Kingdom Parliament.'[138] As Professor Geoffrey Marshall puts it:

> The fundamental question raised by an assertion of "autochthony" is whether a legally effective abdication of British legislative authority has been made by the United Kingdom. If it has, further local operations, proclamations, and breaches of continuity are superfluous. If it has not, they are ineffective.[139]

Professor Hogg notes that the Canada Act 1982 contains an express abdication of British legislative authority over Canada. For example, section 2 provides that: 'No Act of the Parliament of the United Kingdom passed after the Constitution Act, 1982 comes into force shall extend to Canada as part of its law.'[140] This language may plausibly be read to mean the termination of imperial authority over Canada. In the final analysis, however, it is the fact of Canadian independence, which was completed with Canada's undertaking full custody of its Constitution by relocating the power to amend its Constitution from the United Kingdom Parliament to the Federal Parliament in Canada, that effected the patriation of the Canadian Constitution.

The simple lesson gleaned from the foregoing discussion of the patriation of the Canadian Constitution is that political independence results in the effective termination of British sovereignty over a territory and the emergence of a *new* sovereignty in that territory. In Kelsenian language, that territory, which was previously a subordinate part of the British legal and political order, now becomes the 'sphere of validity' of a *new* legal and political order. On this view, then, the constitution of this *new* sovereign state, whether or not it was in its origin an imperial/colonial statute, is effectively *patriated* at political independence. That is to say, the *new* sovereign state has full custody of its constitution. This is precisely the case of Barbados and of every other Commonwealth Caribbean state. That is to say, Canada has finally achieved by the patriation of its Constitution what every single Commonwealth Caribbean state had successfully achieved 'at the moment of independence'. From that moment, they each had full custody of their *Constitution*. There was nothing left in Britain to be patriated. How, then, are we to understand the term 'patriation' in the context of the current project of constitutional reform? What special sense are we to make of it given that there is no part of the *West Indian Independence Constitution* left to be 'brought home' from Britain?

The term 'patriation of the constitution' is now widely understood to mean 'bringing the constitution home.' In other words, we should wish to be able to say that our constitution has the force of law and if necessary of supreme law through its own native authority and not because it was enacted or authorised by the Parliament of the United Kingdom; that it is, so to speak, 'home grown', sprung from our own soil, and not imported from the United Kingdom. This speaks to the principle of 'autochthony', which is a characteristic of the origin, not necessarily the content, of constitutions. As Kenneth Robinson explains, 'A constitution might originally have been "made in Britain" in the sense that it was given the force of law by an Act of the British parliament, it might indeed be the exact replica of the British constitution, but it would nonetheless be autochthonous if subsequently embodied in a document which owed its validity and authority to no country or institution outside that to which it applied.'[141]

On the other hand, a constitution which bears no resemblance in the political arrangements it prescribes to that of the British constitution would yet fail to achieve autochthony if 'enacted' by a Commonwealth country by any method whatsoever authorised by a law passed by a legislature whose authority might be argued to be 'derived' from a United Kingdom statute. On this view, it has been argued, 'the 1956 Constitution of Pakistan evidently fails, that of the Indian Union probably passes but only the Irish Constitution of 1937 indubitably succeeds.'[142]

> The Constitution of Pakistan of 1956 was "in fact and in law enacted by the Constituent Assembly with the assent of the Governor-General and it derived its force of law from the Indian Independence Act of 1947;" the Constitution of India did not receive the Governor-General's assent and accordingly if such assent was under the Indian Independence Act requisite for the completion of the process of enacting constitutional measures, as the Federal Court of Pakistan later held, the Constitution of India does not owe the force of law to the Indian Independence Act and India achieved constitutional autochthony with its "enactment;" the Irish Constitution of 1937 was merely approved by the Dail Eireann and thereafter submitted to the people in a referendum but the Act which provided for

this plebiscite was studiously silent about what effect an affirmative vote might have. The Constitution was an act of the people as declared in its preamble and its "enactment" constituted a revolution in law.[143]

It bears emphasis, however, that the method by which a constitution has come about is not conclusive of its 'legal validity,' for a constitution could not logically be treated as if it were the product of a legislature, since there could not logically be some pre-existing rule of positive law in terms of which a constitution could be enacted. For to say that a constitution, the supreme and fundamental law, may derive legal validity from some pre-existing law, is first to deny that it is the supreme law, and second, to hold as a theoretical possibility that the constitution might itself be declared to be unconstitutional – which would be an obvious absurdity. Therefore, even if the Constitution were 'reenacted' by the Barbados Parliament, it would not derive legal validity from that act and it would not be a creature of Parliament.

In a strictly juridical sense, therefore, there is no need to make the break in the continuity of British sovereignty in the sense envisaged by the Barbados term of reference, since the break would already have been made by the appropriate Independence Act, the effect of which was to renounce forever the power of the Parliament of the United Kingdom to make laws for the country. In other words, the Independence Act had effected a valid and irrevocable redefinition of the power of the British Parliament so far as concerned the making of laws for the country, and the link with the United Kingdom legal system was thereby severed and a separate grundnorm came into existence.

Still, such a change in the legal form in which the constitution has been prescribed is critical, not so much because of any practical consequences it might have, but rather because of the symbolic significance which is attached to it; for the effect it is expected to have on the way in which the constitution, and the political system as a whole, 'excites and preserves the reverence of the population.' That is to say, if the memories of the 'source' of our constitution in a historical sense offend nationalist sentiments, then it may be a matter of some moment to secure specific proclamations of our identity as an independent sovereign people in a 'symbolic' re-enactment of the constitution, less redolent of British colonialism, and to remove once and for all the 'stigma' that the constitution derives its validity and the force of law from an Act of the British Parliament. In sum, then, there is need for a broader philosophical understanding of the meaning and importance of the patriation term of reference in the context of constitutional reform.

It bears repeating that the patriation of the *Independence Constitution* anticipates that the constitution would be given a 'local root of title' by resting its *validity* and *authority* on an Act of the local parliament, thus replacing the British Order-in-Council. But the mere re-enactment of the *Constitution* by the local parliament would not necessarily involve the people as a whole, in any meaningful way, in the revision of their constitution. Rather, it merely repeats the central feature of the British model of parliamentary democracy in the use of a 'legal' process, which does not directly involve the people at large, but only their elected representatives, to conclude or amend the charter on which their polity is based. What is more, the question of the *validity* of a democratic constitution is, at bottom, a question about its *grounding* and *authority*; and, in a democratic polity, the people are presumed to be the font of that authority, the analytical necessity for explaining the validity of the constitution.[144] This expresses the ideal of democratic constitutionalism: the idea of the people of a country enacting for themselves the laws that organize and regulate their political association.

To repeat, the *political* process by which Commonwealth

Caribbean countries have gained their independence from Britain is known in the relevant literature as the 'lawful devolution of sovereignty', in contrast to revolution, such as obtained on the North American Continent in the 1700s. By this process of lawful devolution of sovereignty, Britain grants political independence to or devolves sovereignty upon a colony – meaning, the colony now becomes an independent sovereign state. Political independence, then, and revolution are two momentous political events from which a new sovereign state may emerge. As one writer puts it: 'The revolutionary act par excellence is ... the founding of a new order.'[145] In other words, political independence, as does revolution, always appears as an end and a beginning: the *end* of an *old* legal order and the beginning of a *new*. 'What occurred before the revolution no longer speaks with the authority of law.'[146] As Professor Paul Kahn notes,

> One of the earliest documents of the American Revolution provides a concise statement of this position: "Whereas ... the American Colonies are declared to be in a state of actual Rebellion, we conceive that all Laws and Commissions by, or derived from the authority of the King or Parliament, are annulled and vacated, and the former civil Constitutions of these Colonies for the present wholly suspended."[147]

Similarly, the Mauritius Independence Statute states that 'the achievement of independence should in itself be understood as having liberated the legal order of Mauritius from its hierarchical subordination to that of the United Kingdom, so that the omnicompetence of the United Kingdom Parliament ceased to prevail in the local legal system.'[148] In the final analysis, therefore, 'That which continues across the revolutionary breach [or political independence] survives not because it is law but because it is affirmed or validated in a new act of choice.'[149]

When, therefore, the *truth* of political independence is grasped: that it is the process of *creating* a new sovereignty or political order, we come to appreciate the jurisprudential axiom that there can be no rule of positive law by which sovereignty is established. This is obviously so because the sovereign is itself the source of law, including the constitution as the original *legislation* of civil society, or the fundamental law of the political order. In other words, 'Law appears to us as the expression of sovereign's will; the sovereign is the normative origin of the legal order conceived as a single subject acting at a particular moment in time.'[150] On this view, then, it would be a contradiction in terms to say that the constitution of a *new* legal and political order continues to derive authority and validity from an imperial colonial law of Britain. We therefore need an alternative 'grammar of thought' by which we might reconceptualize the legislative process by which Britain chooses to devolve sovereignty upon its colony.

One plausible account might be to say that the process in question is a special political process, cast in terms of law, by which Britain, the imperial power, reconstitutes its relationship with its colony, so that, at the conclusion of the process, the relationship between Britain and its colony is no longer one of 'imperial power qua colony'; rather, it is one of 'sovereign power qua sovereign power.' On this view, it means that at the very moment the Independence Constitution takes effect as the constitution of the new sovereign state, it loses that reality as a legislative enactment of imperial Britain. We then search for the ground of the authority and validity of the new constitution where is generally found the validity and authority of the constitution of any democratic society: in the 'political acceptance' of the people of that society.

Equally, it would be a contradiction to say that the constitution derives its validity and authority from an Act of the local parliament, since the constitution, as the most superior norm and the ultimate validating rule of a legal order, cannot itself be the enactment of another positive rule or law. As Professor Richard Kay puts it, when we ask questions about the validity of the constitution and what makes it law, we have left the universe of positive law.[151] For given that the constitution is the ultimate validating rule of a legal system, then whatever makes it valid law must itself be something other than law.[152] It means, then, that the Barbados Constitution, say, would derive no more authority and validity than it already has from an Act of the Barbados Parliament. What is more, the Parliament is a creature of the Constitution; it derives its authority and validity from the Constitution.

But if the foregoing analysis is correct, then precisely what sense does patriation of the Constitution make? What special significance could there be to the re-enactment of the Constitution by the Parliament of Barbados? Such questions force critical reflection on the true meaning of patriation, in the context of the current enterprise of constitutional reform.

It is submitted that patriation might have that special *office* of removing, once and for all, certain errors from our constitutional jurisprudence: that our Independence Constitutions derive *legal validity* from the statutory enactments of the British Imperial Parliament, and that we have 'retained' the monarchy, thus remaining subjects of the British Crown. In other words, some legal significance attaches to the idea that West Indian Independence Constitutions were statutory enactments of the British Imperial Parliament, and that Britain, in theory at least, could repeal those enactments and reclaim its sovereignty over these territories. This error in our thinking is compounded by the belief that, in most cases, ours are monarchical constitutions and we have remained 'subjects' of the British Crown. In the circumstances, therefore, re-enactment of the *Constitution* by the local parliament would carry tremendous purchase in that it would help to remove all doubts about authorial origin, and make it seem *as if* the *Constitution* now has a 'local root of title'. But more important, this idea of the enactedness of the *Constitution*, though according to Professor Michelman of the sheerest banality, 'is nevertheless with us for the duration, because perception of the Constitution's enactedness figures crucially in the country's acceptance of it as supreme law.'[153]

In what, then, must patriation consist if it is to accomplish its mission? It is submitted that, in the circumstances, patriation must consist not only in the re-enactment of the *Constitution* by the local Parliament, it must also consist in something that gives the people a more direct participatory role in the re-enactment of their Constitution. For although Parliament may legitimately claim the authority to speak on behalf of the people, we are reminded that what we are engaged in here is nothing less than the fundamental task of constitution making. It means, then, that patriation should consist in both the political process of referendum and the *legislative act of re-enactment*. In other words, the people having spoken through the referendum process, Parliament meets as a special Constituent Assembly or Constitutional Convention to give *legal* formality to the People's constituent power, to their adoption of the Constitution as their Supreme Law; and to leave a permanent reminder that, in a constitutional democracy, the rule of law must also be the rule of the people. For to leave it as a possibility that the Constitution may derive its authority and validity solely from the consent of the Legislature is to make it vulnerable to the challenge of a right of legislative repeal. Thus, the very possibility of a challenge of this nature, 'proves the necessity of laying the foundations of our national government deeper than in the mere section of delegated authority.'[154]

On this understanding of patriation, we grasp its signal importance. Patriation, to repeat, becomes a symbolic act by which we affect to make our Constitution *our* very own; to give to it 'a local habitation and a name', or, in Professor Hart's elegant phrase: 'a local root of title' – 'title' here being used analogically in the Blackstonian sense to signify 'the legal ground of possessing that which is our own.'[155] On this view, patriation becomes a legitimate or justifiable act of appropriation. And this 'grammar' of common law property, in the circumstances, becomes eminently apropos, given that our *Republican Constitution* stands for: *res publica, res populi*. The Constitution therefore stands as an expression of the sovereign's will; a representation of the popular sovereign.

Patriation, then, conceived as popular referendum and legislative re-enactment, becomes an act of *inscription* by which each citizen appends his/her signature to the Text to signify *assent* and authorship: '*We the People do ordain and establish this Constitution.*' This then becomes the clearest and surest expression of the sovereignty of the people written into the Constitutional Text, and of the idea that, in a Republican State, the 'People' is the fount of all political authority. On this view, the Constitution becomes the *enacted* law of '*We, the People*', the intentional production of our political will. And, as Professor Michelman reminds us, to think of a people living under a fundamental-legal regime that they themselves have made or adopted is already to confer upon them an identity of their own making.[156] This is the democratic ideal: 'the idea of a country's people being the authors of the fundamental laws that constitute their polity; the laws, that is, that fix the country's 'constitutional essentials' – charter its popular-governmental and representative-governmental institutions and offices, define and limit their respective powers and jurisdictions, and thereby express a certain political conception [of themselves].'[157] For, in the final analysis, political democracy or popular political self-government is first of all the ongoing social project of authorship of a country's fundamental laws by the country's people, in some non-fictively attributable sense.[158]

Of West Indian Monarchies and Constitutional Absurdities

An oath is of no moment, being not took
Before a true and lawful magistrate
That hath authority over him that swears – Shakespeare

It is still our wont in the Commonwealth Caribbean, on the view that Queen Elizabeth II of Britain continues to be our queen, to pledge allegiance to her. Our governors-general, prime ministers, members of parliament, judges, *et al*, must swear allegiance to Her Majesty, her heirs and successors upon assuming office. This idea has been given currency by our interpretation of certain language in virtually every West Indian Independence Constitution vesting the 'Executive authority of [the State] ... in Her Majesty, her heirs and successors.'[159] This language is commonly taken to mean that ours are monarchical constitutions (or that we are monarchies) and that Queen Elizabeth II is not simply our 'head of state', she is rather our queen – and, of course, we continue to be her 'subjects'.

The question whether the British Monarch is indeed queen of those Commonwealth Caribbean states of which she is the head and, therefore, whether ours are monarchical constitutions, is one of the most important interpretive issues in Commonwealth Caribbean constitutional jurisprudence, for it goes to the heart of the issue of our constitutional and political identity. It is at the heart of the story we tell of ourselves: a defining category of our rhetorical self-representation. That is to say, we have chosen to define ourselves one way, as 'subjects' of the British Monarch, rather than as we authentically are: the citizens of Independent States. It therefore bears emphasis that the continual retelling of this story functions critically in the ongoing construction of our constitutional identity. Witness, for example, how one Barbadian intellectual, the late Sir James Tudor, has told the story in respect of Barbados:

We are a nation state because, together with our other attributes of sovereignty, [Queen Elizabeth II] is our Queen. Ours is a territory that came into history neither by conquest, nor by cession, nor by an exchange, but as a realm discovered by Englishmen and settled in the name of an English King, long before the designations 'Great Britain' or 'United Kingdom' ever entered the history books. The Crown is therefore the oldest institution in Barbados, with Parliament coming next.

It is this understanding that Barbados entered history as an English realm which makes me a monarchist. Had I not understood and accepted this as an indefeasible truth, I could not have had a career in the politics of my country, and a place in its Parliament. I could never have taken the Oath of Allegiance to the Queen if she were only Queen of the United Kingdom and nothing else.[160]

Arguably, then, one of the more critical terms of reference for constitutional reform is that which charges a commission '*to advise and make recommendations concerning the appropriateness or otherwise of maintaining [our] links with the British Crown.*'[161] To repeat, this idea of continuing 'links' with the British Crown is taken to mean that, at independence, the monarchy was 'retained' and that we are, like Britain, constitutional monarchies. What, therefore, is critically needed is an adequate explanation of the Crown's continuing presence in the post-independence Commonwealth Caribbean constitutional order.

This idea that the British Crown may in some way be abstracted from its *native* constitutional order, in order to continue to serve as 'the Crown' to Britain's former dominions and colonies, was first given purchase in 1926 with the Balfour Declaration, which was issued at the conclusion of an imperial conference. The Declaration recognized the political independence of the self-governing members of the British Commonwealth – Australia, Canada, Eire, New Zealand, and South Africa. In essence, the Declaration recognized the equal status of these territories to that of Great Britain. It stated that

> They [the United Kingdom and the dominions] are autonomous communities within the British Empire, equal in status, in no way subordinate one to another in any aspect of their domestic or external affairs, although united by a common allegiance to the Crown, and freely associated as members of the British Commonwealth of Nations.[162]

But the Balfour Declaration was not a formal legal document. It merely expressed a political understanding reached by the prime ministers of the countries concerned. In a word, it established a political convention. It was then given formal legislative expression in 1931 with the enactment of the Westminster Statute by the British Imperial Parliament. The Westminster Statute was the Act declaring the political independence of Britain's dominions; defining, once and for all, the process of 'lawful devolution' by which Britain would henceforth grant independence to its colonies. What is of the utmost importance is that the Declaration and the Statute would have essayed Britain's peculiar gloss on the fundamental political concepts of political independence and sovereignty: the colony would become a sovereign state, but 'remain in allegiance to the Crown.'

Indeed, our most distinguished student of Commonwealth Caribbean constitutional law, A.R. Carnegie, would seem to share in this standard interpretation. In accounting for what is entailed at independence, Professor Carnegie submits that British legislative power over a territory disappears in a single event at the moment of independence. There therefore remains, he reasons, the theoretical problem of giving an explanation in legal theory of the manner in which a power ceased to exist when it was intrinsic to the theory that the power could not be abdicated. But we know that this has happened even if we cannot explain how it happened.[163] And legally, in respect of those countries 'where the monarchy has been retained', 'all this meant no change in the legal power of the Crown, but merely in the identification of the sources of the advice the Crown takes.'[164] On this view, it would seem, the Crown has virtually the same status in the post-independence West Indian political order as it had in the pre-independence political order. This view has been amply supported by recent statements in the Barbados press. Witness, for example, the comment by Mr. Edmund Hinkson on the question of Barbados's relationship with the British Crown:

> On Barbados attaining political independence from Great Britain in 1966, the decision was taken by the then Government to continue to vest the executive authority of the country in the British Monarchy, as represented by the Governor-General. Under this system, the Queen of England, and subsequently her heirs and successors by birth, continues to be the Head of State of Barbados.
>
> No Barbadian, under the present monarchical system existing in Barbados, can ever become Head of State, no matter how worthy he or she is. Presently, the Head of Barbados' Statehood has been settled by a British Act of Parliament passed in 1701, by virtue of which the House of Windsor will rule as royalty in Great Britain and, consequently, in Barbados.[165]

The foregoing statement is as representative an explanation yet seen of the standard or 'received' understanding of Barbados' and, indeed, most of the region's 'links with the British Crown.' With the possible exception of Dominica, all the independent countries in the Commonwealth Caribbean had supposedly 'retained the monarchy' on becoming independent of Britain.[166]

It means, then, that for all intents and purposes, the British Crown remains one of the most potent symbols of Commonwealth Caribbean constitutional identity. For in each incantation of the 'Oath of Allegiance to Her Majesty the Queen', whether by a governor-general, a prime minister or a member of parliament, we are all joined together in 'a corporate confession of prayer', giving 'credal affirmation' of our 'constitutional faith' in the monarch of a foreign nation; in a 'confession of belief' in the shared proposition that we are still the 'subjects' of Her Britannic Majesty. When, therefore, this idea is fully grasped, we would come to appreciate the overriding importance of removing the British Monarch as head of state. In a word, the issue becomes one of redefining our constitutional identity by settling once and for all our relationship with the British Crown and removing from the Constitution, as much as is feasible, every conceivable reminder of subordination to British sovereignty. Put differently, patriation must 'kill the Queen' in order to show that the people can create a new political order for themselves.

It has been noted earlier that the *political* process by which Barbados and the other Commonwealth Caribbean countries gained their independence from Britain is known in the relevant literature as the 'lawful devolution of sovereignty', in contrast to revolution, such as obtained on the North American continent in the 1700s. By this process of lawful devolution of sovereignty, Britain grants political independence to or devolves sovereignty upon a colony – meaning, the colony now becomes an independent sovereign state. Political independence, then, and revolution are the two momentous political events from which a new sovereign state may emerge. But Commonwealth Caribbean constitutional scholars seem rather to understand this process of lawful devolution as one which leaves an unbroken relationship between Britain and its former colonies. Such a reading, in my view, of an unbroken continuity in the constitutional relationship between the independent Commonwealth Caribbean and the British Crown rather betrays a passive acquiescence in an unargued doctrinal position, which is the product of an historically situated discourse of power-relation – of imperial power and colony – that has managed to impose its own normative categories on West Indian constitutional thought to the point of silencing the claims of critical reason and hermeneutic reflection.[167]

The problem is fundamentally jurisprudential: how to explain the end of imperial rule in a territory and the conceptualization of that territory 'as if' it has been reconstituted as an independent sovereign state. More simply put, the problem is one of explaining the removal of British sovereignty from the Commonwealth Caribbean at the time of political independence and, therefore, their reconstitution as sovereign states. In other words, any adequate historical/political narrative or explanandum that would be faithful to the cognitive values of its genus, and which affects to explain our advance from colonial status to political independence, must inevitably take account of the corresponding shift in the constitutional position of the British Crown vis-à-vis its former colonies. For it is precisely this sort of shift that we want explained, and an explanandum describes not only an event – something that happens, political independence, say – but rather a 'change.'[168] On this view, Commonwealth Caribbean constitutional theory must apply its best efforts to the task of rational reconstruction in order to explain what is conceptually entailed in this movement from colonial status to political independence; and this requires that reason be allowed full scope for the exercise of a critical hermeneutics that distances itself from the currency of accepted ideas and the unthinking doctrinal adherence to the 'imperial' reading of our constitutional texts. Thus, one may ask, why is it intrinsic to 'the theory' that British legislative power (over the Commonwealth Caribbean) cannot be abdicated? Even if one were to concede that Britain's granting of independence to its former West Indian colonies constitutes an 'abdication' of its sovereignty over those territories, it remains to ask why such sovereignty over the West Indies could not be abdicated.

The explanation is rather simple. As colonies, the West Indies were 'possessions' of Britain. They were never the constituent parts comprising the Nation-State known as Britain. This explains why in 1707, Barbados, for example, as a colony of England, had no say in England's joining with Scotland in political union to form the United Kingdom. Therefore, as a 'possession' of Britain, Barbados was subject to Britain's power of 'ownership' and could have been 'disposed' of accordingly. This is in sharp contrast to the idea of Britain claiming to abdicate itself of its own sovereignty. This would indeed be jurisprudential nonsense since it is indeed intrinsic to the theory of sovereignty that it cannot be abdicated of itself. On this issue, one can do no better than to recur to Professor Hart's eloquent account of what is entailed in the process of lawful devolution of sovereignty by which Britain grants independence to its colonies, and of the consequent shift in the location of the ultimate rule of recognition following upon a devolution of sovereignty to a colony. Professor Hart notes that the recent history of the Commonwealth is in fact an admirable field of study of this process of lawful devolution by which 'a new legal system emerges from the womb of the old one.' In this event, he reasons, 'we find that the ultimate rule of recognition has shifted, for the legal competence of the Westminster Parliament to legislate for the former colony is no longer recognized in its courts.' Thus, even though much of the constitutional structure of the former colony is to be found in the original statute of the Westminster Parliament, this remains only an historical fact, for it is no longer the case that the former colony owes its contemporary legal status to the authority of the Westminster Parliament.[169]

Professor Hart's narrative argues compellingly that, at a minimum, a significant consequence of political independence to a colony is the 'rupture' in the continuity of British sovereignty over that colony. And given that the monarchy is an 'essential moment'[170] of the constitution of the state, then it remains to be explained on what basis the monarchy, *sans* British sovereignty, can be said to have been retained. For, at a minimum, it must mean that the monarchy has been expressly reconstituted as an 'essential moment' of the independent Commonwealth Caribbean political order. But, alas, it is impossible, against settled and entrenched meanings of the relevant key concepts in political theory, for an independent Commonwealth Caribbean political order to 'reconstitute' the British Monarchy as an 'essential moment' of its constitution. In other words, if the idea that the monarch is an essential moment of the state is correct, then, on any plausible conceptual analysis, the monarch is removed from the territory upon the lawful devolution of sovereignty to that territory. That is to say, upon independence, the British Monarch is no longer the sovereign of the territory. It is therefore senseless to speak of our having retained the (British) Monarchy, since we could not plausibly conceive of ourselves as having any constituent power over a British political institution. It remains, then, to argue that, rather than appropriating the British Monarchy, in the sense of making it our own, what we have in fact done is to establish our own monarchies in each of our independence constitutions. Now, although it might be argued that there is not in the history of political theory any fixed process that determines the method of founding a monarchy, still, the monarchy is a human institution and must therefore be conceived as having been established – even though in the history of England, say, one may not be able to date its origin. And considering that the monarchy is an essential moment of the state, then the intention to establish a monarchy must be affirmatively taken at the moment of political founding. At a minimum, then, one must find in the (Commonwealth Caribbean) constitutional text the appropriate constitutive language which affirmatively establishes a monarchy as the essential moment of the emergent state. Such a central political institution could not be said to be affirmatively established by language in the constitutional text affecting to vest the executive authority of the state in 'Her Majesty the Queen, Her Heirs and Successors.' For the illocutionary force of such language would extend only to naming the Queen our (formal) 'chief executive' – our Head of State. But not our Queen![171]

Still, we purport to define ourselves as a political community in terms of our links to the British Crown. We live, we say, in a monarchical society. And this is no simple political status, for it has all sorts of social, cultural, and even psychological implications.[172] For example, as clarified by Sir Edward Coke and other jurists in the seventeenth century, 'the allegiance an English subject owed his monarch is a personal and individual matter.'[173] And William Blackstone has observed that since the King was the '*pater familias* of the nation', 'to be a subject was to be a kind of child, to be personally subordinated to a paternal dominion.'[174] 'In its starkest theoretical form, monarchy ... implied a society of dependent beings, weak and inferior, without autonomy or independence, easily cowed by the pageantry and trappings of a patriarchal King.'[175]

But, at all cost, the British Monarch's continuing presence in the post-independence Commonwealth Caribbean constitutional order has to be explained against the necessary presupposition of constitutional discontinuity; for constitutional discontinuity must be conceived as the inevitable consequence of the devolution of sovereignty upon these former colonies. It bears emphasis that the question of constitutional discontinuity is not simply one of historical or empirical inquiry. Rather, it is fundamentally conceptual and addresses itself – at least in the context of this work – to the problem of defining the current constitutional status of the Commonwealth Caribbean against the background of political independence and its logical implications for the sovereign status of these former British colonies. The principle of discontinuity is therefore used here heuristically as a regulative idea for understanding and explaining the British Monarch's position *vis-à-vis* post-independence Commonwealth Caribbean.

As has been earlier intimated, the theory of discontinuity asks when, and under what circumstances, might it be said that a legal system has ceased to exist and a new one created in its stead? Or, what events might be considered disruptive of the continuous existence of a legal system and the substitution of a new one in its stead?[176] To repeat, however, in the immediate context of this work, the theory of discontinuity addresses itself to the problem of establishing the 'creation' of a national legal order in a territory that formerly had not been the 'sphere of validity of a constitution and a national legal order based on it.'[177] The theory, as formulated, assumes the close identification of the state and the legal order, with their foundations rooted in the constitution. Otherwise stated, for purposes of analysis, the constitution is presumed to be the foundational basis of the legal order and the laws that comprise that order. The metaphor of 'sphere of validity' speaks to the political and conceptual question as to the *'locus'* of sovereignty; specifically, whether the independent territory is deemed to possess a 'local root' of sovereignty or constitutional authority.[178]

To speak, then, of a 'new' political state in the Commonwealth Caribbean is to be led inexorably back to one of the principal concepts in political theory: the concept of the 'state.' The concept is, however, used here in its narrowly juristic sense, as referring to an 'authority' in a defined territory, which fixes the norms of all law, and beyond which there is no higher positive legal and political authority. The state is that which has no legal or political superior, and all other forms of social organization are subject to its control.[179] *'Jus est quod jussum est* is of the essence of the state.

There must be in every organized political community some definite authority not only habitually obeyed, but also itself beyond the reach of authority.'[180] In every political society this entity of sovereignty assumes its form in an elaborate and specified system of governmental institutions. 'The final power in the community is thus collected at a single point within its institutional structure';[181] and in modern political theory it is the constitution of the state which determines the particular institutional structure. For example, the so-called constitutional monarchy that obtains in Britain is a particular form of political state, characterized by its own peculiar institutional structure, wherein the constitutional monarch is at the center or apex of an elaborate and specified system of governmental institutions and therefore plays a role in the constitution of the state.[182] Thus, in an Hegelian sense, the monarch is an essential moment of the state, notwithstanding its mere formality and virtual lack of jurisdictional competence, functioning simply as the symbolic culmination of the decision-making process.[183] In fine, the monarchy is itself an institution of the political state, regulated by the constitution.

Still, the idea that the monarch (the monarchy) is an essential moment of the state is critical. Thus, the concept of constitutional monarchy must reflect and express the idea of the monarch as the central organ of the state's sovereign institutional structure, and is therefore politically inalienable in the sense that sovereignty is deemed to be inalienable. That is to say, sovereignty cannot be alienated from itself. In other words, the conceptualization of this kind of 'alienation' is impossible and cannot be communicated into constitutional law by any form of implementable principle. To repeat, this is why it amounts to jurisprudential nonsense to speak of the independent Commonwealth Caribbean as having retained the monarchy. At best, we have retained the British Monarch as our Head of State, as a vestigial reminder of our former colonial status, because, in some sense, we surmise that we are ennobled by some continuing association with monarchy.

Of Monarchies and Constitutional Republics

The above argument suffices as an adequate corrective to the view that the independent states of the Commonwealth Caribbean are constitutional monarchies, with the British Monarch serving as their Queen. Still, the operative, though erroneous assumption that the Queen of England is also our queen and that we are constitutional monarchies, blinds us to the essential image in terms of which our Independence Constitutions may be cast. Indeed, we are blinded to the very republican nature of the British Monarchy itself. For, on the premise that we are, like Britain, constitutional monarchies – and not republics – the term of reference regarding our relationship with the British Crown is commonly understood to ask whether we should become republics by removing the Queen as our head of state and replace her with a native or citizen of the country – as Trinidad and Tobago, say, has already done. This is an understanding which seems to be shared by all on both sides of the monarchy/republic divide. Prime Minister Patterson of Jamaica, for example, has recently stated that he wishes an amendment to the Constitution abolishing the 'Oath of Allegiance to Her Majesty', and that Jamaica should become a Republic.[184] Prime Minister Arthur of Barbados wishes something similar for his country. As a Barbadian lawyer, Mr. Edmund Hinkson, puts it: 'All that is now required to make Barbados a republic is that the British Monarch should be replaced as its head of state by a Barbadian citizen.'[185] Those opposed to the change in Barbados, for example, simply wish that Queen Elizabeth II would remain head of state. This is a rather simplistic understanding of the essential nature of constitutional monarchies and republics, and of the close correspondence between the two.

A constitutional monarchy is a form of political state, established on the authority of, and regulated by, a constitution – written or unwritten – and in which a monarchy has been constituted as a constituent part of the constitutional structure of the state. That is to say, the monarchy, like every other political institution of the state, is a *creature* of the constitution. Britain and Spain are two outstanding exemplars of constitutional monarchy: the former with a constitution generally considered to be unwritten; and the latter with a written constitution which clearly defines the powers of the monarchy *vis-à-vis* the other political institutions of the Spanish State. Also, a very critical feature of a constitutional monarchy is that it is always some form of representative parliamentary democracy, in that the political rulers are elected by the people, to serve for a constitutionally specified term, in accordance with the principle of universal adult suffrage. A constitutional monarchy is a state based on the principle of popular sovereignty, and under the law of the constitution.

A constitutional monarchy is therefore a form of republican government. 'Republic', which derives from the Latin *res publica*, expresses the idea of government resting on the consent of the people and directed by the public will expressed through representative institutions. Put differently, the term 'republic' refers to a sovereign state in which the 'rulers' are the representatives of a widely-inclusive electorate; and its philosophic principle, 'republicanism', bespeaks a form of political rule in which the people as a whole are conceived of as the true constituent power, and this power is inscribed in a (written) constitution which at once establishes the institutional framework of government for the pursuit of the general good, but within such 'marked and settled boundaries' as would conduce to individual liberty and the rule of law. In a word, republican government is limited, constitutional government. Most importantly, the very definition of republic emphasises that a republic does not consist merely in the absence of a monarch but rather involves the people in government and what we might describe as a representative parliamentary democracy.[186] According to Professor Gordon Wood, republicanism was the ideology of the Enlightenment, which offered nothing less than new ways of organizing society.[187] 'No longer was political society to be conceived as a purely natural entity whose patterns are established through a kind of unthinking and instinctive necessity, but rather as a rationally constituted order – the formulation of social and political institutions on the basis of reason – for the realization of the freedom of the individual.'[188] Otherwise put, the state itself is conceived as an organic ordering of free rational individuals, structured around a shared commitment to and an identification with certain goals and principles.[189]

It is on the foregoing understanding of republican government that the republican nature of the 'Westminster Constitution' is grasped, and that a similar idea attaches itself to the *West Indian Independence Constitutions* which, in the main, are patterned on the Westminster model. With the sole exception of Guyana, all Commonwealth Caribbean states are appropriately classified as representative parliamentary democracies. But we would have a deeper appreciation of this after a more extended discussion of republicanism and republican government.

Republicanism: A Theory of Freedom and Government

Republicanism as a political philosophy expresses a commitment to a particular form of government which carries a compelling claim to moral distinction. It is a form of government which takes justice and liberty as its forming principles and is therefore predicated on the idea of equal citizenship. Republicanism is committed to the development and maintenance of a democratic and pluralist society established on principles of justice, liberty and equality. In a republic people are recognized as citizens, as bearers of rights and freedoms, and not as 'subjects' of a monarch. The most plausible conception of republicanism consists in the conviction that political power is properly the preserve of the people and not of a monarch – that is, an absolute monarch. Moreover, such power is taken to require for its organisation a republican form of government where the people are defined as citizens and not as subjects.[190]

Republicanism as a political philosophy is said to have had its proximate origins in the ancient Greek city-state, which was also the earliest form of democracy.[191] Republicanism and democracy might therefore be said to have been linked in their origin. Republicanism therefore came to express the idea of government by the people in the pursuit of justice and the common good. It bears reminding that the essence of Plato's ideal republic was justice: the idea that 'no ... government provides for its own benefit, but ... it provides and prescribes what is for the benefit of the subject, seeking the advantage of him who is weaker, not the advantage of the stronger.'[192]

But in the eyes of Polybius, the ancient Roman historian, ancient Athens, the home of the Greek city-states, was like 'a ship without a captain, buffeted by the storms of popular opinion.'[193] The problem of Athenian republicanism was traced to excessive reliance on pure democracy which, despite its egalitarian claims, nourished the seeds of faction, demagoguery, and the tyranny of the majority. Thus, according to scholars like Philip Pettit and M.N.S. Sellers, ancient Athens hardly served as a model for English and, ultimately, American republicanism. Rather, it was from the Roman republican constitution that James Madison and his colleagues drew their inspiration for framing the American Constitution. They saw the Roman republic as a constitution in which government was built on a democratic foundation but better devised to guard against problems of faction and demagoguery and tyranny.[194]

The principal devices they celebrated in the Roman constitution were the dispersion of democratic power across different assemblies, adherence to a more or less strict rule of law, election to public office, limitation on the tenure of public office, rotation of offices among the citizenry, and the like.[195] These devices provided the checks and balances whereby a republic might hope to constitute a government that was at once popular and stable.[196] The key idea in this neo-Roman tradition is republican freedom, for it is the ideal of freedom that furnishes the arguments, ultimately, for recourse to such institutions.[197]

What, however, is the most attractive conception of freedom or liberty on which this idea of republican citizenship rests? Professor Philip Pettit defends a conception of 'liberty as non-domination' over and above 'freedom as non-interference' and 'freedom as self-mastery.' For him, freedom as non-domination subsumes freedom as self-mastery or autonomy.[198] A state which is oriented to non-domination will also facilitate the achievement of autonomy. And freedom as non-interference is inadequate since it does not suggest the circumstances under which the law may legitimately interfere in the lives of the citizens. In view of the fact that all law is a form of interference, then we need a discriminating principle that would explain what forms of interference are legitimate and which are not. In the event, those who are subject to another's arbitrary will are unfree, even when that other does not actually interfere with them. A classic example of this was that of British rule in the North American colonies. It was generally believed that the British Parliament was non-interfering in its North American colonies. Still, that Parliament had arbitrary power over the colonists; that is to say, it had the capacity to interfere on an arbitrary basis in the choices of its colonists. Domination in this sense only requires the capacity to interfere, not the actual interference. Thus, although there might be no interference in such a case, unfreedom still exists since the non-interfering master remains a source of domination.[199] On the contrary, actual interference need not result in loss of liberty where the law is non-arbitrary and the interference in question is legitimate.[200]

Pettit therefore considers freedom as non-domination the regulative ideal of the republican state. By this he means a situation in which one is not subject to the arbitrary will of another – whether that other be an individual or the political state itself.[201] A conception of freedom as non-domination requires that no one is able to interfere on an arbitrary basis in the choices of the free person. This, he believes, is the conception of freedom that has been espoused in the long republican tradition. Freedom as non-domination is therefore a republican ideal.[202]

This freedom, according to Pettit, is distinguished from liberty as non-interference and also from liberty as democratic participation.[203] It is a negative form of liberty, but it requires something other than the absence of interference. It requires the absence of dependency upon the will of another and the absence of vulnerability to interference at the will of that other. It requires the absence of mastery or domination by any other.[204] For instance, republicanism, as the ideology of the Enlightenment, would have challenged the primary assumptions and practices of monarchy and of the monarchical society in which, according to Blackstone, the King stood in a position of 'pater familias of the nation', and in which to be a subject was to be a kind of child, to be personally subordinated to a paternal dominion.[205] 'In its starkest theoretical form, monarchy, as Americans [would] later ... describe it, implied a society of dependent beings, weak and inferior, without autonomy or independence, easily cowed by the pagentry and trappings of a patriarchal King.'[206] Republicanism, in contrast, 'offered new conceptions of the individual, the family, the state, and the individual's relationship to the family, the state, and other individuals.'[207]

Freedom as non-domination differs from freedom as non-interference in two ways. They differ in the judgments made about those who are dominated but not actually interfered with – for example, the subjects of a kindly master – and about those who are not dominated but are interfered with – for example, the citizens who are bound by a regime of law, the legitimacy of which they endorse and is contrary to arbitrary interference.[208] Pettit suggests that this was the conception of republican freedom associated with the English commonwealthmen tradition and, ultimately, with the sort of republicanism shared by the American founders. The commonwealthmen would have insisted that being the subject of another made a person unfree, even if the other was not disposed to interfere.[209] As Algernon Sydney would write in the late 1600s, 'he is a slave who serves the best and gentlest master in the world, as well as he who serves the worst.'[210]

And there is the question of the relationship between the foregoing conception of republican freedom and the public institutions through which such liberty is secured for the citizens of an ideal republic.[211] These institutions, almost all of a Roman provenance, include the rule of law to which even a monarch is subjected, a dispersion of the powers given to those who make and administer the law among many hands; a restriction on the tenure with which public office is held; a dispensation that allows for public discussion of important issues; for public deliberation over how to resolve them, and for a degree of public participation in their resolution; an arrangement for the appointment of certain officers by a system of voting or lottery or a mixture of both.[212] This intimate connection between these republican institutions and the freedom they support is indeed constitutive of the free society. That is to say, freedom as non-domination does not exist independent of those institutions that would ensure its effective possibility.[213] The freedom of the citizens is therefore constitutively tied to those participatory and other institutions whereby it is supported.

There is also a close connection between republican freedom

and certain forms of civic virtue.[214] For example, the effective rule of law is only possible in a society where the laws themselves are supported by actively sustained social norms.[215] In addition, laws will be effective in protecting citizens against each other and in empowering them against the state, only insofar as they enjoy allegiance among the populace at large; that is, if the people generally believe in the rightfulness of the state, in its authority to issue commands, so that those commands are obeyed not simply out of fear or self-interest, but because they are believed in some sense to have moral authority, because subjects believe they ought to obey.[216]

Freedom as non-domination – the emancipation or liberty from subordination to any potentially capricious or arbitrary will of another – is taken to be a supreme political value, which has institutional implications for organizing our political life, given its linkages with equality, community, and civic virtue, and the emphasis on constitutionalism and on the checking of government.[217] In short, freedom as non-domination supports a certain conception of democracy in which it is possible for the people to be part of the very process of constitution-making and to contest whatever government does. This idea of freedom as non-domination is associated with the long republican tradition of thought that has shaped many of the most important institutions we have come to associate with democracy.[218] In other words, the republican ideal would necessarily have led to the establishment of a constitutionalist democratic state, given that constitutionalism and democracy are indispensable requisites of republican government.

Certainly, seventeenth and eighteenth century Americans would have embraced freedom as non-domination as an ideal in their fight against British rule. So, even though the traditional commonwealthmen and the American republicans of the seventeenth and eighteenth centuries hailed the ideal of freedom as non-domination as extending only to an élite of propertied, white males, it was nonetheless possible for the ideal to have been reappropriated and reintroduced as a universal ideal of contemporary society. Indeed, this ideal has already been inscribed in many of our more important political institutions and can serve to articulate a compelling account of the institutional forms of a just society.[219] In other words, freedom as non-domination – the end to which the true republican state is constituted – furnishes the appropriate standard by which to judge the constitution and other basic social and political institutions of a community.[220]

Republicanism, Constitutionalism and Democracy

To repeat, republicanism is a normative principle that speaks to a form of political rule in which the sovereign power of the state is said to be located in the people as a constituent whole, but is exercised by their representatives, elected on the principle of universal adult suffrage. A republic is therefore understood to be a representative, democratic state, in which the state's power is constitutionally limited. A republic is distinguished from a true democracy in that, in the latter, the entire populace participates directly in governmental affairs. In contrast, in a republic, power is said to *derive* from the people but is exercised through representative institutions. Therefore, the people are excluded from participating in the day-to-day governance of the country.[221]

Also, the very idea of republican government is predicated on certain values that claim universal validity: citizenship, equality, justice and liberty. Citizenship underscores the fact that, in a republic, citizens are not the 'subjects' of a monarch, but rather hold their citizenship as equals, and as a matter of fundamental, inalienable right, on par with the monarch himself, assuming that there is one.[222] Republican citizenship therefore does not depend on some act of allegiance to a monarch. The republican constitution constitutes a constituency of citizens, not the 'subjects' of a monarch. Republican citizenship therefore entails the virtues of Justice, Liberty, and Equality. The question therefore remains as to the form the republican state must assume if it is to realize the ideals of Justice, Liberty, and Equality.

Indeed, one of the most critical issues in contemporary republican debate concerns the appropriate form of the republican state. Essentially, the question is as to the forms the republican state must necessarily assume if the republican ideals of justice and liberty are not to be seriously compromised. Put differently, how should the republican state be organized so that the republican ideal of freedom as non-domination be realized? What fundamental principles of political philosophy should inform the ordering of the republican state?

It is submitted that the constitutional democratic state is the only possible form of political state in which the republican ideal of freedom as non-domination can best be realized. The constitutional democratic state makes the strongest claim to moral distinction above other forms of political rule. Republicanism and constitutionalism are therefore the twin concepts of the just state. In other words, republicanism necessarily entails constitutionalism and democracy. As we have noted, the *true* republican state is a constitutional democracy; constitutionalism being a normative principle which expresses the idea of government limited and regulated according to the fundamental norms of a society's settled constitutional arrangements. The constraints in question may or may not be recorded in a formal constitutional text.

The term democracy is used here in its modern conceptualizations to denote, first and foremost, the idea of government based on the consent of the people; meaning, government by the elected representatives of the people. Democratic government on this view embraces the idea that the people have the power to hold government accountable by contesting whatever it does – whether legislatively, administratively, or judicially.[223] This means that decision-makers are accountable to the ordinary people whom they affect.[224] It also means that public decisions must be made on a basis of reasoned deliberation in which the relevant considerations appropriate to the issue in question actually determine the outcome. In the case of legislative decisions, for example, the relevant considerations are likely, and ought to be, what all can agree to as pertinent, under accepted canons of reasoning.[225] Whereas, in administrative and judicial decisions, they will be the more specific considerations that are established as relevant under the laws that govern the operation of those arms of government.[226]

In a word, then, in a republic, public decisions are taken in a deliberative way in accordance with the ideal of a 'republic of reasons.' As Professor Cass Sunstein puts it, the traditional republican vision, in particular the vision which inspired Americans in the eighteenth century, was that of a polity within which citizens have equal claims and powers, and public matters are decided by deliberation on the basis of considerations that have common appeal, meaning, they are not biased in favour of any group, or even in favour of the status quo, and agreement serves as a regulative ideal as to how things should be decided.[227]

So, the constitutionalist, democratic republic is necessarily the form that a state must inevitably assume if it is to promote justice and the ideal of 'freedom as non-domination', and minimise, as much as is feasible, the presence of arbitrary will in the coercive apparatus of the state.[228] It means, then, that the separation of powers is indispensable to the realisation of a just state, for it is only through the separation of powers principle that the authorities are made accountable in various ways to one another and are subject to mutual sanctioning. For example, the legislature can censure the executive for failing to execute its laws properly, and the judiciary can expose the legislature to criticism by finding that the laws it makes are in contravention of certain constitutional provisions.[229] As Kant has reasoned, the ideal constitution is a *republican constitution*; one that is founded on the principle of separation of powers and thereby allows for the greatest possible human freedom in accordance with laws by which the freedom of each is made to be consistent with all others. Kant therefore endorsed the idea of the doctrine of separation of powers as an indispensable principle of the rational republican constitution. In other words, Kant's endorsement of the republican constitution as the only truly legitimate constitution, rests on the view that the rational state under the rule of law is a democratic state which serves the ideal of justice, and whose very nature can be conceived and grasped only by the language of right and freedom.[230] And, for Kant, 'no state can fulfil its genuine task of the realisation of right and the protection of freedom if it does not adhere to the principle of separation of powers as an indispensable basis of its constitution.'[231] As he puts it:

> Every state contains three powers, i.e. it contains the generally united will in three persons (*trias politica*): the sovereignty personified by the legislator; the executive power personified by the head and members of the government and administration under the rule of law; and the judicial power and administration of justice which determines the right of everybody according to law.[232]

To this Professor Wolfgang Kersting's insightful gloss may be added:

> The unitary power of the state which is founded in the united general will divides itself for the purpose of the rational organization of the realization of justice into three different areas of competence which combine the tasks of the legislative in establishing rules, the judicial use of rules in making judgments and the executive

implementation of rules and judgments. For Kant, separation of powers is obviously the functional and institutional becoming ... of the three conceptually separable moments of the process of the realization of justice.[233]

To repeat, the republican state is a constitutionalist, democratic state. It is a state limited and regulated according to the fundamental norms of society's settled constitutional arrangements. In a word, it is a state defined by the normative principle of constitutionalism. Which is to say, it is a state regulated by the rule of law and whose architectonic principle is the separation of powers. But, above all, the republican state is a form of democratic state in which the citizens exercise a fundamental and inalienable right to choose the political rulers who would exercise the powers of the state.

Today, the republican state is understood to include a bill of fundamental rights in its constitution; rights that protect certain fundamental interests that are constitutive of human personhood, and in the absence of which protection, no republican regime can claim to live up to the ideals of justice and liberty. This means that the constitutionalist, democratic republic is wedded to the counter-majoritarian principle, that is, the idea that there are certain areas of law not governed by the majoritarian principle; not subject to majority will. This constitutionalist condition, it was earlier noted, is predicated on a certain conception of democracy that is representative in nature and in which public matters are decided by deliberation on the basis of considerations that all in principle can agree to, and in which citizens have the power to challenge any public decision, be it legislative, administrative, or judicial. It means, then, that the republican state is a state under the rule of law; which means that all agencies of government are constrained to act only under the authority of law, and only in a way that accords with the requirements of law; that is to say, in fidelity to the due process of law.

The Modern British State: A Monarchical Republic

The foregoing discussion of republicanism and republican government frames the appropriate context for consideration of the true nature of the modern British State. When 'republic' is defined in terms of its core 'principles' rather than in terms of the title assigned to the head of state, the modern British State will be understood to be, in essence, a republican state.

Today, the United Kingdom of Great Britain is at once a formal monarchy and a representative, parliamentary democracy. As the term United Kingdom implies, Britain is formally a monarchy, and its governmental officers are officially described as agents of the 'Crown', tracing back to a time when England was an absolute monarchy and governmental officers were literally agents of the Crown. But, as Professor B.O. Nwabueze notes,

> The Queen's position in the British Constitution is largely the product of historical evolution. The monarch once embodied in himself the entire sovereign power of the state, which he exercised at his discretion as a personal ruler. The government was his in every sense of the word, and he was synonymous with the state. He possessed and exercised over his ministers, other public servants and subjects generally, a power that was at once absolute and complete. However, in the course of centuries of constitutional evolution, the monarch has lost his personal discretion in the exercise of sovereignty. In law, sovereign power still reposes in him, the government is still his own, but he no longer governs personally, most of his powers having devolved upon elected ministers, yet these ministers still regard themselves, as of old, as the

Queen's ministers, and the government which they administer as Her Majesty's Government.[234]

In essence, then, the British monarchy is now anachronistic in substance. The House of Lords is equally anachronistic, consisting mainly of hereditary descendants of landed aristocrats who, in feudal times, constituted the primary structure of political organization.[235]

Britain is also considered a representative, parliamentary state because of the existence of a representative political institution, at the heart of the state system.[236] Deriving from this practice of a representative institution functioning as the central institution of the state are the historic principles of representation, consent, limited and legitimate government. Over the past three centuries, Parliament – specifically, the House of Commons – has emerged as the necessary and defining institution of the modern UK State. As the British political scientist David Judge remarks, although due regard must be paid to the historical and continuing significance of the monarchy and the House of Lords within British political culture, what distinguishes them from the House of Commons is that they are essentially unnecessary; that is to say, they are not *necessary* or *defining* institutions of the modern UK State.[237]

The Glorious Revolution of 1688 and the attendant constitutional settlement of 1689 are deemed to have been the momentous events marking the emergence of the modern UK State. The centuries-old conflict between the crown and the parliament had come to a head with the Revolution of 1688 and, with the success of its forces over those of the King's, parliament was able to spell out precisely the conditions under which the monarchy was to continue.[238] According to Professor Jeffrey Goldsworthy, 'After James II fled to France, a Convention of the two Houses was convened in January 1689 to settle the terms on which the monarchy would continue. The Houses established committees to draft a Declaration of Rights, which was read to William and Mary, James's daughter, during the ceremony at which they were offered the Crown.'[239] Further, Professor Goldsworthy notes, the Bill of Rights (1689), which enacted most of the Declaration of Rights, restricted many important royal prerogatives. Most importantly, it controlled the royal succession, and the so-called inseparable prerogatives of the Crown, especially the disputed power to dispense with statutes. It placed the dispensing power firmly under the control of Parliament, providing that no statute could be dispensed with, except as allowed by the statute itself, or by the special provision of a bill 'to be passed during this present session of parliament.'[240] And, finally, to reinforce the Crown's subjection to statute, the Coronation Oath Act (1689) was passed, which required William and Mary, and subsequent kings and queens 'in all times to come', to swear 'to govern the people of this Kingdom ... according to the statutes in parliament agreed on, and the laws and customs of the same.'[241]

With the acceptance by William and Mary of the gift of the crown on the terms and conditions set by parliament, the foundations for the ultimate sovereignty of Parliament were unmistakably laid. Thus, after 1689, as C.R. Munro points out:

> Parliament was to be its own master and free from interference ... Parliaments were to be held frequently, and the election of their members was to be free. The Crown's power to levy taxes was made subject to parliamentary consent, its power to keep a standing army made subject to statute, and powers of suspending or dispensing with laws ... were declared illegal.[242]

To repeat, then, 'what was asserted and accepted in 1689 was the principle of *parliamentary sovereignty*, whereby parliament secured legal supremacy amongst the institutions of the state. Thus, not only was the monarchy subordinated to parliament, but, also, the last vestiges of the claim of the courts that parliament could not legislate in derogation of the principles of the common law were removed. Constitutional theory was at last reconciled to the legal practice that had been developing for nearly a century.'[243]

In the years following the Glorious Revolution of 1688, according to Professor Gordon Wood, the English had become increasingly aware of the marvelous peculiarity of their limited monarchy. 'The constitution of our English government (the best in the World)', they told themselves, 'is no arbitrary tyranny, like the Turkish Grand Seignior's, or the French King's, whose wills (or rather lusts) dispose of the lives and fortunes of their unhappy subjects.'[244] In essence, then, with the Glorious Revolution, the English had radically transformed their monarchy: they had executed one King and deposed another, written charters and bills of rights, regularised the meetings of their parliaments, and even created a new line of hereditary succession.[245] Representation in the House of Commons had allowed for the participation of His Majesty's subjects in the affairs of government.[246] The Bill of Rights of 1689 had finally affirmed that the Monarchy was subject to the law. Not only was the Crown forced to govern through Parliament, but also, the right of the individual to be free of unlawful interference in his private affairs was established. In a word, the monarchy was brought under the 'rule of law'; and, to the English, theirs was a constitution specially dedicated to liberty. The Glorious Revolution had therefore firmly established the concepts of liberty and the rule of law as the basic principles of the state. So, although the British practice never fully realised the republican model of popular sovereignty through elected senators and magistrates, still, according to the English 'Cato', England's constitution was 'a thousand degrees nearer akin to a commonwealth', than to absolute monarchy.[247]

With the clear acceptance of William and Mary that the

Crown was only one of several institutions that shared political power in England, there began in earnest the reconstitution of the English political system. Their having accepted the gift of the Crown on the terms and conditions laid down by Parliament, it became obvious that it was the invitation of Parliament, and not hereditary claims, that constituted the legitimising foundation of their monarchical status. Moreover, the provisions of the Bill of Rights, which comprised a principal part of the terms on which the invitation to the Throne was extended to William and Mary, and which they accepted as a binding specification of the conditions of their rule, embodied the principle of *limited* royal authority. This limitation on royal authority was in due course reinforced by further legislation, such as the Act of Settlement of 1701, entitled 'An Act for the further Limitation of the Crown and better securing the Rights and Liberties of the Subject.' This Act increased the accountability of ministers to the Commons and provided the terms of appointment for judges that secured their independence from the Crown.[248]

By the seventeenth century, notwithstanding the rise of monarchical absolutism in France, constitutional government was clearly the ascendant political doctrine in England and on much of the continent.[249] England, in fact, is considered to have played the dominant role in the development of the doctrine of modern constitutionalism. In this respect, Professor Scott Gordon notes that a remarkable proportion of today's democracies have derived their political systems directly, or indirectly via the United States, from England.[250] For instance, even in countries whose peoples differ greatly from the English, such as India and Pakistan, the period of British colonial rule seems to have been sufficient to establish constitutionalism as a widely accepted political ideology.[251] Witness also the fact that English political forms and principles were transplanted to America, thus creating a large transatlantic communion of political philosophy that has led to the development of constitutionalism in the modern world. It may then be said that modern constitutionalism, in both practice and theory, had its main origins in seventeenth century England.[252]

English constitutionalism, as was intimated, developed out of the political conflicts of the seventeenth century between King and Parliament. Out of the protracted struggle for power between these two political institutions, the idea of a polity composed of countervailing powers became clearly defined.[253] However, it was not until the nineteenth century that the idea had taken hold that the populace at large could be safely permitted to share in the exercise of state power.[254]

Still, the events of the seventeenth century did in fact establish the principle of constitutional government in the nation;[255] with the Glorious Revolution of 1688 being construed by some to have been the most crucial event in the development of English constitutionalism.[256] In opposition to the doctrine of monarchical absolutism there developed the idea that England was a pluralist polity in which political authority is shared by a number of independent institutions – with the King, House of Lords, and the House of Commons conceived as representing, respectively, the classical monarchical, aristocratic, and democratic elements of the constitution. In addition, there was also the development of the English judiciary as a distinct center of political authority independent of both the Crown and Parliament.[257] England was thus regarded as a compound of the three primary forms of government noted by Aristotle, with the King, Lords, and Commons embodying, respectively, the basic elements of monarchy, aristocracy, and democracy, and the English constitution was said to consist of the King, the two houses of Parliament, and the independent judiciary.[258] Thus, England was said to have had a mixed government with the King and the two houses of Parliament all participating in performing the law-making function of the state; that is to say, they constituted 'three concurrent powers' in legislating. The principal objective of this form of government is the preservation of the people's liberties.[259] In other words, this desired end was understood to be attained only by a constitutional structure that permits each estate to act as a buffer against the excesses of another.[260]

During the eighteenth century, the concept of mixed government had become commonplace in English political thought. The English political system continued to develop in the direction it had taken following the Glorious Revolution. When Robert Walpole became the first lord of the treasury and chancellor of the exchequer in 1721, he chose to remain in the House of Commons, which initiated the practice that the prime minister, and other high officers of the Crown, be selected (mainly) from the elected membership of the Commons and remain there to participate directly in parliamentary debate.[261] In addition, the power of the House of Lords was reduced by both statute and practice, and by the reign of George IV, the role of the monarch had become largely ceremonial.[262]

These developments made the House of Commons – the elected, representative body – the dominant institution in English government; and political thinkers of the eighteenth century had come to view the political system as pluralistic, with independent institutions that had the power to constrain each other.[263] Thus evolved an English political system that Baron de Montesquieu, a Frenchman with very strong leanings toward republicanism, would praise in his celebrated text, *The Spirit of the Laws*. Here, Montesquieu praised the English system of governance as one of the few in history that had effectively secured the liberty of the citizenry.[264] According to Professor Scott Gordon, Montesquieu considered the English system of government to be admirable for two reasons: because it conformed to the fundamental spirit of English society, and because that spirit is worthy of admiration in

itself.[265] The English nation had 'for the direct end of its constitution political liberty.' In England, liberty had attained 'its
highest perfection.'[266] And by 'liberty', Montesquieu meant
'political liberty', under which the citizen is constrained by laws,
and the authorities who make and administer the laws are also
constrained.[267] The genius of the English constitution thus laid
in its having solved the problem of power. 'The hand of the state,
necessary to protect members of society from each other and
from foreign enemies, was strong in England; the citizens were
protected *by* the state; but they were also protected *from* the state:
they had *political* liberty.'[268]

For Montesquieu, the English political system he observed
revealed all the fundaments of republican government. England,
in his view, 'may be justly called a republic, disguised under the
form of monarchy.'[269] The *functional* separation of powers had
now become an essential feature of the English constitution. And
although this was not precisely the *institutional* separation of
powers that would later become the hallmark of the American
Constitution, Montesquieu nonetheless interpreted the English
constitution in terms of the countervailance model of institutional 'separation', which requires that the several entities be
invested with sufficient independence to enable them to impose
constraints upon each other.[270] This, in his view, was what was
necessary in any state, republican or monarchical, whose animating 'spirit' was civic liberty.[271]

Montesquieu regarded the 'institutional' separation of the
state functions – the legislative, the executive, and the judicial –
as being essential to the control of the coercive authority of the
state.[272] There was, however, some contradiction here given that
he had construed the judiciary as part of the executive. His insis-
tence was that the legislative and the executive functions must
not be institutionally combined if liberty were to be preserved.[273]
For if the legislative and the executive functions were performed

by the same persons, 'there would be an end then of liberty.'[274] Furthermore, he praised the English constitution for dividing the legislative branch into two bodies, which 'check one another by mutual privilege of rejecting' the proposals of each.[275]

Professor Scott Gordon stresses that Montesquieu's concept of 'separation' was not meant to denote a complex of *completely independent* institutions. Rather, as he had stated, the preservation of liberty requires that the executive and legislative organs of the state be dependent on each other. It is not separation in itself that protects liberty, but the arrangement of the separated powers in a system of mutual control.[276] Thus he writes:

> Democratic and aristocratic states are not in their own nature free. Political liberty is to be found only in moderate governments; and even in these it is not always found. It is there only when there is no abuse of power. But constant experience shows us that every man invested with power is apt to abuse it, and to carry his authority as far as it will go. Is it not strange, though true, to say that virtue itself has need of limits? To prevent this abuse, it is necessary from the very nature of things that power should be a check to power.[277]

And,

> To form a moderate government, it is necessary to combine the several powers; to regulate, temper, and set them in motion; to give as it were ballast to one, in order to enable it to counterpoise the other. This is a masterpiece of legislation, rarely produced by hazard, and seldom attained by prudence.[278]

It meant that Montesquieu's view of England as being essentially a republic, despite its having a monarch, was predicated on the notion that a monarchy, too, *can* be a 'moderate government'

– if the monarch is constrained in the exercise of his authority. And such constraints can only be effected through the construction of a constitutional machinery, which, as was the case in England, produced 'a republic under the form of monarchy.'[279] In addition, he thought, constraints on the monarch can also be effected through non-governmental institutions such as churches, by the existence of a powerful nobility, and by long-standing customs that induce the monarch to respect established practice.[280]

It is fair to say that Montesquieu's comments on the English system of government in *The Spirit of the Laws* would have done much to enhance the wide admiration that that system enjoyed in the later eighteenth century. His comments were closely studied by Americans who, after the Revolutionary War had been won, faced the task of constructing a constitution that would bind the thirteen former colonies into one nation.[281] Thus, when the Americans began in earnest to devise a (federal) constitution for themselves, there was no better model to emulate. 'They constructed a political system that differed greatly from the English one in its structural details, but one that was guided by the same basic view of the purposes, and dangers, of political power.'[282]

Today, Britain is understood to be a form of representative, limited government; it is a parliamentary democracy. It is not commonly referred to as a republic since it has retained the monarchy at the apex of an elaborate complex of institutions comprising the state. Thus it is otherwise referred to as a 'formal monarchy.' All governmental officers, Prime Minister *et al*, are officially described as agents of the 'Crown.' The Crown, along with the House of Lords and the House of Commons, comprise the Parliament of Britain. However, today, Parliament is generally understood to mean the House of Commons. So the principle of parliamentary government, which rather implies that Parliament, the representative institution, directly elected by the great body of the people, is the most important institution in the British political system, means the House of Commons.[283]

As David Judge observes, historically, the triumvirate of monarch, lords and commons was of immense importance. However, the settlement that was reached after the Revolution of 1688 permanently established Parliament's central role in the British government. In other words, the constitutional settlement of 1689 has clearly demonstrated that while the monarch retained prerogative powers and the House of Lords residual legislative powers, it was the House of Commons that had successfully asserted its legislative and financial primacy within the state. Thereafter, there were no doubts that the 'sovereignty of parliament' resided in the lower chamber. Therefore, although due regard is paid to the historical and continuing significance within British political culture of the monarchy and the House of Lords, what distinguishes them from the House of Commons is that they are essentially unnecessary; that is to say, they are not the *necessary* or *defining* institutions of the modern UK State.[284] And, with the independence of the judiciary guaranteed within a system of the functional separation of powers, the fundamental question remains whether the British political system can be validly interpreted as an exemplification of the republican constitution. Britain, today, is essentially a republic.

Of Constitutional Monarchies and Parliamentary Republics

It is rather unfortunate that, in contemporary political and constitutional analysis, monarchical and republican government are distinguished solely on the fact that one has a monarch as head of state and the other does not. Thus, on this view, Britain and Spain are not generally considered to be republics, notwithstanding that they exemplify the core principles of republican government. We might therefore be aided in our appreciation of the republican character of the British monarchical constitution if we were to consider briefly Hegel's defense of constitutional monarchy in his political philosophy.

The parliamentary model of government has been historically associated with the monarchical system of Britain. Britain is a constitutional monarchy, and theorists who favour a constitutional monarchy over a presidential system, for example, argue that the sovereignty (and unity) of the state is best guaranteed *formally* by the single, human self of the monarch. In other words, a monarch is necessary to symbolise and give reality to the unity of the state. Stephen Bosworth, for example, in his work, *Hegel's Political Philosophy : The Test Case for Constitutional Monarchy*,[285] reasons that an hereditary head of state is an essential part of the most rational constitution; a constitution which is democratic, is written, has a 'parliamentary form', an independent judiciary headed by a supreme court, a prime minister and a council of ministers selected by arrangements similar to those provided by the fundamental law of Germany, namely, 'constructive vote of no confidence' procedure, and, finally, a parliament composed of two houses – an elected chamber, chosen by universal adult suffrage, and a non-elected chamber.[286]

In the *Philosophy of Right*, Hegel praises constitutional monarchy as the most rational constitution; as the constitution corresponding to the highest stage of historical development with respect to the idea of freedom.[287] Hegel's constitutional (or democratic) monarchy is in fact likened to the British Constitution – 'a parliamentary democracy with cabinet government'. The hereditary head of state formally appoints the prime minister, who then appoints the cabinet, but the prime minister and his cabinet are made fully accountable to an elected chamber elected by universal adult suffrage. It therefore bears emphasis that the Hegelian description of the architectonic of a constitutional monarchy is very much consistent with the proper conceptual understanding of 'republican government'. That is to say, Hegel's 'Constitution of the Rational State' is in reality a republican constitution. His monarch is a constitutional monarch, whose function in the well-constituted state is essentially formal, as the substantive roles of creating and executing laws are given over to the other two powers of the legislature and the executive.[288] The monarch is bound by the concrete content of the advice he receives, and if the constitution is firmly established, he often has nothing more to do than to sign his name.[289] But despite the formality, the role of the monarch is an essential one; it functions symbolically as the culminating point of the decision-making process of the state.

Professor Paul Reading advises that Hegel's theory of monarchy may be better appreciated if we were to consider it more as a historical solution to the problem of the unity of the rational state, in the context of early nineteenth-century European politics. In this regard, Hegel conceived of the monarch as giving 'embodiment to the institutional structure of the society itself and so personifies the coexistence of the universal law uniting all citizens with the irreducible singularity marking each of them.'[290] Put differently, the personality of the rational state can only be fully actualized in the concrete, natural person of the monarch. That is to say, the monarch is an essential moment of the state embodying in his person the organic unity of the other constituent parts comprising the state.

As the political philosopher Peter J. Steinberger observes, for Hegel, the problem of individual and society can only be resolved by conceiving of political society as an organism. 'In this organism, the identity of the parts and the whole are deeply dependent upon one another in a way that parallels, at least metaphorically, the seamless identity of the infinite world as it must be rationally comprehended.'[291] But political society, so conceived as a single thing, is one entity, and not merely a conglomerate of several entities; therefore, its various aspects or 'moments' are them-selves to be understood as developments or elaborations of *it*.[292] This thought is clearly articulated in Hegel's consideration of the state as an entity of sovereignty; as an 'organic' whole and not a mere aggregate of independent and self-subsistent parts.

But the idea of the fundamental unity of the state denies any claim that either the monarch or the majority is sovereign over against the rest of the state. Therefore, 'if we wish to say that the state acts, we must conceive of this not in terms of one particular part of the state but, rather, the state as a single, irreducible whole.'[293] However, the state, as the centralized institution of political authority in society, is very much an abstraction and can only *act* through its agents who, for Hegel, can only be persons, not 'fictional' persons or collectivities, but 'real' persons.[294] Hence, Hegel concludes, there is a sense in which the state cannot act except in the form of a single person.[295] That is to say, we need some single individual at the culminating point of the process of political decision-making in society in order to intelligibly ascribe actions to the state. Simply put, sovereignty requires that all the autonomous power centers of a society converge toward a single point of public authority: the monarch.

Put differently, 'sovereignty', this central concept of modern political thought, is another term for the unity of the state. It is the distinctive attribute of the modern state, and expresses the idea of the unity of the constituent parts. Thus, the sovereignty of the state is not to be identified with any single element in the state; rather, it is an attribute of the ensemble that includes the legislative and executive as well as the princely powers. But for Hegel, it is the person of the monarch which is uniquely suited to express the radical unity and ideality with which he identifies the sovereignty of the state. The state ultimately has to act as an individual, as a unified 'personality' whose 'simple self supercedes all particularities, cuts short the weighing of arguments and counterarguments ... and *resolves* them by its "I will", thereby initiating all activity and actuality.'[296] 'The personality of the state has actuality only as a *person, as the* monarch'; for 'personality ... has its *truth* ... simply and solely as a person ...'[297]

Of course, as Professor Paul Franco observes, it is not clear why the 'personality' of the state must ultimately be embodied in a single person. Nor is it clear why the state's manifest need to act as a unit requires that an actual individual pronounce the 'I will' that resolves and concludes all political deliberation. After all, he reasons, modern democracies seem to get along well without this element of monarchical decision; they do not fall apart or show themselves incapable of unified action in the absence of a single person's pronouncing the 'I will'. Also, even when one concedes the role of monarch in Hegel's constitutional scheme as symbolizing the moment of subjective will, of which only the human being is capable, it is still unclear why the principle of subjective will is any better represented by reposing the power of ultimate decision in a single human being rather than in a group of human beings.[298]

Still, it might be said that, from a practical standpoint, the hereditary, non-elected monarch, in virtue of the tenure of office, is able to exercise the prerogatives of sovereignty when no other person elected by majority vote is available. That is to say, in the event that the full range of the more obviously democratic institutions have temporarily failed, the monarchical element of the constitution is called upon to act to foster the effective return to democracy.[299] The non-elected head's ability to function in this substantive role turns on the fact that the tenure of office would generally survive any prolonged electoral divisiveness which may plague a society or its representative assembly.

But, in the final analysis, Hegel's political state, like that of his predecessor Kant, is the constitutional state, which, in reality, is the republican state. For Kant, as we have earlier noted, the ideal constitution is a *republican constitution*, which allows the greatest possible human freedom in accordance with laws by which the freedom of each is made to be consistent with that of all others. Thus, in defense of the republican constitution, Kant writes that

> All forms of state ought to be ... based on the ideal of a constitution which is compatible with the natural rights of man, so that those who obey the law should also act as a unified body of legislators. And if we accordingly think of the commonwealth in terms of concepts of pure reason, it may be called a *Platonic ideal* (republica noumenon), which is not an empty figment of the imagination, but the external norm for all civil constitutions whatsoever and a means of ending all wars. A civic society organized in conformity with it and governed by laws of freedom is an example representing it in the world of experience (republican phenomenon), and it can only be achieved by a laborious process, after innumerable wars and conflicts. But this constitution, once it has been attained as a whole, is the best qualified of all to keep out war, the destroyer of everything good. Thus it is our duty to enter into a constitution of this kind; and in the *meantime*, since it will be a considerable time before it takes place, it is the duty of *monarchs* to govern in a republican ... manner ... In other words, they should treat the people in accordance with principles akin in spirit to the laws of freedom which a *people of mature rational* powers would prescribe for itself, even if the people is not literally asked for its consent.[300]

Similarly, the Hegelian constitution of the rational state is, at bottom, a republican constitution, a constitution established on some version of popular sovereignty and which recognizes freedom of property and persons as fundamental principles. On this view, 'a properly Hegelian appraisal of his theory of the monarch would have to be open to the very collapse of the institution of monarchy as a historical solution to the problem of the unity of the rational state.'[301] For Hegel's constitutional monarchy refers to a state in which the legislative, executive, and 'princely' powers are differentiated but ultimately united under the head of a monarch who rules in accordance with the constitution and the decisions of his ministers. 'Such a constitution represents the peak of constitutional development', according to Hegel, 'because it alone is able to reflect and accommodate the subjective freedom that constitutes the great achievement of the modern world.'[302]

In sum, then, Hegel's conception of the political state recognizes the critical importance of the division of powers in the state as 'the guarantee of public freedom.' Thus, notwithstanding his repudiation of what he considered to be the negative and mechanical doctrine of the separation of powers most famously articulated by Montesquieu in *The Spirit of the Laws* and adapted to the democratic circumstances of the United States by Madison, Hegel has nonetheless, in common with his predecessor Kant, endorsed the idea of the doctrine of separation of powers as an indispensable principle of the rational republican constitution. For, as we have earlier noted, Kant's endorsement of the republican constitution as the only truly legitimate constitution, rests on the view that the rational state under the rule of law is a democratic state which serves the ideal of justice, and whose very nature can be conceived and grasped only by the language of right and freedom.[303] And, for Kant, 'no state can fulfil its genuine task of the realization of right and the protection of freedom if it does not adhere to the principle of separation of powers as an indispensable basis of its constitution.'[304]

In every political society the sovereignty of the state assumes its form in an elaborate and specified system of governmental institutions. 'The final power in the community is thus collected at a single point within its institutional structure';[305] and in modern political theory it is the constitution of the state which determines the particular institutional structure. For example, the so-called constitutional monarchy that obtains in Britain is a particular form of political state, characterized by its own peculiar institutional structure, wherein the constitutional monarch is at the center or apex of an elaborate and specified system of governmental institutions and therefore plays a role in the constitution of the state.[306] Thus, in an Hegelian sense, the monarch is an essential moment of the state, notwithstanding its mere formality and virtual lack of jurisdictional competence, functioning simply as the symbolic culmination of the decision-making process.[307] The monarchy is itself an institution of the political state, regulated by the constitution.

American Republicanism

As we have earlier indicated, in his classic work, *The Spirit of the Laws*, Montesquieu emphasized that the English system of governance of the eighteenth century was notable as one of the few in history that had effectively secured the liberty of the citizenry.[308] He considered England to be the 'one nation ... in the world that has for the direct end of its constitution political liberty.'[309] It was a system of political liberty in which the citizen was constrained by law, but the authorities who made and administered the laws were also constrained. This idea of political liberty meant that members of society were protected from each other, but they were also protected from the state.[310] Thus, for Montesquieu, England was essentially a republic despite having a monarch, given that the power of the English monarch was limited by 'the rule of law.'

Also central to Montesquieu's thought was the notion of a *functional* separation of powers: the idea that the different functions of the state should be performed by different institutional organs, but each having the authority to act as a check upon the other. For him, the separation of the legislative and executive powers was necessary in any state, republican or monarchical, whose animating 'spirit' was civic liberty, since this was essential to the control of the coercive authority of the state.[311] In addition, Montesquieu thought that the English constitution further protected liberty by dividing the legislative branch into a lower and upper house, which 'check one another by the mutual privilege of rejecting' the proposals of each.[312]

In the final analysis, for Montesquieu, the genius of the English constitution laid in its having solved the problem of political power.[313] This was effected by a constitutional arrangement of 'mixed government' – a combination of monarchy, aristocracy, and democracy; in addition to a constitutional mechanism of a functional separation of powers: the idea that the different functions of the state should be performed by different institutional organs, but arranged in such a way that they limit the powers of each other within their respective jurisdictional boundaries. To repeat, then, on Montesquieu's analysis of the English constitution and political system, it was concluded that England was essentially a republic, despite having a monarch. As between 'monarchy' and 'republic', Montesquieu clearly favoured the latter over the former. Still, in his view, a monarchy can be a 'moderate government', if the monarch is constrained in the exercise of his authority. And such constraints, he thought, can only be exercised by the construction of a constitutional machinery, which, as in the case of England, produced 'a republic under the form of monarchy.'[314]

We have also noted that the English system of government was widely admired in the later eighteenth century, particularly by the Americans, who, when, following their successful War of Independence over the British, had come to devise a constitution for themselves, in order to bind the thirteen former colonies into a single union, thought that there was no better model to emulate.[315] True, they constructed a political system that differed greatly from the English one in structural details; still, it was one that was guided by the same basic view of the purposes, and dangers, of political power.[316] Montesquieu was thus regarded as 'the oracle who is always consulted and cited on this subject' of how the liberty of the people may be secured against the power of the state.[317] Indeed, it was Montesquieu's theory of partial separation of powers that guided the construction of the several state constitutions, and the same principle was also followed in the proposed federal Constitution.[318]

Today, the United States is widely regarded as the primary exemplar of democratic republican government. The American Constitution is self-consciously republican; and it guarantees republican government to every constituent state of the United States of America. The idea of monarchical government was therefore expressly rejected. The American pursuit of the republican ideal is expressly stated in the Constitution's Preamble: 'We the People of the United States do hereby ordain and establish this Constitution in order to secure the blessings of *Liberty* for ourselves and our posterity...' These words are an articulate expression of the fundamental principles of republican constitutionalism. They give expression to the fundamental idea of popular sovereignty, and to the end to which the people aspire: 'to secure the blessings of Liberty', and to provide for the 'common good'.

The classic exposition of American republicanism, as it existed when the United States Constitution was debated and ratified, has been given by James Madison, Alexander Hamilton and John Jay, writing under the name of Publius. In their collection of essays, *The Federalist Papers*, they articulated the same central elements of republican constitutionalism that had dominated the state conventions, and the writings of English and Roman republican thinkers since Cicero and Polybius.[319] These included popular sovereignty, a senate, independent magistrates and a (quasi-) democratic assembly, seeking to establish 'justice' and the 'common good' on the basis of 'liberty', 'virtue' and the 'rule of law.'[320]

Above all, then, one of Publius' principal concerns was how to curb and control the excesses of popular government in light of the fact that republican governments are also given to arbitrariness, injustice, and disorders that had plagued other forms of government. Both Federalists and Anti-federalists were therefore united in the common view that the purpose of republican government is to establish 'justice' and the 'common good' on the basis of 'liberty' and 'virtue' through the 'rule of law' in a mixed and 'balanced' government.[321] Therefore, the distinctive challenge facing American republicans in the establishment of a federal republic was how to frame a constitution on the basis of justice, liberty and the pursuit of the public good whilst avoiding the vices and corruption to which the Roman republic had succumbed, or the Cromwellian dictatorship on which the English republic had floundered.[322] The central lesson said to have been drawn by Cicero and Montesquieu from Rome's destruction was that republican government required that sovereignty should rest ultimately in the hands of the *populus*, but that the people should never exercise it directly, as they had at times in Rome.[323] American republicans therefore embraced the idea of a bicameral legislature, the rule of law, the independence of the judiciary, and the sovereignty of the people, but this sovereignty was expressed through a system of elected representative government in which the people did not have a direct say. The idea was to curb the 'turbulence and follies of democracy' that had beset the Roman republic where the people approved the laws.[324] And the idea of a senate was to secure a check upon the popular assembly. That is to say, the senate would have a veto power over legislation coming from the popular assembly and the legal prerogative to advise and consent to certain executive actions.[325]

To repeat, then, American republicans, in particular John Adams, James Wilson and the Federalist Publius, all shared a common American conception of republicanism, which they drew from the literature and experience of the Roman and English republics.[326] They sought to realise Liberty, Justice, Virtue and the Common Good through popular sovereignty and the rule of law under a mixed and balanced constitution comprising elected magistrates, a deliberative senate and a representative popular assembly.[327] In a word, this re-echoed the consensus among Rome's great historians that the substance of republican government consisted in a search for the common good, pursued under the rule of law, through a sovereign people acting in a popular assembly, subject to the authority of a senate and the discipline of elected magistrates. It bears emphasis that the popular assembly stood first among the balanced institutions of any republican government, to confirm the republic's fundamental commitment to popular sovereignty and the 'imperium populi.'[328]

The republican government ultimately defended by Publius and other American republicans was one consisting of a legislature divided into separate houses to 'check the intemperate passions' of the popular assembly and one from which the people were excluded in their collective capacity, an independent executive separate from the legislature, and an independent judiciary separate from the executive and the legislature. This, the Americans had reasoned, was the best institutional arrangement for securing the republican virtues of Justice, Liberty, and the Rule of Law.[329]

In the American republican tradition, the idea of independent self-governance is underscored, first and foremost, in the Declaration of Independence. Indeed, the very first paragraph of the *Federalist* poses the question, whether the abiding principles of the Declaration of Independence can be realized in practice. By raising the question whether a 'society of men are really capable or not of establishing good government from reflection and choice, or whether they are forever destined to depend for their political constitutions on accident and force', Publius was in fact asking whether the people are really capable of exercising in practice the fundamental right proclaimed in the Declaration, namely, 'to institute new Government, laying its Foundation on such Principles, and organizing its Powers in such form, as to them shall seem most likely to effect their Safety and Happiness.'[330] In other words, there is no incompatibility between Publius' overriding purpose and the basic values of the Declaration. Thus, acceptance of the fundamental principles of the Declaration would explain the rejection of the English monarchical tradition in the Federal Constitution and, in its stead, the enactment of the principle of republican citizenship.[331]

The Federal Republican Constitution, in contrast to the British Constitution, has enacted the idea of 'popular government'; that is to say, a system of government that is an 'unmixed' republic, one whose foundations are wholly popular, 'with no qualifications of wealth, of birth, of religious faith, or of civil profession' for elective office.[332] The path to elective office is open to 'every citizen whose merit may recommend him to the esteem and confidence of his country.'[333] The electorate for members to the House was to be 'the great body of the people of the United States', comprised of those who are eligible to vote for members of the lower chambers in the states – 'not the rich more than the poor; not the learned more than the ignorant; not the haughty heirs of distinguished names, more than the humble sons of obscure and unpropitious fortune.'[334]

The republican remedy for the diseases – majority factions – most incident to republican government was to be found 'in the extent and proper structure of the Union' – separation of powers, federalism and limited government – and, subsequently, in the Bill of Rights.[335] Far from being incompatible with republicanism, Publius maintained that separation of powers was indispensably necessary. For Publius, the history of republics was scarcely encouraging given their demonstrated incapacity to control the violence of faction. In the final analysis, therefore, Publius' most enduring and significant contribution to the practice of self-government resides in the degree to which he was able to show how and why republicanism could be reconciled with the complex and interrelated elements of constitutionalism broadly defined, such as the principle of separation of powers and the idea of limited government. Separation of powers and limited government are not only compatible with but are supportive of republicanism.[336]

From our earlier discussion of English republicanism, it is quite obvious that republicanism can take different forms, even though in the final analysis all constitutional republics embody the notion of popular sovereignty. Also, the principle of separation of powers does not tell us how the powers and authority are divided, nor does limited government inform us about the substance and nature of the limitations.[337] For example, Publius argued for a separation of the three competences of the state: the executive, the legislative, and the judicial, far beyond the partial separation in the English constitution. Still, the overriding objective was to secure individual liberty, order, and the rule of law; and to minimize, as much as was feasible, the possibility of arbitrary and capricious government.[338] Thus, in Federalist 10 Publius writes: 'To secure the public good and private rights against the danger of [majority factions], and at the same time to preserve the spirit and form of popular government, is then the great object to which our inquiries are directed.'[339]

So among the subjects Publius addressed was 'the conformity of the proposed Constitution to the true principles of republican government.' He defines republican government as one 'which derives all its powers directly or indirectly from the great body of the people, and is administered by persons holding their offices during pleasure for a limited period, or during good behaviour.'[340] For a government to be truly republican, 'it is essential ... that it be derived from the great body of the society, not from an inconsiderable proportion or favored class of it.' And this, it bears emphasis, did not mean immediate or direct rule by the people; it is enough, according to Publius, that those who govern are ultimately accountable, directly or indirectly, to the people. Publius therefore defined republican government in terms of those principles relating to the derivation and exercise of power.[341] A republic, in opposition to pure democracy, say, is 'a government in which the scheme of representation takes place.' For Publius, then, 'mixed' regimes which recognize and institutionalize the claims and interests of 'favored' classes – e.g., the 'hereditary aristocracy and monarchy' in England – simply did not fit the republican category.[342]

The proposed Constitution of 1787 therefore fitted nicely into Publius' conception of republicanism. The very process of constitutional founding spoke to that. It was a constitution ordained by the People of the United States for their own Happiness and designed to secure the Blessings of Liberty to themselves and their posterity. It was therefore a constitution established on the idea of the sovereignty of the people. However, there was the modern innovation of 'representation' which Publius and his fellow federalists believed would save the American republic from the avarice, ambition, factions and corruption that had ruined the English Commonwealth and Rome.[343] Thus, for Madison, the great difference between the American and other republics consisted in the principle of representation.[344]

In the American context, this meant, as we have earlier noted, 'the total exclusion of the people in their collective capacity from any share in the government, and not in the total exclusion of the representatives of the people, from the administration of the government.'[345] Therefore, unlike the Roman Republic, the new American constitutions saw to it that the people had no direct role in administration or legislation at all.[346] The 'right of suffrage' was therefore considered a fundamental article of representative government.[347]

This idea of representative government replaced the 'pure democracy' of the ancient polity: the ancient conception of a popular or democratic assembly in person. This, the federalists believed, was the most effective way to secure justice and the public good – the essential virtues of republican government. The genius of republican liberty required that all power be derived from the people, but the people's representatives must be carefully controlled and balanced to avoid an 'elective despotism' by the legislature.[348] This meant a balance and separation between the different departments of government, and a bicameral legislature.

For Publius, the 'dispersion-of-power' or separation of powers principle was an indispensable article of republican government. Simply, the principle requires that the principal governmental powers or functions of making law, of executing or administering law, and of adjudicating those cases where the law has to be applied, must be dispersed among different hands.[349] A consolidation of functions in the hands of one person or group would, more likely than not, conduce to arbitrary government. As James Madison writes in Federalist 47: 'The accumulation of all powers, legislative, executive, and judicial, in the same hands, whether of one, a few, or many, and whether hereditary, self-appointed, or elective, may justly be pronounced the very definition of tyranny.'[350]

The separation of powers principle simply means that those who must determine whether legislation does conform to constitutionalist constraints are not the legislators themselves. Also, if those who execute the law are to be required to conform to existing laws in their mode of execution, then it is important that they are not their own judges. It is important that the relevant judicial power, by which the execution and making of law may be sanctioned, be in other hands.[351] So then, the separation-of-powers constraint is indispensable to the promotion of the just state, because it means that the authorities are accountable in various ways to one another and are therefore subject to mutual sanctioning; that is to say, the legislature can censure the executive for failing to execute its laws properly, and the judiciary can expose the legislature to criticism by finding that the laws it makes are out of keeping with certain constitutional provisions.[352] To repeat the Kantian injunction: 'No state can fulfil its genuine task of the realization of right and the protection of freedom if it does not adhere to the principle of separation of powers as an indispensable basis of its constitution.'[353]

American Republican Constitutionalism

But this relationship between separation of powers and republicanism merits special attention, given that, to some, the American version of the separation of powers principle may seem to have compromised the republican principle or the idea of popular control of government. In particular, the American introduction of a bill of fundamental rights in the Constitution had made it even more compelling that the more basic and fundamental laws not be subject to excessively easy, majoritarian amendment. Thus, on this view, the republican conception of the just state would reject a concept of law that would locate 'the ultimate source of law in public opinion and the will of the legislature.'[354] In other words, the idea of fundamental rights underscored the fact that law, in particular constitutional law, is legitimated by something other than the fact of enjoying popular majority support. Law is legitimated to the extent of its justness. It is essential, therefore, in order to preserve the integrity of the fundamental law and to make effective the idea of constitutional constraints on the law and on the powers of the state, that the fundamental law not be subject to the will of majority faction.[355] It therefore bears emphasis that Publius' alleged compromising of the republican principle by his advocacy of the institutional separation of powers was to secure the rule of law and the values associated with it, not the least of these being liberty under the law.[356] Thus, central to the relationship Publius draws between republicanism and separation of powers is the need for checks on the legislature in particular, considered to be the most powerful branch of government and therefore the most dangerous to liberty and the rule of law. It is the legislative assembly, he thought, that most bears watching because its powers are broader 'and less susceptible to precise limits' than either the executive or the judicial powers. What is more, in a republic, the legislature enjoys 'full discretion ... over the pecuniary reward of those who fill the other branches.'[357]

The real challenge facing Publius was to show how constitutionalism – understood in terms of the values to be served by separation of powers such as freedom from governmental oppression, liberty, and a steady and impartial execution of the laws with regard to both ruler and ruled – could be combined with his conception of republicanism, which, in the final analysis, involved rule by deliberative majorities.[358] In the round, however, Publius' ultimate aim was to secure limited government. Thus he writes:

> By a limited Constitution, I understand one which contains certain specified exceptions to the legislative authority; such, for instance, that it shall pass no bills of

attainder, no *ex-post facto* laws, and the like. Limitations of this kind can be preserved in practice no other way than through the medium of courts of justice, whose duty it must be to declare all acts contrary to the manifest tenor of the Constitution void. Without this, all reservations of particular rights or privileges would amount to nothing.[359]

Publius' conception of 'limited constitution' was therefore made evident in the remarkable development of the practice of judicial review: the power of the courts to review democratically enacted legislation. This is one of the most critical mechanisms of constitutional constraint in the republican polity to which the citizens might agree in the *original* act of founding.

By granting to [the Court] a non-legislative body that is not electorally accountable the power to review democratically enacted legislation, citizens provide themselves with a means for protecting their sovereignty and independence from the unreasonable exercise of their political rights in legislative processes. ... By agreeing to judicial review, they in effect tie themselves into their unanimous agreement on the equal basic rights that specify their sovereignty.[360]

In other words, constitutional constraints may be regarded as forms of democratic precommitment that a people may take against their own imperfections.[361]

Constitutionalism secures the rule of law. It brings about predictability and security in the relations of individuals to the government by defining in advance the powers and limits of that government.[362] It binds government by rules laid down in advance of its actions – even when these actions are the results of majority decisions. In other words, constitutionalism presupposes that there are good moral reasons for a people to posit in advance concrete determinations about what morally ought to be done, even though these determinations may from time to time conflict with majority *democratic* decisions.[363]

The words of the Preamble to the American Constitution are unmistakably an articulate expression of the fundamental principles of republican constitutionalism. They give expression to the fundamental idea of popular sovereignty and to the ends to which the people aspire in the establishment of the Constitution: 'to secure the blessings of Liberty', and to provide for the 'common good.' The resulting structure would further support this claim. This means, therefore, that the separation of powers is clearly the central architectonic principle of the Constitution. Both the presidency and Congress are representative political institutions of *'We the People.'* The Supreme Court is less obviously so, but it is nonetheless a *representative* institution of the Sovereign People, since it was *they* who spoke it into existence. In other words, the institutional arrangements resulting from the Constitution's architectonic plan assigned the legislative, executive and judicial powers or functions of the State to the respective specialized institutions. This was the institutionalization of the separation of powers principle, whose principal office in any constitutional arrangement is to control the coercive authority of the state. In other words, the institutional, and by extension the functional, separation of powers was understood as serving to protect the liberties of the people from the power of the state.

As Professor Scott Gordon explains, the political theory of the Constitution as expounded by Publius in the *Federalist Papers* clearly reveals that an overriding concern of the Framers was the protection of the liberty of the citizen by the prudent control of political power. Consequently, the *Federalist* repeatedly employs the concepts of separation of powers and checks and balances. It describes a design of government in which the several institutions were both independent and interconnected, in such a fashion that each could exercise constraints upon the others, but without one dominating another.[364] For example, the Bodinian proposition that sovereignty resides in the institution that makes law was transmuted into the view that legislatures are only derivative repositories of sovereign authority, exercising it *pro tempore* on behalf of the people.[365] So, in the final analysis, what would ultimately guarantee that the state would not become tyrannous are the positive institutional conditions that would constrain the exercise of political power. As was stated in the instructions given to Boston's representatives to the Massachusetts Bay Assembly in 1776:

> 'Tis essential to liberty that the legislative, judicial, and executive powers of government, be, as nearly as possible, independent of and separate from, each other; for where they are united in the same persons, then would be wanting that mutual check which is the principal security against the making of arbitrary laws, and a wanton exercise of power in the execution of them.[366]

Also, the critical problem of protecting minorities from the will of the majority must be solved if the republican ideal of political liberty is to be made a reality. It is a question of protecting the legitimate interests of minorities in a political system based on popular sovereignty. This was a particular concern for many Americans given that the proposed Constitution of 1787 did not include a specific statement of basic citizen rights.[367] In the *Federalist* 10, Madison proffers the solution to the problem of reconciling majority rule with minority rights. As one commentator puts it, 'The essence of Madison's greatness as a theorist and a politician lay in his insight into how to reconcile the rights of individuals and minorities with the necessity of majority rule. The solution he embraced was the extended compound republic, an idea that turned prevailing theory on its head.'[368]

But, perhaps, the critical auxiliary mechanisms for protecting the legitimate interests of minorities in a political system based on popular sovereignty were to come from the addition to the Constitution of the 1789 Bill of Rights and the subsequent development of the practice of judicial review. Today, the Bill of Rights is regarded as an integral part of the Constitution of the United States, even though it was not included in the initial proposal. 'Specific statements of civic rights that were not to be infringed by government were contained in most of the state constitutions, and the inclusion of a similar statement in the proposed national Constitution was strongly urged at the Philadelphia Convention by George Mason of Virginia. But this idea received no support and was rejected.'[369] However, it was the very absence of a specific statement of civic rights that were not to be infringed by the federal government that constituted one of the main grounds of the Anti-Federalists' attack on the proposed constitution.[370] Therefore, it was in consequence of a compromise reached over the inclusion of a specific statement of civic rights that ratification by the states was secured. The Constitution was therefore amended to include a statement of rights.

But a constitutional Bill of Rights would hardly serve to effectively constrain government in the absence of the positive institutional conditions that would secure the legal enforcement of the stated rights. This underscores the critical importance of the separation of powers to the rule of law and, in particular, an independent judiciary that would make possible the exercise of judicial review: the power of courts to review the constitutionality of legal norms enacted by democratic organs of the state. This doctrine of judicial review was given canonical expression by Chief Justice John Marshall in the seminal case of *Marbury v. Madison*. And, although *Marbury* was not itself about the enforcement of a fundamental right against governmental encroachment, the doctrine has nonetheless expanded over time to this area so that, today, the history of American constitutional development is seen, in large part, as the history of the role of the federal courts as guardians of the rights specified in the amendments to the Constitution that are aimed at constraining the power of the federal and state governments.[371]

Marbury may therefore be read as a classic exposition of American republicanism. In constructing an opinion that would ultimately lay the philosophical foundations for the role of the Supreme Court as the final arbiter of the Constitution, Chief Justice Marshall read the Constitution as a whole as an articulate expression of the fundamental principles of limited republican government. That is to say, he understood the polity constituted by the written constitutional text to be a 'government of law and not of men'; and the Constitution itself as an expression of a sovereign people. In a word, the idea of the rule of law based on a constitution established by the people.[372]

A polity under the rule of law is one in which ruler and ruled are alike subject to the law's commands. So whether it be the President of the United States or the King of Great Britain, they are equally answerable in law where the vested legal right of the citizen has been violated.[373] For, '[t]he very essence of civil liberty certainly consists in the right of every individual to claim the protection of the laws, whenever he receives an injury. One of the first duties of government is to afford that protection. In Great Britain the King himself is sued in the respectful form of a petition, and he never fails to comply with the judgment of his court.'[374] And Marshall further added: 'The government of the United States has been emphatically termed a government of laws, and not of men. It will certainly cease to deserve this high appellation, if the laws furnish no remedy for the violation of a vested legal right.'[375]

Moreover, Marshall understood the rule of law as a system of representation. That is to say, in a system of political belief that takes popular sovereignty as its first principle, the rule of law is deemed to make its appearance as the representation of the sovereign people. As Professor Paul Kahn puts it, the authoritative source of law is always outside of law itself. Law appears to us as the expression of the sovereign's will; the sovereign being the normative origin of the legal order conceived as a single subject acting at a particular time.[376] For Marshall, the sovereign people have an original right to establish, for their future government, such principles as, in their opinion, shall most conduce to their own happiness. 'The exercise of this original right is a very great exertion; nor can it, nor ought it to be frequently repeated. The principles, therefore, so established, are deemed fundamental. And as the authority from which they proceed, is supreme, and can seldom act, they are designed to be permanent.'[377] Moreover, 'This original and supreme will organizes the government, and assigns, to different departments, their respective powers.'[378] The rule of law therefore makes its appearance through the *representative* institutions created by the sovereign's will. Therefore, the Supreme Court, whose judicial office is to enforce the Constitution and the laws of the United States, is also a *representative* institution of the sovereign people.

Commonwealth Caribbean Republican Constitutionalism

It is a common sentiment among political scientists and students of constitutional theory that Great Britain and the United States represent two of the most outstanding and successful models of constitutional democratic government. As one student of constitutional theory puts it, 'the story of modern constitutionalism may in many ways be depicted as a great debate between American and British principles.'[379] As was earlier noted, when the Americans came to the task of fashioning a national constitution, 'in order to form a more perfect union and to secure the blessings of liberty', they found an exemplary model in the British Constitution; though England was by no means the *fons et origo* of constitutional theory and practice.[380] True, the Americans have established a form of government structurally different from that of Great Britain; still, it is a system of government that rests on the same foundational principles of democratic republican government: government based on popular sovereignty, under the rule of law, and checked and balanced by the separation of powers, including an independent judiciary.[381] The ultimate end of this form of government is the political and civic liberty of the citizenry. Thus, we have said, the British Constitution, despite its inclusion of monarchic and hereditary - aristocratic institutions, may properly be seen as belonging to the genus of republican government. So then, Great Britain and the United States are two outstanding exemplars of democratic, republican government.

Commonwealth Caribbean constitutionalism is properly located somewhere between the 'unwritten' constitutionalism of the United Kingdom and the 'written' constitutionalism of the United States. The British colonies in the West Indies had existed for centuries. Their development from colonies to independent sovereign states was consequent upon their nurturing in British constitutional forms and principles. In other words, the political forms and underlying principles of governance, which were developed in England (and ultimately in Britain), following the 1688 Glorious Revolution, were in fact transplanted to these West Indian colonies. Commonwealth Caribbean constitutionalism has obviously developed under the nurturance of English/British constitutionalism. It is therefore understandable that the *West Indian Independence Constitution*, which was the product of negotiations conducted by colonial leaders and British imperial officials and subsequently legislated as an order in council of the imperial parliament, would bear a distinctly British cast. Modeled after the British Constitution, the *West Indian Independence Constitution* is otherwise referred to as a written version of the Westminster-style constitution, with a judicially enforceable Bill of Rights appended.

The critical importance of the colonial experience in shaping the model of constitution and form of governmental organization that these former colonies have adopted at the time of political independence can never be overstated. Therefore, with the single exception of Guyana, all Commonwealth Caribbean states have a governmental structure similar to that of Britain: the Cabinet system headed by a prime minister, and chosen from amongst the persons elected to the House of Representatives; an unelected, nominated upper house, the Senate and, most importantly, a judiciary that is institutionally independent of both the executive and legislative branches. On this view, Commonwealth Caribbean constitutionalism shares with British and American constitutionalism the philosophical position that good government means constrained government, and that the only way of achieving this is by structuring the 'frame of government' as a pluralistic compound of separated and mutually controlling institutions.[382]

But this may in fact overstate the separation of powers under the *West Indian Independence Constitution*. For the nearly complete fusion of the legislative and executive powers, which Bagehot has identified as a defining feature of the English constitution, has nearly been perfected in the Commonwealth Caribbean constitutional arrangements where, in the instance of a small legislature, almost the entire majority in parliament might well comprise the entire Cabinet. This underscores the critical importance of the separatedness and independence of the judiciary to the notion of limited government and the rule of law as the foundation of civic liberty and protection from arbitrary political power. As Blackstone has emphasized in the *Commentaries*:

In this distinct and separate existence of the judicial power in a peculiar body of men, nominated indeed, but not removable at pleasure, by the crown, consists one main preservative of the public liberty; which cannot subsist long in any state, unless the administration of common justice be in some degree separated both from the legislative and from the executive power. Were it joined with the legislative, the life, liberty, and property, of the subject would be in the hands of arbitrary judges, whose decisions would be then regulated only by their own opinions, and not by any fundamental principles of law; which, though legislators may depart from, yet judges are bound to observe.[383]

But the force of the separation of powers principle under Britain's largely unwritten constitution must be found in the conventions and 'spirit' of the constitution, interpreted in the light of the requirements of the rule of law.[384] With the *partial* agency of House of Lords and judiciary in each other, the separation and independence of legislature and judicature has been judicially described as a constitutional convention of the highest importance. For if as judge, legislator, member of Cabinet, and head of an administrative department, the Lord Chancellor is 'the spectacular exhibit in the museum of constitutional curiosities', he is rightly subject to firm conventions governing his various roles.[385] He is expected to divorce his judicial from his political roles. Also, the convention which constitutes the Judicial Committee as an impartial and independent court of law suffices to preserve the separation of powers. As was stated in *British Coal Corporation v. R.*, 'According to constitutional convention it is unknown and unthinkable that His Majesty in Council should not give effect to the report of the Judicial Committee, who are thus in truth an appellate court of law....'[386]

Under the written *West Indian Independence Constitution,* however, the separation of powers – in particular the separation of legislature and an independent judiciary – need not be a matter of constitutional convention, since writing allows for the institutional crafting of the judiciary separate and apart from the legislature and executive branches. This raises the question of the strength of the analogy drawn by Lord Diplock, in *Hinds v. The Queen,*[387] between the Jamaican Constitution, based on the 'Westminster model' and 'the basic concept of separation of the legislative, executive and judicial power as it had been developed in the unwritten constitution of the United Kingdom.'[388] In other words, one wonders whether the separation of powers under the Jamaican Constitution which Lord Diplock has celebrated in *Hinds* does not in fact bring that Constitution into a closer kinship with the American Constitution, thereby making *Hinds* the *progeny* of *Marbury v. Madison,* rather than the product of British constitutionalism. In a word, the Jamaican Independence Con-stitution, though modeled after Britain's, is, in some respects, probably more like that of the United States.

It bears repeating that the essential values of law, liberty and democracy are best protected if the three primary functions of a government under law are discharged by three distinct institutions.[389] This idea was firmly grasped by the Englishman John Locke who wrote in his Second Treatise of Civil Government:

> It may be too great a temptation to humane frailty, apt to grasp at power, for the same persons who have the power of making laws, to have also in their hands the power to execute them, whereby they may exempt themselves from obedience to the laws they make, and suit the law, both in its making and execution to their own private advantage.[390]

The doctrine of the separation of powers was developed further by the French jurist, Baron de Montesquieu, who based his exposition on the British constitution of the early 18th century, in his work, *De L'Esprit des Lois*. And although Montesquieu did not by any means originate this idea of the separation of powers, it is generally accepted that the *Laws*, more than any other document, was responsible for the importance it attained in later-eighteenth-century constitutional theory.[391] He wrote:

> When the legislative and executive powers are united in the same person, or in the same body of magistrates, there can be no liberty ... Again, there is no liberty, if the judiciary power be not separated from the legislative and executive. Were it joined with the legislative, the life and liberty of the subject would be exposed to arbitrary control; for the judge would then be the legislator. Were it joined to the executive however, the judge might behave with violence and oppression. There would be an end to everything, were the same men, or the same body, whether of the nobles or of the people, to exercise those three powers, that of enacting laws, that of executing the public resolutions, and of trying the causes of individuals.[392]

But it is understood that Montesquieu's was more of a *functional* separation of powers, since he reduced the effective functional entities to two, construing the judiciary as part of the executive.[393] That is to say, in the chapter of *The Spirit of the Laws* dealing with the English Constitution, he emphasized the role of the executive and the two branches of the legislature as checks on one another, and dismissed the judicial power as 'in some measure next to nothing.'[394] The judges were 'only the mouth that pronounces the words of the law, inanimate beings who can moderate neither its force nor its rigour', and the legislative power would not 'bow before the tribunals of law, which are lower than it.'[395] As Professor Jeffrey Goldsworthy observes, in most theoretical writings of this period, the judicial power was treated as merely one aspect of the executive power, which was acknowledged to be vested in the Crown and subordinate to the legislature.[396]

So it was in Madison's and Hamilton's interpretation of Locke and Montesquieu that we were to find a clearer articulation of the structural principle of institutional and functional separation of powers. That is to say, by 'separation of powers', Madison and Hamilton meant to refer to the establishment of the executive, the judiciary, and the two houses of Congress as separate *institutions* each with its own constitutional status and none subservient to another.[397] Note, for example, Hamilton's statement on the independence of the judiciary in *Federalist* no. 78:

> The complete independence of the courts of justice is peculiarly essential in a limited constitution ... [i.e.] one that contains certain specified exceptions to the legislative authority; such, for instance, as that it shall pass no bills of attainder, no *ex-post-facto* laws, and the like. Limitations of this kind can be preserved in practice no other way than through the medium of courts of justice, whose duty it must be to declare all acts contrary to the manifest tenor of the Constitution void. Without this, all reservations of particular rights and privileges would amount to nothing.[398]

In this statement, Hamilton has drawn the intimate connection between the *institutional* separation of powers and the practice of judicial review and, above all, the critical importance of the writtenness of the constitution – a fact that Chief Justice John Marshall would later make a great deal of in articulating the doctrine of judicial review in *Marbury v. Madison*. So, although in every other respect but the structure of their governmental systems, the British and the United States constitutions may be said to 'rest upon the same notions of law, of justice, and of the relation between the rights of individuals and the rights of the government, or the state',[399] the fact of the writtenness of one constitution and the unwrittenness of the other has made for different important constitutional practices in the two. Writing makes possible the institutional crafting of the judiciary as a coordinate branch of government, with the judicial office defined in such a way as to allow for the practice of judicial review. Thus, the reduction of constitutional principles to written form was seen to be a crucial development for, as Justice William Patterson put it in 1795, '[i]t is difficult to say what the constitution of England is; because not being reduced to written certainty and precision, it lies entirely at the mercy of the Parliament ... there is no written constitution, no fundamental law, nothing visible, nothing real, nothing certain, by which a statute can be tested.'[400] And, as Professor Richard Kay has more recently observed, under a written constitution the extent of state power can, in the first instance, be ascertained by the ordinary judicial process of construction of a legal enactment. But English judges respond to challenges to the validity of acts of Parliament by putting forward the rule of parliamentary supremacy as an axiom of the legal system:[401]

> What the statute itself enacts cannot be unlawful, because what the statute says is itself the law, and the highest form of law that is known to this country. It is the law which prevails over every other form of law, and it is not for the court to say that a parliamentary enactment, the highest law in this country, is illegal.[402]

It follows, then, that no matter how ineradicable the independence of the judiciary and of the judicial process as features of the 'Westminster model' constitutions, in the absence of a single, venerated document, legal reasoning must depend on 'what, though not expressed, is none the less a necessary implication from the subject-matter and structure of the constitution....'[403] But as Justice Iredell has said, a constitution should not be 'a mere imaginary thing, ... but a written document to which all may have recourse.'[404] In sum, the principle of parliamentary sovereignty, which Dicey refers to as 'the dominant characteristic of [British] political institutions' and which means that Parliament has 'the right to make or unmake any law whatever and, further, that no person or body is recognized by the law of England as having a right to override or set aside the legislation of Parliament',[405] is denied as the dominant principle of the written Jamaican Constitution. Thus, whereas in Britain, the absence of a single written constitutional text has resulted in the absence of a tradition of review of primary legislation, thereby leaving ultimate responsibility for reconciling individual rights with the needs of the public interest largely in the hands of the legislature, under the Jamaican Constitution, as *Hinds* has clearly established, judicial review of primary legislation that supposedly threatens individual rights is advanced as a necessary requirement in the enforcement of a written superior law against the legislative and executive branches of government.[406] In other words, Lord Pearce's statement, in giving the court's advice in *Liyanage v. R.*, that any analogy with the British Constitution must be indirect since an unwritten constitution could provide no helpful guidance in interpreting a written document, would seem quite apropos.[407]

The *Hinds* case involved the establishment of the Gun Court at the height of a wave of gun crimes in the 1970s. One of the provisions of the Gun Court Act, by which the Court was established, affected to confer jurisdiction on resident magistrates to hear firearm offences, previously triable only by Supreme Court judges. Another provision concerned the establishment of a Review Board to determine the length of sentences of persons convicted under the Act. The Review Board consisted of five members: a judge of the Supreme Court or Court of Appeal, serving as the Chairman, and four other persons (the director of prisons, the chief medical officer, a nominee of the Jamaica Council of Churches, and a psychiatrist appointed by the Prime Minister after consultation with the Leader of the Opposition). It means, then, that the majority of the Review Board were not persons appointed in accordance with Chapter VII of the Constitution, which relates to the appointment of persons exercising judicial powers.

Lord Diplock, who delivered the decision of the Judicial Committee, remarked on the separation of powers principle, which he said is a fundamental principle of all Westminster-model constitutions, of which the Jamaican Constitution is an example. He described the written constitutions, established by United Kingdom statutes or orders in council, as 'drafted by persons nurtured in the tradition of that branch of the common law of England that is concerned with public law and familiar in particular with the basic concept of separation of legislative, executive and judicial power as it had been developed in the unwritten constitution of the United Kingdom.'[408] He further noted that

> The chapter dealing with the judicature invariably contains provisions dealing with the method of appointment and security of tenure of the members of the judiciary, which are designed to assure to them a degree of independence from the other branches of government.
>
> What, however, is implicit in the very structure of a constitution on the Westminster model is that judicial power, however it be distributed from time to time between various courts, is to continue to be vested in persons appointed to hold judicial office in the manner

and on the terms laid down in the chapter dealing with the judicature, even though this is not expressly stated in the constitution.[409]

The legislature might provide for the establishment of new courts, in the exercise of its power to make laws for the 'peace, order and good government' of the state. When, however, under a constitution on the Westminster model, a law is made by the parliament which purports to confer jurisdiction on a court described by a new name, the question whether the law conflicts with the provisions of the constitution dealing with the exercise of judicial power does not depend on the label which the parliament attaches to the judges when exercising the jurisdiction conferred on them by the law whose constitutionality is impugned.[410] Rather, the question must be: What is the nature of the jurisdiction to be exercised by the judges who are to compose the court to which the new label is attached? Does the method of their appointment and security of their tenure conform to the requirements of the constitution applicable to judges who, at the time the constitution came into force, exercised jurisdiction of that nature?[411]

It bears emphasis that those provisions pertaining to the higher judiciary are deeply entrenched in the Constitution and, therefore, any alteration thereto must be according to the procedures specified in the Constitution, which, in some cases, might include 'a direct vote of the majority of the people themselves.' 'The manifest intention of these provisions is that all those who hold any salaried judicial office in Jamaica shall be appointed on the recommendation of the Judicial Service Commission and that their independence from political pressure by Parliament or by the Executive in the exercise of their judicial functions shall be assured by granting to them such degree of security of tenure in their office as is justified by the importance of the jurisdiction that they exercise.'[412]

As Professor Allan notes, it would seem to follow from the foregoing that the separation of powers and, in particular, the independence of the judiciary and of the judicial process are ineradicable features of the 'Westminster model' of constitutions – including, of course, the constitution of the United Kingdom. It could not be too strongly emphasised that the British constitution, though largely unwritten, is 'firmly based on the separation of powers: Parliament makes the laws, the judiciary interprets them.'[413] However, in the absence of a single, venerated document, legal reasoning must depend on 'what, though not expressed, is none the less a necessary implication from the subject-matter and structure of the constitution ...'[414] Still, in the absence of any judicially enforceable formal limitation on the legislative power, too much is left to legislative self-restraint – a 'constitutional convention of the highest importance' in the United Kingdom.[415] It is therefore instructive that in *Hinds*, particular regard was had to the written provisions of the Jamaica Constitution in order to determine whether the Jamaican Parliament had exceeded the bounds of its constitutional authority.

Parliamentary or Presidential Republics?

On the understanding that all the independent sovereign states in the Commonwealth Caribbean, with the single exception of Guyana, are representative parliamentary republics, issue is joined on the question of the more appropriate style of republican constitution and government for these island-republics. That is to say, one of the outstanding questions for constitutional reform is whether these island-republics should retain the current model of republican constitution, with the appropriate emendations, or should they rather adopt the republican model similar to that of the United States of America?

'Prime Minister or President?'[416] This is how the question was put in recent years in respect of India, the world's largest democracy, and also the first of the so-called republics within the Commonwealth of Nations. Upon independence from Great Britain back in 1948, India adopted (or retained) the prime-ministerial system of government under which it was tutored during its long tenure of colonial rule by Britain. The question whether India should now reconsider that system of parliamentary government has been raised in response to recent instability in government resulting from the 'rainbow coalition governments being cobbled together and then held hostage by threats of defection.'[417] Many now believe it is time to have a government led by a directly elected executive president; to throw out the parliamentary system and bring about a seminal change in the format of political leadership. In a word, there is a growing section of political opinion in India favoring a largely US style of presidential government. The assumption is that this form of government would be more stable, that the president and chief executive will be directly elected and political technocrats can be brought in as members of the president's cabinet to help run the government.[418]

The question of the suitability of the US inspired presidential model over the Westminster inspired parliamentary model for the Commonwealth Caribbean merits careful consideration. Fortunately, in the Commonwealth Caribbean, where the experience with democratic institutions is of reasonably long standing, democracy is not especially challenged as a form of government by alternative ways of organizing the political community.[419] It is therefore instructive that the overriding objective behind this civic enterprise of constitutional reform is the strengthening of democratic institutions and governance, and the enhancement of citizen-participation in the affairs of the State. On this view, then, the question of the particular configuration in the constitutional design of our democratic political institutions assumes central importance. For it is now understood that political institutions contribute to the consolidation and stability of democracy.[420] That is to say, although it is conceded that institutional forms are not magic formulas capable of solving all problems, it is none the less the case that constitutions, governmental institutions and the rules of the game have considerable impact in shaping political behaviour. In other words, the formal and informal political architecture of democratic regimes and the social and economic contexts in which they operate have tremendous implications for the success or failure of democratic governance. Countries in the Commonwealth Caribbean, embarking upon the enterprise of constitutional reform, must therefore take account of this salient fact.

According to the American political theorist, Robert Dahl, there is no one universally best way to structure the constitutional arrangements of republican governance. Therefore, in the absence of one universally best solution to this problem, specific solutions may be adapted to the social, historical and economic conditions and experiences of the particular country.[421] In other words, the political institutions of a nation must be considered in relation to their broader social environment; they must be articulated consistent with the cultural and social-psychological characteristics of the society. The issue of the constitutional arrangements of political institutions may therefore be resolved by considering the likely pattern of social and economic developments in the society and the impact of the choice of political forms on such developments.

The two forms of constitutional democratic government referred to here are identified in the philosophical literature by the concepts: 'parliamentarism' and 'presidentialism', of which Great Britain and the United States are, respectively, the two most successful examples. They are in essence republican although Britain, as was earlier noted, rightfully bears the title of 'constitutional monarchy.' For the purposes of this work, then,

Carl Friedrich's observation, that 'the story of modern constitutionalism may be depicted as a great debate between American and British principles',[422] should carry considerable purchase. In other words, given the choice between these two outstandingly successful models of republican government, the question for us is which of the two we would consider the more appropriate to our particular social and economic circumstances? Which of the two, having regard to our size, our political history and the level of our social and economic development, offers a better fit with the aspirations, characteristics, and relatively conservative nature of Caribbean peoples?

These two paradigm examples of constitutional democratic government: 'parliamentarism' and 'presidentialism', are each defined by two fundamental characteristics. Alfred Stepan and Cindy Skach, for example, define the 'pure' parliamentary model of democracy as a system of mutual dependence in which the chief executive power must be supported by a majority in the legislature and can fall if it receives a vote of no confidence; and the executive power (normally in conjunction with the head of state) has the capacity to dissolve the legislature and call for elections.[423] And they define the 'pure' presidential model of democracy as a system of mutual independence in which the legislative power has a fixed electoral mandate that is its own source of legitimacy; and the chief executive power has a fixed electoral mandate that is its own source of legitimacy.[424] On their reasoning, 'these necessary and sufficient characteristics are more than classificatory. They are also the constraining conditions within which the vast majority of aspiring democracies must somehow attempt simultaneously to produce major socioeconomic changes and to strengthen democratic institutions.'[425] In view of this, therefore, these two models are considered in further detail, and their appropriateness to our circumstances in the Commonwealth Caribbean. We begin with the presidential model.

Presidentialism

Perhaps the most instructive angle from which to undertake a comparative analysis of presidential and parliamentary government is the constitution of the executive authority of the state and the consequent structure of the executive-legislative relations. The typical presidential model, such as that of the United States, is distinguished by the famous doctrine of 'the separation of powers', which, according to the American interpretation, requires that there be no overlap of personnel between the three branches of government – the legislative, the executive, and the judicial.[426] More importantly, it excludes any branch from acting on its own in selecting or replacing the people who hold offices in one of the other branches.[427] In consequence, under the presidential system, the president (the executive officer) is elected directly by the electorate, independent of the election of the legislature, and is both the holder of executive power and the symbolic head of state. Under the US Constitution, for example, '*The executive power shall be in a President of the United States of America. He shall hold his Office during the Term of four Years, and, together with the Vice President, chosen for the same Term, be elected as follows....*'[428]

Under the presidential system, the president is not only the holder of executive power, he is also the symbolic head of state. He or she is elected directly by the people for a fixed term, and cannot be dismissed, except in the exceptional case of impeachment, between elections. In short, his tenure in office is not dependent on the formal vote of confidence by the democratically elected representatives in parliament.[429] The president therefore has considerable powers in the constitution, and generally has virtually exclusive control of the composition of the cabinet and the administration.

The related outstanding feature of the presidential system is that the legislature, like the president, is also elected directly by the electorate for a fixed term, and its tenure or survival in office is independent of the president, in the same way that the president's tenure in office is independent of the legislature.[430] It means, then, that both the president and the legislature enjoy democratic legitimacy and owe their accountability directly to the people and not to each other. In consequence, the resulting structure of executive-legislative relations is often marked by the problem of 'deadlock' between the president and legislature since the two may not be of the same political party. Indeed, even when the majority party in the legislature is also of the president's party, 'deadlocks' may arise, thus resulting in enormous economic, administrative and social costs. This is compounded by the 'rigidity' of the presidential system. As Professor Juan Linz puts it:

> The ... main institutional characteristic of presidential systems is the fact that presidents are elected for a period of time which under normal circumstances cannot be modified nor shortened; and sometimes due to provisions preventing re-election, not prolonged. The political process therefore becomes broken into discontinuous rigidly determined periods without possibility for continuous readjustments as political, social and economic events might require. The time of the mandate of a president becomes an essential political factor to which all the actors in the political process have to adjust and this has many important consequences.[431]

In sum, then, this rigidity in the political process makes adjustment to changing situations extremely difficult, not allowing for the replacement of a leader who has lost the confidence even of his own party.[432] In other words, the rigidity of the system does not allow for the substitution of the president by someone more able to make a compromise with the opposition when polarization (either in the legislature or in the country at large) has reached an intensity that threatens to erupt into a political or constitutional crisis.[433] In the circumstances, the extreme measure of impeachment, in the event of a constitutional crisis, has proven far more difficult to use compared to a vote of no confidence. And barring impeachment, there are no mechanisms to change the president without violating the constitution, unless he or she is willing to resign. Note, for example, that in relatively recent times, US President Richard M. Nixon, in the wake of the 'Watergate crisis', resigned from office rather than face the possibility of impeachment. This, however, was virtually a unique situation in American politics. President Bill Clinton, even more recently, refused to resign office, and the country was faced with a long drawn out impeachment battle that eventually resulted in his 'acquittal.'

It is generally believed that the mutual independence of the presidential system, which creates the possibility of political impasse between the chief executive and the legislative body and for which there is no constitutionally available impasse-breaking device, is the single most outstanding weakness of the presidential system.[434] Presidential systems bear the great danger of political deadlock. Presidentialism systematically contributes to impasses and democratic breakdown. Because the president and the legislature have separate and fixed mandates, and because presidents often find themselves frustrated in the exercise of their power due to their lack of a legislative majority, they are more likely to be tempted to bypass the legislature and rule by decree. Also, given that it is extremely difficult to remove a president who has virtually no consensual support in the country or who is acting unconstitutionally, this is likely to result in both the president and the opposition seeking military involvement to resolve the crisis in their favour.[435] Military coups are therefore a strong possibility in presidential systems.

Parliamentarism

In sharp contrast to a *pure* presidential system, such as the United States, a *pure* parliamentary regime, such as Great Britain, is defined by a system of mutual dependancy relationship between the executive and the legislature.[436] That is to say, the chief executive power of the state is chosen from, and must be supported by, a majority in the legislature, and can fall if it receives a vote of no confidence. As Professor Juan Linz puts it,

> in parliamentary systems the only democratically legitimated institution is parliament, with the government deriving its authority from the confidence of parliament, either from parliamentary majorities or parliamentary tolerance of minority governments, and only for the time that the legislature is willing to support it between elections, and as long as parliament is not able to produce an alternative government.[437]

It means, then, that in a parliamentary system there is a virtual fusion of the chief executive authority – the Cabinet headed by a prime minister – and the legislature. The prime minister is appointed by the head of state, and the former in turn appoints the members of the Cabinet from among the elected members of his or her party in the legislature. This means that the prime minister and his government cannot survive without at least the passive support of a legislative majority. The government is therefore accountable to the legislature, given that, by a vote of no confidence, the legislature can bring down the government. Of course, the prime minister (normally in conjunction with the head of state) has the authority to dissolve the legislature and call for fresh elections.

This defining condition of mutual dependence between executive and legislature is considered the essence of pure parliamentarism. According to Alfred Stepan and Cindy Skach, 'from this defining condition a series of incentives and decision rules for creating and maintaining single-party or coalitional majorities, minimizing legislative impasses, inhibiting the executive from flouting the constitution, and discouraging political society's support for military coups predictably flows.'[438]

It is generally conceded that parliamentarism introduces much greater flexibility into the political process and allows for changes *within* government to meet changing circumstances. For example, in a parliamentary system, it is highly possible to change the head of the executive, the prime minister, without necessarily bringing down the government. That is to say, where a prime minister has lost the support of his or her party, and whose continuation in office is likely to erupt into a serious political crisis, he or she might be replaced by his or her party, or by the formation of a new coalition, or by the withdrawal of support by parties tolerating the minority government, without a major constitutional crisis.[439] It is more often than not possible for parliament to produce a new prime minister and a new government. Of course, in the most extreme cases, there is always the alternative of calling for new elections. In the final analysis, the inherent mechanisms of parliamentarism are deadlock-breaking devices, which tend to discourage resort to military involvement in order to resolve a political or constitutional crisis.[440]

Constitutional Choice

As was earlier intimated, the fundamental political-institutional question for the Commonwealth Caribbean, of a choice between the two paradigmatic models of parliamentarism and presidentialism, must ultimately be determined on the basis of their suitability for sustaining and strengthening democratic governance, and for facilitating the momentous task of economic and social restructuring facing our island-democracies. The political and psychological importance of the right constitutional choice cannot be overstated. After all, as Alfred Stepan and Cindy Skach remind us, constitutions are 'institutional frameworks' that in functioning democracies provide the basic decision rules and incentive systems concerning government formation, the conditions under which governments continue to rule, and the conditions by which they can be terminated democratically.[441] In other words, more than simply one of many dimensions of a democratic system, constitutions create much of the overall system of incentives and organizations within which the other institutions and dimensions found in the many types of democracy are structured and processed.[442]

Professor Juan Linz concludes from his study of parliamentary, presidential, and semi-presidential regimes that, with the outstanding exception of the United States, most of the stable democracies of Europe and the Commonwealth have been parliamentary regimes and a few semi-presidential and semi-parliamentary, while most of the countries with presidential constitutions have been unstable democracies or authoritarian regimes.[443] The United States of America is in fact the only historically stable purely presidential system in the world. It is therefore significant that, with the notable exception of Latin American countries, few democracies have opted for the US model of presidentialism. But it is instructive that in Latin America the presidential system has rarely ever produced political stability.[444] Of course, this fact does not necessarily speak to the intrinsic merit of one system over the other, given that there are many social, economic, cultural and political factors that may contribute to the success or failure of democracy in countries around the world. Still, our consideration of the fundamental characteristics of the two is instructive in informing a reasoned constitutional choice.

Perhaps the single most important factor that would commend the choice of a presidential system is the apparent stability of the executive: the president is elected for a fixed term of years and cannot, except in very extraordinary circumstances, be removed from office between elections. This is often contrasted with the instability experienced in some parliamentary democracies which undergo frequent crises and changes in the prime ministership; particularly multiparty democracies, such as European democracies, including Italy, Portugal, Israel and India.[445]

But despite the experience of unstable parliamentary governments, parliamentarism has none the less had a remarkable success story over presidentialism. This is believed due to the fact that the 'rigidity' in the political process, occasioned by the fixed mandates of the presidential executives and legislatures, makes adjustments to changing situations extremely difficult. In consequence, the occasion of executive-legislative deadlock, which is so easy an occurrence in presidential democracies where, more often than not the president fails to get a legislative majority, often results in constitutional crises and also frustrates the government in its efforts to implement any economic restructuring and austerity plans it may consider necessary for its development projects.[446]

In contrast, in parliamentary democracies, especially in countries of two-party systems, the executive's party often enjoys a majority of seats in the legislature. And in instances of minority governments, parliamentary executives are often motivated to form coalition governments and party alliances in order to attract the necessary support to remain in office and to survive any possible votes of confidence. For it bears reminding that the absence of fixed mandates and the safety devices of the parliamentary institutional framework allow for the calling of rapid new elections, the constitutional removal of unpopular, unsupported governments through the vote of no confidence, or simply the withdrawal from the government of a vital coalition partner.[447]

It means then, that 'even though parliamentary systems can create political paralysis or instability in the presence of many weak, non-programmatic, personalistic, and opportunistic parties unable to form stable coalitions, various constitutional formulas are available to reduce the danger of such occurrences.'[448] In other words, whereas the decision rules of parliamentarism do not assure government stability, or that any particular government will be efficient in formulating policies, still, the decision mechanisms available in the parliamentary framework do provide constitutional means for removing deadlocked or inefficient governments – both executives and parliaments.[449] For our island parliamentary democracies, with fragile economies and facing critical developmental problems, this is bound to be the most appealing factor in favour of retaining our parliamentary model of government. The flexibility inherent in the constitutional parliamentary framework would allow for greater ease in the implementation of policies designed to facilitate major socioeconomic changes and at the same time avoid the economic, social, and even psychological costs of executive-legislative deadlocks.[450]

The 'rigidity' of the presidential system, particularly where the president and the legislature are likely to be of divided 'loyalties', argues against its acceptability for our small island states, which already have a strong tradition of parliamentary democracy. The overriding factor, therefore, in favour of maintaining the parliamentary system of government is that it affords the government a greater measure of ease in having its policies adopted by the legislature, and ultimately implemented for the good of the society. This is of obvious critical importance to small and fragile Commonwealth Caribbean economies. A 'deadlock' between the executive and the legislature which results in the 'shutting down' of government could have irreparable economic and social consequences for a small island state. If, therefore, a choice between the two systems would be informed by our political tradition and our particular social and economic circumstances, then we are well advised to maintain our current model of government. The question now remains as to those reforms which may be necessary in order to deepen and strengthen the process of democratic constitutional governance. An adequate response to this question must include reconsideration of the office of head of state in our parliamentary constitutional scheme.

The President and Head of State

As was earlier intimated, one of the positive characteristics attributed to presidentialism concerns the identifiability and accountability of the executive office. The president, who serves as both the chief executive and the symbolic head of state, is elected directly by the electorate and is therefore directly accountable to the people. At an election the people know precisely for whom they are voting for the presidency, and this invests the office with a measure of democratic legitimacy not available to a prime minister and the head of state in a parliamentary system.[451]

We must be careful, however, not to overstate these advantages deriving from this feature of the presidential system. For given the case of a stable, two-party system in a parliamentary democracy, such as Barbados, say, the people already know that the leader of the party winning the election will be the prime minister. What is more, the people also know who are likely to be members of the cabinet. That is to say, either the voters are going to return the incumbent to office, or they are going to vote the opposition party into office. Either way, given the practice of 'shadow ministries' in a parliamentary system, the voters know they are not only voting for a candidate to be a member of parliament; they are more likely than not voting for a prospective minister of government. This might indeed be an overlooked characteristic of the parliamentary system, but the fact that voters are likely to know aforehand who the members of the entire cabinet are likely to be is certainly a basis for a more informed choice at election time.

True, under the presidential system, the successful presidential candidate has virtually absolute freedom in the composition of his cabinet. He is free to appoint members from the opposition party. In a parliamentary system, the prime minister must appoint (most of) his cabinet from among the successful candidates in his party. This means, however, that the voters have an indirect say in the composition of the cabinet. On this view, one could say that the entire cabinet is accountable to the electorate, in that if the government as a whole does not perform satisfactorily, it would be voted out at the next election. Under the presidential system, in contrast, it is only the president who is accountable to the electorate and, assuming the possibility of reelection, only the president, and not the members of his or her cabinet, would be facing the voters.[452] But, above all, a prime minister can be made 'accountable' to parliament and to his own party by a vote of no confidence at any time, with the party coming to the voters at the end of the period or even earlier, should the leadership crisis in parliament or in the governing party lead to anticipated elections.[453]

Then there is the question of the relationship between the chief executive and the office of head of state. In a presidential system, the president is both the chief executive and the head of state. Because the president is democratically elected, he or she is the representative of a clear partisan political option in the country, or at least of his or her party within the coalition that may have brought him or her to power.[454] This means that the president must combine, or at least reconcile, what Bagehot, in his account of the English Constitution, so aptly described as the 'dignified' and 'efficient' parts of the constitution.[455] The fact remains that a president representing clear ideological and partisan interests could hardly avoid the partisan political fighting necessary to have his or her policies adopted by the legislature.[456] This, it must be emphasized, is not in keeping with the role of a head of state, who must exist somewhat above partisan politics and be a symbol of the unity and continuity of the state and the nation. The Westminster parliamentary model of government would therefore seem to have an advantage of a 'dual executive', in which the head of state is presumed to represent the 'dignified' office of the constitution, with the prime minister representing the 'efficient.' This is to say, the head of state is supposed to be a non-partisan figure uniting the nation in his or her person and symbolizing the continuity of the state. The prime minister, in contrast, is the effective head of government and is therefore responsible for the day-today governance of the country.

It is easy to underestimate the critical importance of this state of affairs to good governance. By standing in the constitutional scheme above the complex of offices constituting the 'efficient' part of the constitution, the head of state – be it the monarch, governor-general or president – can play an important and decisive role at that critical moment when the society is faced with the breakdown of democratic institutions or political and civil strife.[457] Consider, for example, the critical role played by King Juan Carlos of Spain, both in the country's transition to democracy (1975-79) and at the time of the February 23, 1981 coup attempt. The King's role in the traumatic hours following the sequester of the entire government and legislature on February 23, 1981, clearly shows the importance of the division of roles and of the 'reserve' powers of a legitimate and popular head of state.[458]

But it is not only in the extreme cases that the critical importance of the office is revealed; it is also revealed in the ways in which the office can function as a 'check' on executive and legislative excesses. We have earlier intimated that the parliamentary/cabinet model of government lends itself to a highly centralized, executive-dominated form of government. By requiring that the executive be directed by leaders of the majority in the legislature, it fuses executive and legislative power, which makes the cabinet the central legislative and executive organ in the Westminster-type parliamentary system.[459] In our small island-states this translates into the accumulation of both legislative and executive authority in the office of prime minister. This is compounded by the substantive powers of appointment vested in the prime minister – such as the appointment of the head of state, judges, and the members of the public service commission. Now given this scenario, a properly constituted office of head of state can play an indirect, yet critical, role in the practice of good democratic governance. First, the dignity and importance of the office could be honoured by changing the method of appointment, thereby making appointments to the office seem less a 'gift' of the prime minister's office. Next, the office could be invested with a veto power over legislation thereby warning parliament against hasty and ill-conceived legislation. But, above all, one of the most effective ways to curb the extensive powers of the prime minister is to remove from that office the exclusive grant of the public power of appointment to such critical offices as the judiciary and the public service commission, and assign that power to the office of head of state. This would go a long way toward reinforcing the principle of the political independence of the judiciary and ensuring that it functions critically in the protection of the fundamental rights of the citizen, and in constraining the political excesses of 'an elective despotism' of prime ministerial government.[460] It is therefore well advised to reconstitute the office of head of state by investing it with greater 'energy' and regular substantive authority.

This is a matter of telling importance, for it puts in issue the fundamental question of the role of the head of state, and of the relationship between a head of state and a prime minister, in a parliamentary regime.[461] This question was raised in sharp relief by recent events in Trinidad and Tobago. The question whether a prime minister has the constitutional authority to name whomever he wishes to the cabinet, with which the president is compelled to comply, embraces this broader question of the correct understanding of the role of the head of state in the parliamentary regime and of the consequent nature of the presidential-prime ministerial relationship.

It bears repeating that, in a parliamentary democracy, the prime minister enjoys the lion's share of constitutional powers. What is more, the head of state (president or governor-general) is constitutionally obliged to act on the advice of the prime minister. This is necessary because the prime minister is the head of government and is therefore responsible for the day-to-day functions of government. In normal times, this relationship between head of state and prime minister can be one of trust and counsel. The head of state can play the role of adviser or arbiter by bringing prime minister and leader of opposition together and facilitating the flow of information among them.[462] The reigning assumption, as Professor Thomas Baylis puts it, 'is that the respective roles of the two executives are complementary and closely defined and distinguished in practice as well as theory: the president undergirds legitimacy and represents state or national continuity, while the prime minister exercises policy leadership and takes responsibility for the day-to-day functions of government.'[463]

But it is commonly understood that this enormous grant of prime ministerial powers is precisely the source of the greatest potential danger and of possible conflict between the head of state and prime minister. Barring personality differences – something clearly evident in the recent Trinidad and Tobago presidential-prime ministerial conflict – disputes between the head of state and the prime minister are in essence struggles over power, or at least in their respective understanding of the grant of their powers.[464] Presidents or heads of state, in seeking to make full use of what they understand to be their legal prerogatives, may be inclined to interpret their powers broadly thus giving rise to the accusation of presidential encroachment on prime ministerial turf: that the president has exceeded his or her legal authority or at least has violated the norms of the appropriate presidential role.[465]

This, quite interestingly, was precisely the nature of the charge levelled by the Prime Minister and the then Attorney-General of Trinidad and Tobago against President Robinson when the latter initially refused to sign the Prime Minister's appointment of seven defeated candidates in the last general elections to top cabinet posts. It is rather instructive that the dispute has arisen over the appointment of cabinet ministers given that, according to Professor Thomas Baylis, disputes between the head of state and prime minister frequently concern the appointment or removal of cabinet ministers and other high state officials.[466] Opinion is divided as to whether the Prime Minister acted judiciously in naming seven defeated candidates to top cabinet posts, although the weight of the learned law opinions tended to favour his constitutional authority to do what he did.[467]

But disputes over the appointment of cabinet ministers rarely escalate into open conflict that ultimately lead to a constitutional crisis. Still, the Trinidad and Tobago *case* has come at a most propitious moment as we ponder the question of constitutional reform. For given the 'elective dictatorship' of the prime ministerial office in our island-democracies, the *case* has certainly put in high relief the issue of the appropriate institutional changes to these two executive offices in order to ensure the enhancement of democratic governance and the rule of law. How, for example, are heads of state to be chosen; what formal powers are to be accorded them, and the circumstances under which prime ministers and cabinets can be forced from office?[468]

Such issues of constitutional details are instructive when we consider that in an ethnically divided society one possible source of presidential-prime ministerial dispute can be the question of who has authority over the armed forces – the head of state or the prime minister?[469] Of course, this is not only important for an ethnically divided society; it is only to say that the potential for danger would seem more urgent in a society marked by ethnic divisions. For assuming that in such a society the major political parties by and large track ethnic lines, it means that a prime minister, having the power to appoint the minister of the armed forces and to decide when to deploy the military in the interest of law and order etc., has at his disposal the means to destroy his political enemies.[470] In view of this, it would seem that the question of the control of the military and, indeed, of the protective and security forces generally, should be the subject of the grant of formal powers to the head of state.

To sum up, it can be said that the *formal* separation of powers between the executive and the legislature in the presidential regime contributes to a *balance* of power between these two branches of government. In theory, at least, this state of affairs should redound to greater deliberative democracy given that the legislature can deal with bills on their merits without the fear of causing a cabinet crisis, and without being 'blackmailed' by the executive into accepting its proposals. In a word, this *formal* separation of powers entails greater legislative independence and a more balanced executive-legislative relationship.[471]

But presidentialism invariably offers fewer chances for consensual politics given the concentration of executive power in one party and in one person. In other words, it is extremely difficult to introduce executive power sharing or coalition governments in presidential systems. As Professor Arend Lijphart puts it, 'presidentialism is inimical to the kind of consociational compromises and pacts that may be necessary in the process of democratization and during periods of crisis ... .'[472] But, by far, maybe the most negative consequence of presidentialism is the executive-legislative deadlock that it encourages. This, as we have already noted, can be devastating for our relatively small democracies with fragile economies.

Parliamentarism, on the other hand, is believed to introduce greater flexibility into the political process and tends to encourage the kind of consociational compromises that would avoid executive-legislative deadlocks. For this reason political scholars have concluded that parliamentarism, by affording greater ease in the implementation of major social and economic policies, is more suited to countries undertaking momentous tasks of economic and social transformation. When these factors are taken in conjunction with the political maxim that people generally prefer a system they know and are familiar with to one they do not know nor understand, it is rather doubtful that the people of the Commonwealth Caribbean would opt for a change from the parliamentary to the presidential system of government. Indeed, in the West Indies, where the British tradition was especially strong, well known and deeply admired, it was never a question at independence, whether to consider adopting the alternative presidential system of government. As Professor Anthony Payne has observed, the historical legacy of British colonialism has shaped the emergent forms of politics in the post-independence Commonwealth Caribbean. Our tutelage under the Westminster system has nurtured a political culture of constitutionalism, that is, the presumption that political change should only occur in accordance with rules and precedents.[473] Indeed, the very process of 'constitutional decolonisation' or lawful devolution of sovereignty, by which these countries gained their independence, was marked by 'an evolutionary process by which the territories of the region were slowly graduated ... along a series of stages toward greater self-government and eventual independence.'[474] A political order has therefore emerged that is based on the working of practices and commitments that manifestly have as their inspiration the Westminster system. The net result is that most Commonwealth Caribbean states either still operate the constitutions they were given at independence, or have conceived of constitutional change as an incremental process of adjustment.[475] Constitutional reform therefore rather consists in the modernisation and modification of the basic model, which does not disturb the essential formulation of the British constitutional inheritance, rather than in a comprehensive revamping of the system.[476]

The Legislature – Bicameral or Unicameral?

It is hardly surprising that, in our 'export' Westminster model of parliamentary democracy, we should have a second, upper legislative chamber which, originally, may have been intended to replicate the British House of Lords – a partially hereditary body. In our current system, this second chamber – the Senate – is a wholly appointed body. The majority of this body are appointed by the prime minister, with the remainder to be appointed by the leader of the opposition in parliament (the opposition senators), and by the governor-general (the independent senators). In most cases, the prime minister and the leader of the opposition may revoke their appointments at will.

Given the manner of their appointment, it is not surprising that most senators feel a sense of loyalty to their principals rather than to the people as a whole. In consequence, voting in virtually every Commonwealth Caribbean senate is always along party lines – consistent with the voting in the lower house. Still, the senate is part of the legislature and shares in the power of Parliament to make laws [which] shall be exercised by bills passed by the Senate and the House of Representatives.

The question whether the senate should be retained should be determined on some ideal conception of democracy and on the senate's role in fostering that ideal. The conception of democracy this work embraces is that of a form of political rule in which the people as a whole are conceived of as the true constituent power. Democratic governance therefore depends for its success on open public deliberation and reflection. Ideally, it entails a process by which citizens consult and deliberate about what options or policies are best for them. But this ideal model of deliberative democracy may only have been feasible in the ancient Greek *polis* in which every citizen assembled in the 'Public Square' to consult and deliberate on matters of public concern. Today, in the modern democratic society, policies of day-to-day governance could not possibly be deliberated upon by a collectively acting citizenry. Deliberations must necessarily take place through representative institutions. The legislature is there-fore the principal agent of deliberative democracy; and its delib-erations must be guided by the ideal of public reason – 'the reason of equal citizens who, as a collective body, exercise final political and coercive power over one another in enacting law and in amending their constitution.'[477] As the political philosopher Joshua Cohen puts it:

> The notion of deliberative democracy is rooted in the intuitive ideal of a democratic association in which the justification of the terms and conditions of association proceeds through public argument and reasoning among equal citizens. Citizens in such an order share a commit-ment to the resolution of problems of collective choice through public reasoning, and regard their basic institu-tions as legitimate in so far as they establish the frame-work for free public deliberation.[478]

It is submitted that it is in terms of the foregoing conception of deliberative democracy that we may critically assess the role of the senate in our constitutional scheme. First, it bears noting that an unelected body with the power to make law is contrary to the democratic ideal. It is one of the central premises of the concept of democracy and democratic government that only a body of elected representatives should have the power to make laws by which the lives of the citizens are to be governed. The problem with an unelected senate having this power readily becomes apparent when one considers that the power to make laws for the governance of society is indeed the most awesome power of the state.

Today, bicameralism is considered a universal feature of modern constitutional governments.[479] Indeed, it is numbered among the central features of republican government. A bicameral legislature is thought to advance the achievement of limited government; it is generally valued as an important component in a checks and balances system of government.[480] In short, the theoretical foundation of bicameralism was the principle of countervailance: the idea that the political power of the state may be organized within a constitutional structure of checks and balances, in order to protect the civic liberty of the citizenry by permitting each estate of government to act as a buffer against the excesses of another.[481] A second legislative chamber is thought to be an essential part of the overall constitutional scheme of checks and balances as a safeguard against legislative abuse; as a security against the making of arbitrary laws.[482]

In English constitutional development, the principle of bicameralism may have been planted with the meeting of the Great Council called by Edward I in 1295, which, according to Professor Scott Gordon, has been enshrined in history as the first of England's parliaments. Later dubbed the 'Model Parliament', it included representatives from the lesser aristocracy, the clergy, and the urban boroughs.[483] From that time on, according to

Professor Scott Gordon, Parliament has been composed of two groups: those entitled to membership by virtue of their aristocratic status, and those who attend in their capacities as *representatives* of other classes.[484] Thus, from very early on, Parliament met as the House of Commons and the House of Lords. Bicameralism was thereby entrenched in the English system of government, dividing the authority of Parliament between two independent bodies with the power to check one another as well as the monarch.[485]

With the Glorious Revolution of 1688, an elected House of Commons, generally construed as representing 'the people', became firmly established as a fundamental feature of the English constitution.[486] Today, with the decline in power of the House of Lords, true legislative authority rests with the House of Commons – or, more accurately, 'the Cabinet in the Commons.'[487] Still, it is considered desirable to preserve the bicameral nature of the British Parliament. The House of Lords, though limited to delaying legislation, is still considered a valuable part of the constitutional scheme of checks and balances.[488]

In the event, however, the principle of representation, which was the legitimating principle of the English Parliament, became institutionalized in the colonial government of British America, and was adopted by them for their states and national governments after they became independent.[489] In American constitutional theory, bicameralism is considered an essential principle of good government, regardless of how the two legislative organs may be constituted. In the American political system, the House of Representatives is said to represent the people, and the Senate is said to represent the states. They are however elected by the same body of electors, and are of relatively equal power. The Senate has been defended as critical to orderly and decent government – as a 'check' upon the 'easy passage of passionate legislation' which a single-house political system tended to facilitate.[490] A classic argument for the adoption of a bicameral system was made by James Madison at the Federal Convention in Philadelphia:

> In order to judge of the form to be given to [the Senate], it will be proper to take a view of the ends to be served by it. These were first to protect the people agst. their rulers; secondly to protect the people agst. the transient impressions into which they themselves might be led. A people deliberating in a temperate moment, and with the experience of other nations before them, on the plan of Govt. most likely to secure their happiness, would first be aware, that those chargd. with the public happiness, might betray their trust. An obvious precaution agst. this danger wd. be to divide the trust between different bodies of men, who might watch & check each other...[491]

And subsequently, in *Federalist* 48, having regard to the fact that, in a republic, the legislature is the *most* powerful branch, its powers being 'less susceptible of precise limits', Madison further defends the adoption of a bicameral system on the grounds that

> [I]n a representative republic where the executive magistracy is carefully limited, both in the extent and the duration of its power; and where the legislative power is exercised by an assembly, which is inspired by a supposed influence over the people with an intrepid confidence in its own strength; which is sufficiently numerous to feel all the passions which actuate a multitude, yet not so numerous as to be incapable of pursuing the objects of its passions by means which reason prescribes; it is against the enterprising ambition of this department that the people ought to indulge all their jealousy and exhaust all their precautions.[492]

It may be said that bicameralism ensures that a 'sober second thought' is brought to bear on the passage of legislation.[493] However, in order to be assured of this gain from the existence of a second legislative house, one must ensure that the members of one house are more virtuous, deliberative, and reflective than members of the other; something it might be nigh impossible to guarantee.[494] However, as was earlier intimated, this might well have been the motivating thought behind the existence of a senate in the Commonwealth Caribbean constitutional scheme.

It is generally understood that the Senate evolved out of the Legislative Council, which patterned its relationship with the House of Assembly in a fashion similar to that of the House of Lords and the House of Commons.[495] The Legislative Council was a standard feature of early British colonial government in the Commonwealth Caribbean through which British-appointed governors ruled the colonies on behalf of the Crown. Generally speaking, the earliest form of colonial governance would have been one in which the power and authority to govern a colony was vested exclusively in the hands of a Governor, assisted by purely nominated executive and legislative councils. This would subsequently have developed into a system consisting of three basic institutions: a wholly elected Assembly patterned after the House of Commons; a nominated council patterned after the House of Lords; and the governor, head of the executive, appointed by and responsible to the Crown. Still, further constitutional development saw the office of chief minister, and subsequently premier, as the head of government, chosen from among the elected members of the House of Assembly and replacing the Governor in terms of the power of nomination. A wholly nominated Legislative Council therefore continued as a second chamber. With political independence, the office of premier was changed to prime minister; and the Legislative Council became the Upper House or Senate, with the power to deliberate over legislation and to delay Bills except money bills.[496]

To repeat, then, in our current constitutional structure, the House of Assembly is said to represent the people, and the Senate, the fully nominated body, is said to represent certain interests in the society, such as labour, private industry, education, the youth, etc. The question for constitutional reform, as was earlier stated, is whether the Senate, as presently constituted, plays any meaningful role in the life of the Commonwealth Caribbean polity.

It is hardly surprising that the Senate, as currently constituted, is considered of minor significance in our constitutional scheme. After all, it is hardly to be expected that, in a constitutional democracy, an entirely nominated part of Parliament would be accorded power comparable to that of the elected part, and thus constitute some safeguard against legislative abuse. Of course, the alternative is to have an elected Upper House which could proclaim its own democratic mandate and challenge the government majority in the elected Lower House.

But the question of an elected Senate with its own democratic mandate actually sharpens the issue of the desirability of preserving the bicameral nature of the Commonwealth Caribbean parliamentary system. This issue might be fruitfully addressed in terms of the 'cost of governance' for an island parliamentary democracy. Put differently, the issue is one of the advantages and disadvantages of bicameral and unicameral systems for our parliamentary democracies.

Virtually all Western constitutions create two legislative chambers based on different principles of representation. The lower chamber typically represents the people, as is the case of the House of Representatives in the US Congress; and the upper chamber represents the states, as is the case of the Senate in the US Congress, or the people, or something else such as the aristocracy, as is the case of the British House of Lords.[497] Also, the two chambers differ in power from one country to another. For example, there may be a strong upper chamber, such as the US Senate, roughly equal in power to the lower chamber in being able to initiate and veto legislation; or there may be a weak upper chamber, such as the British House of Lords or the Spanish upper chamber, with the power to discuss, advise, or even to delay legislation, but not to initiate legislation or veto it.[498]

In contrast, a unicameral system is one in which there is only one legislative chamber, no matter how constituted. On this view, Britain and the Commonwealth Caribbean are said to have bicameral legislative systems. But although parliament consists of two chambers: the popularly elected lower chamber, (the House of Commons or House of Assembly), and the unelected upper chamber, (the House of Lords or Senate), virtually all legislative power belongs to the Lower House. Britain's House of Lords and the Commonwealth Caribbean Senate possess virtually no power. So, in everyday discussion, 'Parliament', in the Commonwealth Caribbean constitution, refers almost exclusively to the House of Assembly. On this view, therefore, this highly asymmetric bicameral system may be called 'near-unicameralism.'[499] Thus, for the purpose of a comparative analysis of the two systems in terms of cost of governance, the West Indian political system will be taken as 'unicameral', and the US political system as the paradigm model of the bicameral system.

According to Professor Robert Cooter, in the situation where both chambers are elected and roughly equal, and enacting legislation requires the concurrence of both chambers, the necessity for bargaining between the two houses increases; and so would the transaction costs of legislation.[500] As a matter of fact, in a bicameral presidential system such as that of the United States, the transaction costs for enacting legislation are expected to be phenomenally high since there may be bargaining not only between the two houses, but also between the president and the two houses – or, more accurately, between the president and legislators in the two houses.[501] In any event, one consequence of a bicameral system is the relatively high transaction cost of enacting new legislation. Thus, Professor Cooter concludes: high transaction costs tend to reduce the speed and quantity of new legislation, and therefore privilege the status quo over changes. A majority in the second chamber preferring to maintain the status quo would, more likely than not, vote to block legislation deemed too 'radical.'[502]

A unicameral system is generally expected to require less bargaining for enacting legislation; although, in a unicameral presidential system, the president is expected to bargain seriously with the legislature over the passage of legislation – especially where the majority in the legislature are not from the president's party.[503] Therefore, it should prove more instructive to compare the unicameral – or rather near-unicameral – parliamentary system, such as Britain or the Commonwealth Caribbean.

To repeat, in a parliamentary system, the government is formed by the party winning the majority of seats in parliament, or, if no party wins a majority, by the party that can assemble a coalition commanding a majority of votes. A government remains in office so long as it commands a majority in parliament, or until it reaches the maximum number of years allowed by law between general elections. A parliamentary system therefore unites executive and legislative powers, since the prime minister and members of cabinet are selected from among the elected members in the lower house. Also, a unicameral parliamentary system unites legislative powers in a single house, as in Great Britain where the House of Commons governs and the House of Lords comments.[504]

It means, then, that in a parliamentary system with tight party discipline, there is hardly any need for negotiation between the executive and the legislature, since the prime minister gives orders to legislators of his own party to enact legislation. In other words, where the cabinet is composed of the leaders of a cohesive party in the House of Assembly, say, it can confidently count on getting its legislative proposals approved without the need for extensive bargaining with the legislators of the party.[505] And even where a coalition government exists, the prime minister would still be able to count on the support of the coalition majority in the House since the members of the coalition would have a stake in the government remaining in office.

It might therefore be said that in a unicameral (or near-unicameral) parliamentary system, such as Britain or the Commonwealth Caribbean, which unites executive and legislative powers, transaction costs over the passage of legislation are virtually nil. This could have tremendous implications for any parliamentary state in the Commonwealth Caribbean wishing to enact fresh legislation aimed at redistributing wealth, in order to effect a major social and economic transformation of the society. For example, we may take the case of Barbados, which is unquestionably the outstanding exemplar of a stable, near-unicameral parliamentary system in the Commonwealth Caribbean.

Prime Minister Owen Arthur has stated categorically that one of the overriding objectives of his Government is the eradication of poverty in Barbados. To this end, he has established a Ministry of Social Transformation from the very onset of his second term. Among other things, his ambition is to grow the economy and effect an equitable distribution of wealth, so that no sector of the society should feel marginalised or 'left out.' Assume, then, that the Prime Minister and his Cabinet were to embark on a series of ambitious legislation towards their objectives, which might include, say, major amendments to the Tenantries Act in order to secure such primary social goods as land and housing to those who are least well off. Now, with a very secure majority in

Parliament, supported by a very disciplined and cohesive party, the Prime Minister and his Cabinet are assured of the passage of the legislation. They do not have to negotiate with another branch of government or with another party.[506] Any negotiations that occur will take place among the members of the ruling party; that is to say, within the Cabinet. In other words, the cooperation of the executive and legislature required to enact legislation is virtually assured. Not even the unicameral presidential system can boast of this, where the president must negotiate with the legislature; especially where the president belongs to one party and another party controls the legislature.

It has been noted that negotiations over the passage of legislation will be greater in a bicameral, than in a unicameral, political system. Also, it is generally expected that negotiation costs will be higher in a presidential system – whether unicameral or bicameral – than in a parliamentary system.[507] This should further strengthen the case for the retention of the parliamentary model of government. It means, then, that if we should genuinely wish to have a *true* bicameral parliamentary system, the Senate would have to be made into an elected body. But with the Senate having its own democratic mandate, its legislative authority *vis-à-vis* that of the House of Assembly will also increase. This means that the passage of legislation could require negotiations between the two Houses of the Legislature, and also between the prime minister and sections of the Legislature, very much on the level of a presidential system. In other words, as was noted earlier, if the constitution were to give roughly equal power to both houses of the legislature, as in the United States and Australia, say, and that it was necessary for both houses to agree in order to enact legislation, then when the two chambers disagree, they must bargain to a solution.[508] They may iron out their differences through a 'conference committee', which must come up with a final draft of the bill for their vote.[509] In the final analysis, we must consider whether the benefits of a *genuine* bicameral system, which might indeed redound to more balanced legislation, are worth the costs.

We are therefore back to our initial question: whether the Senate should be retained and as a fully nominated body. The recent Constitution Review Commissions of Jamaica and Barbados have recommended that the Senate be retained. The Barbados Commission, for example, has recommended that the Senate's composition be modified 'principally to provide for more representatives for those who do not support the Government of the day and also to give recognition to the fact that there are now more than two established political parties in Barbados and that the number of parties can increase.'[510] In a nutshell, this recommendation would view the Senate as a corrective to the perceived weaknesses in the electoral process. But whatever changes are made to the composition of the Senate, what is clear is that, in a democracy, a nominated chamber cannot be accorded power comparable to that of an elected chamber. It means, then, that a decision to retain a nominated Senate must turn on a conviction that the obvious administrative costs of maintaining that body as part of the political infrastructure are far outweighed by the benefits derived from having a second chamber.

It is generally argued that the Commonwealth Caribbean Senate does enjoy some representative capacity given that it is largely appointed by elected representatives – the prime minister and the leader of the opposition. It is also argued that membership in the Senate is representative of certain important interests or organizations in society, *viz.*, the Chamber of Commerce, Agriculture, Labour Unions, to name a few. These, it is believed, would make substantial contributions to deliberations affecting their interests. Finally, there is the view that, given the limitations of our society, the electoral process cannot be relied on to guarantee that pool of talent in the House of Assembly from which a prime minister might form a capable government. The Senate could therefore be a body from which the prime minister could draw Cabinet members. This, combined with the deliberative character of the Senate, might well be the best way of putting the case for its retention.

The case for the deliberative character of a nominated second chamber, however, would hardly carry much purchase since, lacking a genuine independent voice, a nominated Senate could hardly be expected to bring any significant challenge to proposed government policies. The question of the representation of certain interests in the legislature, through the Senate, raises a moral issue: whether it is contrary to the democratic ideal in that it enhances the quality of the right of certain groups to vote for the government of their choice above a similar right of others. Finally, there is the question of a prime minister's option of filling his cabinet with members from the Senate. This, it should bear emphasis, implies a certain vision of the society and the electorate: that they are lacking in sophistication and integrity and therefore cannot be trusted to exercise proper judgment and elect good men and women who are competent to serve as cabinet ministers and vigilantly guard their actions thereafter.[511] The view is that nominated members can provide specialist advice and be a source of the expertise which may not be secured through a popular election. This process of nomination will bring in valuable members who, because of possible class-race bias of the electorate, would be unable to win an election; and it would further serve to 'correct' the results of any one election, and make the legislature more representative. However, it can never be guaranteed that nominated members of the Senate would prove to be more virtuous, more deliberative, and more reflective than the elected members of the House of Assembly, and therefore contribute more meaningfully to democratic governance. The answer may therefore be for political leaders to choose more worthy candidates to contest elections.

Electoral Reform: 'First-Past-the-Post' or Proportional Representation?

With the possible exception of Guyana, the Westminster majoritarian model of parliamentary democracy remains the standard form of government for the entire Anglophone Caribbean. Consequently, one noted feature of the Commonwealth Caribbean electoral system is the continuing attachment to the 'first-past-the-post' model, which is the electoral model of the British Westminster political system.[512] In a Westminster-type parliamentary system using the 'first-past-the-post' system, the candidate receiving the most votes in an election district wins. This means that if a candidate gets only 40 per cent of the vote in a single district, that candidate wins the election if 40 per cent is the highest among the respective percentages of votes received by the other two or three candidates. Therefore, under such an electoral system, a disciplined political party winning a majority of the votes in every single district could conceivably win an absolute majority of the seats in the legislature, notwithstanding that that party may have won only 40 percent of the popular vote.[513] This is the 'winner-take-all' situation, which is possible in both parliamentary and presidential systems using the 'first-past-the-post' single district rule.[514] This situation has been criticised as having serious implications for the nature of politics in the region, since it tends to over-represent the majority party in parliament and under-represent the others.[515] Indeed, recent election results in places as Grenada, Barbados, St. Lucia, and St. Vincent and the Grenadines have confirmed the truth of this claim. This has therefore prompted the question whether a change to some form of proportional representation is not in fact warranted. In this section, the merits and demerits of the two principal electoral systems – 'first-past-the-post' and proportional representation – and their respective suitability for our island parliamentary democracies will be examined.

The 'first-past-the-post' electoral system is otherwise referred to as the 'single-member district plurality' system or the 'winner-take-all-plurality' rule.[516] Under this rule the party receiving the most of the votes in the majority or all of the election districts wins the elections. In contrast is the pure proportional representation system where the parties receive seats in the legislature in proportion to the popular vote.[517]

From the standpoint of collective theory, Professor Robert Cooter explains that countries using the 'winner-take-all-plurality rule' tend largely to be two-party political systems, where two major parties dominate important elected offices. According to this theory, people tend to vote strategically, that is to say, where there are several candidates, under the 'winner-take-all-plurality rule', citizens tend to vote for candidates whom they think others will vote for, and this behaviour compresses the number of viable parties to two.[518] In other words, the winner-take-all-plurality rule tends to produce two dominant, evenly matched parties located near the center of the political spectrum. And this leads to a very stable situation, since a third party would have very little chance of influencing the outcome of an election, given people's perception that they would be throwing away their votes by voting for minority parties. The net result is that two political parties come to occupy the space of alternatives so as to preclude the entry of a viable or successful third party.[519] Currently, in the Commonwealth Caribbean, Barbados and Jamaica are outstanding examples of the two-party political system.

In any event, a system of at least two strong political parties, at the center of the political spectrum and commanding the allegiance of at least major organized sectors of civil society, channeling political activity through formal legal and political institutions, is a necessary condition of democratic stability in that such a system dampens the influence of any extremist minority parties which could destabilize democracy.[520] It means, then, that a country with multiple political parties having comparable influence in civil society would invariably end up with coalition governments, which, in some instances could be very unstable.[521] In a highly fragmented political system, many different combinations of parties could form the government. A governing coalition must distribute the spoils of office among its members; however, the largest party that forms the coalition government may want to concentrate the spoils of power on its own members, thus causing considerable friction among coalition members.[522]

Equally important is the fact that two-party politics tends to eliminate legislative bargaining, or at least change its character.[523] As we noted earlier, in a parliamentary system (such as Britain or Barbados), the party winning the majority of seats in parliament wins the elections and is invited to form the government. Depending on the margin of victory, the majority party can enact virtually any legislation it wishes without the need to form a coalition that encompasses minority parties. It means, then, that bargaining takes place mainly within the governing party, or between its members and citizens outside of parliament, but not between political parties.[524] Put differently, the most important bargaining over legislation takes place within the ruling party before a bill goes to parliament.[525]

In sharp contrast to the 'winner-take-all' or 'single-member district plurality system', proportional representation aims to represent both majority and minority parties in government by translating votes into seats roughly in proportion to the percentage of popular votes each party receives in a general election.[526] Proportional representation therefore tends to encourage a system with many political parties since each citizen tends to vote for the party whose preferences most closely resemble his or her own, knowing that there is a strong likelihood of the party being represented in the legislature and possibly in government.[527] For these reasons, proportional representation is deemed to be a far more equitable system than the winner-take-all plurality rule.

But proportional representation's virtue of empowering all political parties tends toward a fragmentation, rather than a consolidation, of parties. This means that, in a parliamentary system, each party in the legislature can bargain to join the governing coalition. Depending on the composition of parties forming the coalition – sometimes extremist or less centrist parties – the result could mean a very unstable government.[528] In the event, however, proportional representation creates a greater need for negotiation among parties in the legislature; which means greater transaction costs in enacting legislation and possibly less efficient government.

And there is the matter of choosing the candidates. Under proportional representation, the method generally followed is for each political party to designate a list of candidates and the voters then choose among alternative lists. On any party's list, a voter may like some candidates and dislike others. This means that voters in a particular district would not necessarily be voting for a particular candidate to represent them, but rather for the party slate.[529] Under the single-district plurality rule, however, voters in a particular district get to choose the specific candidate whom they wish to represent them in parliament. This is because, under the plurality rule, only one seat is assigned to each electoral district; therefore, each district is represented by only one legislator.[530] Not necessarily so under proportional representation, since that system would allow for more than one legislative seat to be assigned to each electoral district and, in any event, would allocate seats to parties in accordance with the proportion of votes they receive in the general elections.[531]

In summary, the well-known proposition in comparative politics is that single-member district plurality systems favour two-party systems which are generally believed to be more stable than multiparty systems.[532] Unfortunately, in a Westminster-type parliamentary system, the single-member district plurality rule might result in one party receiving a disproportionate number of seats in the legislature.[533] In some cases, a party receiving only 51 per cent of the popular vote could gain an absolute majority of parliamentary seats – a 'winner-take-all' situation. Proportional representation, in contrast, is deemed to be a more equitable electoral method, since it allows for the allocation of legislative seats to political parties according to their proportion of the popular vote. Under proportional representation, therefore, minority and 'fringe' parties stand a better chance of being represented in the legislature. In other words, proportional representation might result in a wider cross-section of interests in society being represented in the legislature. For this reason, it is an inherently more equitable system of representation, which might encourage wider and more legitimate citizen participation.

Unfortunately, in a parliamentary democracy under proportional representation there is likely to be a greater fragmentation of political parties – which means that coalition governments might be the order of the day. As Professor Arend Lijphart observes, 'proportional representation lacks the restraining influence on third and other weak parties inherent in the single-member district plurality system; therefore, it freely allows the emergence and persistence of multiparty systems. For this reason, it is generally believed that proportional representation, by encouraging a proliferation of parties, promotes instability and, in the long run, could be a danger to the survival of democracy'.[534]

In light of the foregoing discussion, and having regard to our history, political culture and economic circumstances, we can make an informed choice as to whether or not we should retain the current electoral model or adopt some form of proportional representation. It is an undisputed fact that one of the worst dangers to democratic governance in the Commonwealth Caribbean is the potential for abuse of power by the 'elective dictatorship' of prime ministerial government. The 'winner-take-all' situation or 'to the victor the spoils' mentality that our current electoral system indulges compounds the problem ten-fold.[535] As Professor Selwyn Ryan observes, our Westminster-type democracy, under a 'winner-take-all' electoral rule, has encouraged a too destructive competition for political office. It has placed too heavy a concentration of power in the hands of the ruling elites, and has encouraged the marginalisation and alienation of a substantial part of the population from participation in the governance and development of their society.[536] On this view, it would seem that proportional representation is the more attractive electoral system. However, as we noted earlier in this chapter, there are other areas of the constitution in which changes might be introduced to tame the powers of a prime minister and to encourage greater citizen participation in the affairs of the state.

Assuming this to be the case, the question remains whether we would adopt a system of proportional representation, which might indeed result in a wider representation of interests in parliament, but at the possible cost of greater instability. If, therefore, legislative paralysis and political instability are equally frightening prospects, then it must be considered whether political stability, at the cost of not representing all interests and preferences in the society, is the lesser of all evils. In addition, the single-member district plurality method is far simpler and therefore likely to cause less confusion for the electorate than proportional representation. The words of Thomas Jefferson (from the American Declaration of Independence) are the perfect reminder of the human disposition to cling to that which is the more familiar: 'Mankind are more disposed to suffer, while evils are sufferable, than to right themselves by abolishing the forms to which they are accustomed.'[537]

Endnotes

1 See James Boyd White, *When Words Lose Their meaning* 193 (1984).
2 These countries are Jamaica, Barbados, Antigua and Barbuda, St. Kitts and Nevis, and Grenada.
3 Sheldon Wolin, 'Max Weber: Legitimation, Method, and the Politics of Theory,' in *Legitimacy and the State* 63 (William Connolly ed. 1984).
4 Sheldon Wolin, *The Presence of the Past* 2 (1989).
5 *Ibid.*
6 William F. Harris II, *The Interpretable Constitution* 165 (1993).
7 Walter F. Murphy, 'Merlin's Memory: The Past and Future Imperfect of the Once and Future Polity,' in *Responding to Imperfection: The Theory and Practice of Constitutional Amendment* 177 (Sanford Levinson ed. 1995).
8 Stephen Holmes and Cass R. Sunstein, 'The Politics of Revision,' in *Responding to Imperfection: The Theory and Practice of Constitutional Amendment* 285 (Sanford Levinson ed. 1995).
9 Paul W. Kahn, *The Reign of Law: Marbury v. Madison and the Construction of America* 62 (1997).
10 Walter F. Murphy, *supra* note 7, at 183.
11 John Rawls, *Political Liberalism* 238 (1993).
12 *Ibid.* 239.
13 *Ibid.* 228.
14 *Ibid.* 213.
15 *Ibid.*
16 *Ibid.* 226.
17 *Ibid.* 228.
18 Khan, *supra* note 9, at 187.
19 Ulrih K. Preuss, 'Constitutional Powermaking of the New Polity: Some Deliberations on the Relations Between Constituent Power and the constitution,' in *Constitutionalism, Identity, Difference, and Legitimacy: Theoretical Perspectives* 143 (Michel Rosenfeld ed. 1994).
20 *Ibid.* 156.
21 See Ahkil Reed Amar, 'Philadelphia Revisited: Amending the Constitution Outside Article V,' 55 *Univ. of Chicago L. Rev.* 1043 (1988); *idem.*'The Consent of the Governed: Constitutional Amendment Outside Article V', 94 *Col. L. Rev.* 457 (1994).
22 Ahkil Reed Amar, 'Philadelphia Revisited: Amending the Constitution Outside Article V,' 55 *Univ. of Chicago L. Rev.* 1043, 1073 (1988).
23 Quoted in Ahkil Reed Amar, 'The Consent of the Governed: Constitutional Amendment Outside Article V,' 94 *Col. L. Rev.* 457, 462 (1994).
24 *Ibid.* 505.
25 *Ibid.* 499.
26 *Ibid.*
27 Harris II, *supra* note 6, at 203.
28 *Ibid.* 202.
29 *Ibid.*
30 Anne Norton, 'Transubstantiation: The Dialectic of Constitutional Authority,'

55 *Univ. of Chicago L. Rev.* 458 (1988).
31 Quoted in Jon Elster, 'Intertemporal Choice and Political Thought,' in *Choice Over Time* 41 (George Loewenstein and Jon Elster eds. 1992).
32 *Ibid.* 35.
33 *Ibid.* 37.
34 *Ibid.* 41.
35 Jurgen Habermas, *Between Facts and Norms: Contributions to a Discourse Theory of Law and Democracy* 300 (1996).
36 Dennis Lloyd, *Introduction to Jurisprudence, 3d. edn.* 52 (1972).
37 Murphy, *supra* note 7.
38 See Andrew Arato, 'Dilemmas Arising from the Power to Create Constitutions in Eastern Europe,' in *Constitutionalism, Identity, Difference, and Legitimacy: Theoretical Perspectives* 179 (Michel Rosenfeld ed. 1994).
39 Harris II, *supra* note 6, at 168.
40 *Ibid.*
41 *Ibid.*
42 Kahn, *supra* note 9, at 63.
43 *Ibid.*
44 Alan C. Cairns, *Charter Versus Federalism: The Dilemmas of Constitutional Reform* 33 (1992).
45 *Ibid.* 34.
46 *Ibid.* 38.
47 Wolin, *supra* note 4, at 8.
48 *Ibid.*
49 Norton, *supra* note 30, 459.
50 *Ibid.*
51 Wolin, *supra* note 4, at 9.
52 Michel Rosenfeld, 'The Identity of the Constitutional Subject,' 16 *Cardozo L. Rev.* 1049, 1059 (1995).
53 *Ibid.*
54 Harris II, *supra* note 6, at 52.
55 *Ibid.* 73.
56 Rosenfeld, *supra* note 52, at 1053.
57 Harris II, *supra* note 6, at 74.
58 *Ibid.*
59 Quoted in Harris, *supra* note 6, at 79.
60 *Ibid.* 80.
61 *Ibid.*
62 *Ibid.* 79.
63 David A. J. Richards, *Foundations of American Constitutionalism* 92 (1989).
64 *Ibid.*
65 Harris II, *supra* note 6, at 74.
66 Richards, *supra* note 63, at 167.
67 *Ibid.*
68 *Ibid.*
69 Edmund S. Morgan, *Inventing the People: The Rise of Popular Sovereignty in England and America* 59 (1987).
70 *Ibid.* 83.

71 *Ibid.*
72 *Ibid.* 91.
73 *Ibid.*
74 Richards, *supra* note 63, at 93.
75 Samuel H. Beer, *To Make A Nation: The Rediscovery of American Federalism* 309 (1992).
76 *Ibid.* 314.
77 *Ibid.*
78 *Ibid.* 338.
79 See Bruce Ackerman, *We The People: Foundations,* Chapter I (1991).
80 Arato, *supra* note 38, at 166.
81 John P. Diggins, *The Lost Soul of American Politics: Virtue, Self Interest, and the Foundations of Liberalism* 57 (1984).
82 Henry Adams, *The Great Secession Winter of 1860-61* 193-4 (1958); quoted in John P. Diggins, *Id* at 57-58.
83 Beer, *supra* note 75, at 340.
84 Harris II, *supra* note 6, at 178.
85 *Ibid.*
86 *Ibid.* 166.
87 Arato, *supra* note 38, at 179.
88 Quoted in Harris, *supra* note 6, at 108.
89 David A. J. Richards, *supra* note 63, at 42.
90 Harris II, *supra* note 6, at 205.
91 *Ibid.* 172.
92 *Ibid.* 183.
93 *Ibid.* 184.
94 M. J. Detmold, *The Unity of Law and Morality: A Refutation of Legal Positivism* 226 (1984).
95 *Ibid.*
96 *Ibid.* 228.
97 Alf Ross, *On Law and Justice* 83 (1958).
98 *Ibid.*
99 *Ibid.*
100 Harris II, *supra* note 6, at 192.
101 The Barbados Independence Order, 1966.
102 Beer, *supra* note 75, at 337.
103 Richard S. Kay, 'Comparative Constitutional Fundamentals,' 6 Connecticut J. of Int'l Law 445, 449 (1991).
104 *Cheney v. Conn* [1968] All E.R. 779; quoted in Richard S. Kay, *ibid.*
105 *Ibid.*
106 Peter J. Steinberger, *Logic and Politics: Hegel's Philosophy of Right* 214 (1988).
107 See *A. G. of Trinidad and Tobago* v. *McLeod* [1984] 1 W.L.R. 522, 525.
108 Arato, *supra* note 38, at 172.
109 *Ibid.*
110 Richards, *supra* note 63, at 178.
111 Arato, *supra* note 38, at 172.
112 *Ibid.*
113 *Ibid.* 173.

114 *Ibid.*

115 Harris II, *supra* note 6, at 190.

116 *Ibid.* 191.

117 Morgan, *supra* note 69, at 81.

118 Harris II, *supra* note 6, at 167.

119 Holmes and Sunstein, *supra* note 8, at 305.

120 Elster, *supra* note 31, at 35.

121 *Ibid.*

122 *Ibid.* 37.

123 Stephen Holmes, *Passions and Constraint: On the Theory of Liberal Democracy* 135 (1997).

124 *Ibid.*

125 Rawls, *supra* note 10, at 232.

126 Richards, *supra* note 63, at 44..

127 Reported in the *Gleaner* newspaper, (Friday May 17, 2001).

128 See Report of the Constitution Review Commission 2 (1998).

129 From the Address by the then Governor-General, the late Sir Hugh Springer, on the occasion marking the 350th Anniversary of the Barbados Parliament.

130 Hans Kelsen, *General Theory of Law and State* 200 (1961).

131 H.L.A. Hart, *The Concept of Law* 116 (1961).

132 *Ibid.* 116-118.

133 *Ibid.* 118.

134 Peter H. Russell, *Constitutional Odyssey: Can Canadians Be a Sovereign People?* 53 (1992).

135 Peter W. Hogg, *Constitutional Law of Canada* 53 (Third Edition, 1993).

136 *Ibid.* 54.

137 *Ibid.*

138 *Ibid.*

139 Quoted in *ibid.* 55.

140 *Ibid.* 56.

141 Kenneth Robinson, 'Autochthony and the Transfer of Power,' in *Essays in Imperial Government* 250 (Kenneth Robinson and Frederick Madden eds. 1963).

142 *Ibid.*

143 *Ibid.*

144 Harris, *supra* note 6, at *ix.*

145 Kahn, *supra* note 9, at 55.

146 *Ibid.* 60.

147 *Ibid.*

148 Hogg, *supra* note 135, at 57.

149 *Ibid.* Paul W. Kahn, *op. cit.*

150 *Ibid.* 23.

151 Kay, *supra* note 103, at 445.

152 *Ibid.*

153 Frank I. Michelman, 'Constitutional Authorship,' in *Constitutionalism : Philosophical Foundations* 64 (Larry Alexander ed. 1998).

154 *The Federalist* No. 22, quoted in Richard S. Kay, 'The Illegality of the Constitution,' 4 *Const. Commentary* 57, 74 (1987).

155 Eric Cheyfitz, *The Poetics of Imperialism : Translation and Colonization from The Tempest to Tarzan* 49 (1997).

156 Frank I. Michelman, 'How Can the People Ever Make the Laws? A Critique of Deliberative Democracy,' in *Deliberative Democracy : Essays on Reason and Politics* 146 (James Bohman and William Rehg eds. 1997).

157 *Ibid.* 146-7.

158 *Ibid.* 147.

159 See, for example, The Barbados Independence Order 1966, s. 63. Currently, only Dominica, Guyana, and Trinidad and Tobago are considered not to be monarchies.

160 James Cameron Tudor, 'The Queen and Mr. Comissiong', *Daily Nation*, (Thursday November 17, 1992).

161 See, for example, the Terms of Reference of the Barbados Constitution Review Commission (1997).

162 Quoted in Hogg, *supra* note 135, at 49. See also, Russell, *supra* note 134.

163 See A.R. Carnegie, 'Floreat the Westminster Model? A Commonwealth Caribbean Perspective,' (1996) 6 *Carib. L. Rev.* 1.

164 *Ibid.*

165 Edmund Hinkson, 'A Ceremonial President', *Daily Nation* (Monday, November 20, 2000).

166 Both Trinidad and Tobago and Guyana are said to have remained constitutional monarchies at independence, and subsequently changed to republics.

167 Christopher Norris, *Spinoza and the Origins of Modern Critical Theory* 184 (1990).

168 Arthur C. Danto, *Narration and Knowledge* 233 (1985).

169 Hart, *supra* note 131, at 116-118.

170 See Peter J. Steinberger, *Logic and Politics: Hegel's Philosophy of Right* 212 (1988).

171 On the subject of illocutionary acts see William P. Alston, *Illocutionary Acts and Sentence Meaning* (2000); and Natalie Stoljar, 'Is Positivism Committed to Intentionalism? In *Judicial Power, Democracy and Legal Positivism* 175-179 (Tom Campbell and Jeffrey Goldsworthy eds. 2000).

172 Gordon S. Wood, *The Radicalism of the American Revolution* 11 (1991).

173 *Ibid.*

174 *Ibid.* 12.

175 *Ibid.*

176 For an extensive discussion of this concept of 'discontinuity,' see Simeon C.R. McIntosh, 'Continuity and Discontinuity of Law: A Reply to John Finnis,' 21 *Connecticut Law Review* 1 (1961).

177 See Hans Kelsen, *General Theory of Law and State* (1961).

178 See Hart, *supra*, note 131.

179 Harold J. Laski, *Foundations of Sovereignty and Other Essays* 12 (1931).

180 *Ibid.* 17.

181 *Ibid.* 12.

182 Steinberger, *supra*, note 106, at 194.

183 *Ibid.* 212.

184 Reported in the *Gleaner* newspaper, (Friday April 27, 2001).

185 See Edmund Hinkson, 'The Republic Issue – III,' *Daily Nation* (Monday

December 18, 2000).

186 See David Cook, 'Pluralism and the Death of Deference,' in *The Republican Ideal : Current Perspectives* 142 (Norman Porter ed. 1998).

187 Wood, *supra* note 172, at 96.

188 Steinberger, *supra* note 170, at 201.

189 *Ibid.* 210.

190 Norman Porter, 'Introduction : The Republican Ideal and Its Interpretations,' in *The Republican Ideal : Current Perspectives* 19 (Norman Porter ed. 1998).

191 Martin Mansergh, 'The Republican Ideal Regained,' in Porter, *ibid.* 41.

192 *Ibid.*

193 Philip Pettit, *Republicanism : A Theory of Freedom and Government* 286 (1997). I wish to express my indebtedness to Professor Pettit's work on republicanism, from which most of my discussion is drawn.

194 For an understanding of the influence of ancient Roman republicanism on American republicanism see in particular M.N.S. Sellers, *American Republicanism : Roman Ideology in the United States Constitution* (1994). See also, Philip Pettit, 'Reworking Sandel's Republicanism,' 45 *Journal of Philosophy* 73, 83 (1998).

195 *Ibid.*

196 *Ibid.*

197 *Ibid.*

198 Pettit, *supra* note 193, at 273.

199 *Ibid.* 271.

200 *Ibid.*

201 *Ibid.* 272.

202 *Ibid.* 274.

203 Pettit, *supra* note 194, at 83-84.

204 *Ibid.* 84.

205 Wood, *supra* note 172, at 11-12.

206 *Ibid.* 12.

207 *Ibid.* 96.

208 Pettit, *supra* note 194, at 84.

209 *Ibid.*

210 *Ibid.*

211 *Ibid.* 85.

212 *Ibid.*

213 *Ibid.* 86.

214 *Ibid.* 87.

215 *Ibid.*

216 Rodney Barker, *Political Legitimacy and the State* 11 (1990).

217 Pettit, *supra* note 193, at *ix.*

218 *Ibid.* 4.

219 *Ibid.* 6.

220 *Ibid.* 80.

221 Sellers, *supra* note 194, at 200.

222 Cook, *supra* note 186.

223 Pettit, *supra* note 193, at 185.

224 *Ibid.* 186.

225 *Ibid.* 188.
226 *Ibid.*
227 Quoted in *ibid.* 188-9.
228 *Ibid.* 230.
229 *Ibid.* 232.
230 Wolfgang Kersting, 'Kant's Concept of the State', in *Essays on Kant's Political Philosophy* 154 (Howard Lloyd Williams ed. 1994).
231 *Ibid.*
232 *Ibid.* 55.
233 *Ibid.*
234 B.O. Nwabueze, *Constitutionalism in the Emergent State* 56-7 (1973).
235 Scott Gordon, *Controlling the State : Constitutionalism from Ancient Athens to Today* 332 (1999).
236 David Judge, *The Parliamentary State* 2 (1993).
237 *Ibid.* 3.
238 *Ibid.* 20.
239 Jeffrey Goldsworthy, *The Sovereignty of Parliament : History and Philosophy* 159 (1999).
240 *Ibid.*
241 *Ibid.*
242 Judge, *supra* note 236, at 20.
243 *Ibid.*
244 Wood, *supra* note 172, at 13.
245 *Ibid.*
246 *Ibid.*
247 Gordon, *supra* note 235, at 226.
248 *Ibid.* 267.
249 *Ibid.* 224.
250 *Ibid.*
251 *Ibid.*
252 *Ibid.*
253 *Ibid.* 226.
254 *Ibid.* 227.
255 *Ibid.* 228.
256 *Ibid.* 265.
257 *Ibid.* 259.
258 *Ibid.*
259 *Ibid.* 261.
260 *Ibid.*
261 *Ibid.* 277.
262 *Ibid.*
263 *Ibid.* 278.
264 *Ibid.* 279.
265 *Ibid.* 280.
266 *Ibid.*
267 *Ibid.*
268 *Ibid.*
269 *Ibid.*

270 *Ibid.* 282.
271 *Ibid.*
272 *Ibid.*
273 *Ibid.*
274 *Ibid.*
275 *Ibid.*
276 *Ibid.*
277 Quoted in *ibid.* 283.
278 *Ibid.*
279 *Ibid.*
280 *Ibid.*
281 *Ibid.* 278.
282 *Ibid.* 283.
283 Judge, *supra* note 236.
284 *Ibid.* 3.
285 Stephen Bosworth, *Hegel's Political Philosophy: The Test Case for Constitutional Monarchy* (1991).
286 *Ibid.* 17.
287 Paul Franco, *Hegel's Philosophy of Freedom* 306 (1999).
288 Paul Redding, *Hegel's Hermeneutics* 229 (1996).
289 *Ibid.* 230.
290 *Ibid.* 232.
291 Steinberger, *supra* note 170, at 214.
292 *Ibid.*
293 *Ibid.*
294 *Ibid.* 215.
295 *Ibid.*
296 Franco, *supra* note 287, at 314.
297 *Ibid.*
298 *Ibid.* 315.
299 Bosworth, *supra* note 285, at 17. A recent classic example of this is the role played by King Juan Carlos in the restoration of constitutional democracy to Spain.
300 Bosworth, *supra* note 280, at 38.
301 Redding, *supra* note 288, at 232.
302 *Ibid.*
303 Kersting, *supra* note 230.
304 *Ibid.*
305 Harold J. Laski, *Foundations of Sovereignty and Other Essays* 12 (1931).
306 Steinberger, *supra* note 170, at 194.
307 *Ibid.* 212.
308 Gordon, *supra* note 235, at 279.
309 *Ibid.* 280.
310 *Ibid.*
311 *Ibid.* 282.
312 *Ibid.*
313 *Ibid.* 280.
314 *Ibid.* 283.

315 *Ibid.*
316 *Ibid.*
317 *Ibid.* 309.
318 *Ibid.*
319 Sellers, *supra* note 194, at 213.
320 *Ibid.*
321 *Ibid.* 209.
322 *Ibid.* 217.
323 *Ibid.* 219.
324 *Ibid.* 221.
325 *Ibid.* 222.
326 *Ibid.* 233.
327 *Ibid.*
328 *Ibid.* 237.
329 *Ibid.*
330 George W. Carey, *The Federalist Design for a Constitutional Republic* xvii (1989).
331 *Ibid.*
332 *Ibid.* xvi.
333 *Ibid.*
334 *Ibid.* xvii.
335 *Ibid.* xx.
336 *Ibid.* xxv.
337 *Ibid.* xxvi.
338 *Ibid.*
339 *Ibid.*
340 *Ibid.* 21.
341 *Ibid.*
342 *Ibid.* 4.
343 Sellers, *supra* note 194, at 199.
344 *Ibid.*
345 *Ibid.* 199-200.
346 *Ibid.* 200.
347 *Ibid.*
348 *Ibid.* 202.
349 *Ibid.* 177.
350 *Ibid.* 178.
351 *Ibid.*
352 *Ibid.* 232.
353 Kersting, *supra* note 230.
354 Carey, *supra* note 230, at 76.
355 *Ibid.* 77.
356 *Ibid.*
357 *Ibid.* 58.
358 *Ibid.* 133.
359 Quoted in *ibid.*
360 Jeremy Waldron, 'Precommitment and Disagreement,' in *Constitutionalism: Philosophical Foundations* 275 (Larry Alexander ed. 1998).

361 *Ibid.* 277.
362 Larry Alexander, 'Introduction,' in *Constitutionalism: Philosophical Foundations* 4 (Larry Alexander ed. 1998).
363 *Ibid.* 10.
364 Gordon, *supra* note 235, at 309.
365 *Ibid.* 313.
366 Quoted in *ibid.* 298.
367 *Ibid.* 314.
368 Quoted in *ibid.* 316.
369 *Ibid.* 317.
370 *Ibid.* 318.
371 *Ibid.* 319.
372 For a rather thoughtful essay on *Marbury's* central place in American jurisprudence, see Kahn, *supra* note 9.
373 *Ibid.* 247.
374 Quoted in *ibid.* 247, from the opinion of Chief Justice Marshall in *Marbury v. Madison.*
375 *Ibid.*
376 *Ibid.* 250.
377 Quoted in *ibid.* 255.
378 *Ibid.*
379 Quoted in Nwabuze, *supra* note 234, at 65.
380 Gordon, *supra* note 235, at 322-3.
381 *Ibid.* 323.
382 *Ibid.* 288.
383 Quoted in T.R.S. Allan, *Law, Liberty, and Justice: The Legal Foundations of British Constitutionalism* 52 (1993).
384 *Ibid.*
385 *Ibid.*
386 See *ibid.*
387 [1977] A.C. 195.
388 T.R.S. Allan, *op. cit.*
389 See E.C.S. Wade and A.W. Bradley, *Constitutional and Administrative Law* 50 (Tenth ed. 1985).
390 Quoted in *ibid.*
391 Gordon, *supra* note 235, at 281.
392 Wade and Bradley, *supra* note 389, at 51.
393 Gordon, *supra* note 235, at 282.
394 *Ibid.*
395 *Ibid.*
396 Goldsworthy, *supra* note 239, at 201.
397 Gordon, *supra* note 235, at 310.
398 Quoted in *ibid.* 320.
399 *Ibid.* 50.
400 Quoted in Goldsworthy, *supra* note 239, at 209.
401 Kay, *supra* note 103, at 449.
402 Quoted in *ibid.*
403 T.R.S. Allan, *supra* note 282, at 75.

404 See Goldsworthy, *supra* note 239, at 209.
405 See Kay, *supra* note 103, at 449.
406 Allan, *supra* note 383, at 62.
407 See *ibid*. 74.
408 See *Hinds v. R.* [1977] A.C. 195, 212-13.
409 *Ibid.*
410 See Allan, *supra* note 383, at 75.
411 *Ibid.*
412 *Ibid.*
413 *Ibid.*
414 *Ibid.*
415 *Ibid.* 52.
416 See feature article, 'India Ponders "Right" Political System', *Trinidad Guardian* (Thursday September 24, 1998).
417 *Ibid.*
418 *Ibid.*
419 Note the single exception of Grenada which had a Marxist government from 1979-1983.
420 See Juan J. Linz, 'Presidential or Parliamentary Democracy : Does It Make a Difference?' in *The Failure of Presidential Democracy*, Chapter 1 (Juan J. Linz and Arturo Valenzuela eds. 1994).
421 Robert Dahl, *Democracy and Its Critics* 192 (1989).
422 Quoted in Nwabueze, *supra* note 234, at 65.
423 Alfred Stepan and Cindy Skach, 'Presidentialism and Parliamentarism in Comparative Perspective,' in *The Failure of Presidential Democracy* 128 (Juan J. Linz and Arturo Valenzuela eds. 1994).
424 *Ibid.* 120.
425 *Ibid.*
426 Bosworth, *supra* note 280, at 21.
427 *Ibid.*
428 Art. 2, U.S. Const.
429 Linz, *supra* note 414, at 6.
430 *Ibid.*
431 *Ibid.* 8.
432 *Ibid.* 9.
433 *Ibid.* 10.
434 Stepan and Skach, *supra* note 417, at 128.
435 *Ibid.* 130.
436 *Ibid.* 128.
437 See Linz, *supra* note 420, at 5.
438 Stepan and Skach, *supra* note 417, at 128.
439 Linz, *supra* note 420, at 9.
440 Stepan and Skach, *supra* note 423, at 129.
441 *Ibid.* 119.
442 *Ibid.*
443 See Linz, *supra* note 420, at 4.
444 Linz, 'Preface,' *supra* note 420, at *x*.
445 *Ibid.* 9.

446 Stepan and Skach, *supra* note 423, at 129.

447 *Ibid.*

448 Evelyne Huber, 'The Future of Democracy in the Caribbean,' in *Democracy in the Caribbean : Political, Economic, and Social Perspectives* 78 (Jorge Dominguez, Robert Pastor, and Delisle Worrell eds. 1993).

449 Stepan and Skach, *supra* note 423, at 129.

450 See Linz, *supra* note 420.

451 See *ibid.*

452 *Ibid.*

453 *Ibid.*

454 *Ibid.* 7.

455 See Thomas A. Baylis, 'Presidents versus Prime Ministers : Shaping Executive Authority in Eastern Europe,' 48 *World Politics* 297, 301 (1996).

456 Linz, *supra* note 420, at 7.

457 *Ibid.* 46.

458 *Ibid.* 82, note 61.

459 Gordon, *supra* note 235, at 334.

460 See David A.J. Richards, *Foundations of American Constitutionalism* 164 (1989).

461 On this issue, see Baylis, *supra* note 455.

462 Linz, *supra* note 420, at 47.

463 Baylis, *supra* note 455, at 301.

464 *Ibid.* 306, 307.

465 *Ibid.* 307.

466 *Ibid.*

467 See, for example, an opinion by A.W. Bradley in the *Trinidad Guardian* newspaper, (Sunday January 28, 2001). See, also, a rejoinder by Simeon C.R. McIntosh, 'Prudence and Democratic Governance,' in the *Trinidad Guardian*, (Sunday March 4, 2001).

468 Baylis, *supra* note 455, at 300.

469 Linz, *supra* note 420, at 57.

470 *Ibid.*

471 Arend Lijphart, 'Presidentialism and Majoritarian Democracy: Theoretical Observations,' in *The Failure of Presidential Democracy* 96 (Juan J. Linz and Arturo Valenzuela eds. 1994).

472 *Ibid.* 97.

473 Anthony Payne, 'Westminster Adapted : The Political Order of the Commonwealth Caribbean', in *Democracy in the Caribbean : Political, Economic, and Social Perspectives* 60 (Jorge Dominquez, Robert Pastor and Delisle Worrell eds. 1993).

474 *Ibid.* 58.

475 *Ibid.* 61.

476 *Ibid.*

477 Rawls, *supra* note 11, at 214.

478 Joshua Cohen, 'Deliberation and Democratic Legitimacy,' in *The Good Polity* 21 (Alan Hamlin and Philip Pettit eds. 1989).

479 Godon, *supra* note 235, at 232.

480 *Ibid.*

481 *Ibid.* 333.
482 *Ibid.*
483 *Ibid.* 232.
484 *Ibid.*
485 *Ibid.*
486 *Ibid.* 235.
487 *Ibid.*
488 *Ibid.* 332.
489 *Ibid.* 235.
490 See Laura J. Scalia, *America's Jeffersonian Experiment: Remaking State Constitutions 1820-1850,* 107 (1999).
491 From Farrand (ed.), Records of the Federal Convention, vol. 1, p. 421. Quoted in John Elster, 'Intertemporal Choice and Political Thought', in *Choice Over Time* 41 (George Loewenstein and Jon Elster eds. 1992).
492 Quoted in David F. Epstein, *The Political Theory of The Federalist* 132 (1984).
493 Gordon, *supra* note 235, at 298.
494 Scalia, *supra* note 490.
495 See Albert Branford, 'Role of the Senate,' *Sunday Sun* (April 23, 2000).
496 See Lloyd Best, 'Government and Politics in the West Indies,' vol. 20 (Nos. 10-11) *Trinidad and Tobago Review* 27, 32 (November, 1998). For a rather thoughtful essay on this subject see, Ann Spackman, 'The Senate of Trinidad and Tobago,' 16 *Social and Economic Studies* 77 (1967).
497 Robert D. Cooter, *The Strategic Constitution* 185 (2000).
498 *Ibid.*
499 Arend Lijphart, *Patterns of Democracy* 18 (1999).
500 Cooter, *supra* note 497, at 223.
501 *Ibid.*
502 *Ibid.* 213.
503 *Ibid.*
504 *Ibid.* 212.
505 *Ibid.* 215.
506 *Ibid.*
507 *Ibid.*
508 *Ibid.* 223.
509 *Ibid.*
510 See *Report of the Constitution Review Commission* (1998).
511 Scalia, *supra* note 490.
512 See Payne, *supra* note 473, at 57.
513 See Ljphart, *supra* note 499, at 8.
514 *Ibid.*
515 Payne, *supra* note 473, at 57.
516 Lijphart, *supra* note 499, at 146.
517 *Ibid.*
518 Cooter, *supra* note 497, at 28.
519 *Ibid.* 29.
520 *Ibid.* 31.
521 *Ibid.* 75.
522 *Ibid.* 73.

523 *Ibid.* 77.

524 *Ibid.*

525 *Ibid.*

526 Lijphart, *supra* note 497.

527 Cooter, *supra* note 492, at 178.

528 *Ibid.* 179.

529 See Lijphart, *supra* note 499, at 147.

530 See *ibid.* 153-54; see also Cooter, *supra* note 497, at 179.

531 *Ibid.*

532 *Ibid.* 156.

533 Linz, *supra* note 420, at 15.

534 Lijphart, *supra* note 499, at 157.

535 See Selwyn Ryan, *Winner Takes All : The Westminster Experience in the Caribbean*, 266 (1999).

536 *Ibid.*

537 Quoted in Khan, *supra* note 9, at 60.

Chapter 2

The Bill of Rights

Every *West Indian Independence Constitution* contains a Bill of Rights; which is one of the deeply entrenched provisions of the Constitution. The nature of the rights enshrined in a Bill of Rights certainly warrants this. As Mr. Justice Robert Jackson of the US Supreme Court has observed:

> The very purpose of a Bill of Rights [is] to withdraw certain subjects from the vicissitudes of political controversy, to place them beyond the reach of majorities and officials and to establish them as legal principles to be applied by the courts. One's right to life, liberty, and property, to free speech, a free press, freedom of worship and assembly, and other fundamental rights may not be submitted to a vote: they depend on the outcome of no elections.[1]

The philosopher John Rawls has echoed this sentiment when he observed that fundamental rights are a matter of constitutional essentials that are fixed in constitution making beyond tampering by ordinary legislation.[2] The question, then, is one of the nature and provenance of the rights contained in a Bill of Rights that would distinguish them from ordinary legal or political rights which are created by a legislative body and conferred upon the citizens of a society. In other words, the very notion of fundamentality rests on a supposition of rights that are 'natural', in the sense that they are not the product of deliberate legislative acts or explicit social custom or convention, but are rather independent grounds or regulative standards for judging legislation and custom.[3]

It is now commonly understood that constitutional democracy's claim to moral distinction as a form of political rule rests largely on its recognition and enforcement of certain fundamental rights and values which express the idea of the individual as the moral center of society. Put differently, the fundamental rights and freedoms, listed in the Bill of Rights of virtually every written Western constitution, are understood to constitute the moral core of the constitution; their pivotal importance to the ultimate political question of right governance can therefore never be overstated. For, in the final analysis, the rational reason for subsequent generations respecting the terms of the constitutional settlement, made by the founding generation, has less to do with the source than with the content of the constitution.[4] In other words, the very probability of a people venerating their constitution may depend largely on what the constitution contains, and, equally important, on how it is written. This simple, but very important point seems largely to have been missed by the so-called Westminster tradition of constitution writing, out of which West Indian Independence Constitutions have come. The question of the style of constitution writing must therefore be addressed. However, the question of the nature of our fundamental rights and of those which are appropriately constitutionalized in the constitution's text must first be explored.

Fundamental Rights and Freedoms

The fundamental rights and freedoms listed in our constitutions are in fact versions or a species of some of the basic human rights declared in the famous Universal Declarations, such as the Universal Declaration of Human Rights promulgated by the

United Nations in 1948. These basic human rights are often philosophically justified by appeal to some version of natural law theory, such, for example, as the theory articulated by the natural law theorist, John Finnis, in *Natural Law and Natural Rights*.[5] On Finnis' view, our most basic human rights, such as the right not to be murdered, assaulted, tortured, enslaved; the right of freedom of conscience, thought and expression, and to worship, are in fact the elucidation of certain forms of human good that are constitutive of human well-being; our normative conclusions based on a reflective grasp of what is self evidently good for human beings. In contrast, the philosopher John Rawls would base his justification of our fundamental rights and freedoms on some hypothetical construct of an *original contract*[6] – a morally credentialed perspective from which *we* would claim certain fundamental rights and freedoms that are absolutely necessary for the exercise of our basic human capacities to rationally pursue our individual life plans and conceptions of the good.[7] What is evident from these two philosophical approaches is that our justification of basic human rights rests on, or is tied to, some *ideal* conception of the human person as a reflective, self-determining rational agent; a being capable of moral judgments and of making critical choices about his or her own life, and of undertaking practical deliberations about those ends worth pursuing and that would be defining of his or her identity.

One of the more articulate voices on this question of the nature of human rights is that of the distinguished University of Chicago philosopher, Alan Gewirth. According to Gewirth, human rights are rights which all persons have equally, solely by virtue of the ontological fact that they are human rather than belonging to some other kind, and therefore deserve to be treated in certain ways or, more usually, not to be treated in certain ways.[8] He goes on to state that the objects of the human rights, what they are rights to, are certain especially important kinds of goods.[9]

[T]hese goods consist in the necessary conditions of human action, and ... it is for this reason that human rights are supremely mandatory. It is also because the human rights have these Objects that they are uniquely and centrally important among all moral concepts, since no morality, together with the goods, virtues, and rules emphasised in diverse moralities, is possible without the necessary goods of action that are the Objects of human rights.[10]

On this view, Gewirth reasons, human rights are *personally oriented, normatively necessary moral requirements.*[11] They are requirements, first, in the sense of necessary needs; second, in the sense of justified entitlements; and third, in the sense of claims or demands made on or addressed to other persons,[12] to civil society and to the State. They are, in a word, the essential conditions of personhood and this is the normative moral principle that serves to establish the justifying ground of human rights. This feature distinguishes human rights from utilitarian and collectivist norms where rights are consequential upon or instrumental to the fulfillment of aggregative or collective goals.[13]

The ascription of these moral rights to humans is predicated on an assumption of *worth* of all human persons; an attribution of dignity to a being capable of *self-determination*, of framing and executing a rational plan of life. As Gewirth puts it:

An ineluctable element of *worth* ... is involved in the very concept and context of human purposive action. Such action is not merely an unordered set of episodes or events. Rather, it is ordered by its orientation to a goal which gives it its value, its point. This is so even if the action is done for its own sake, so that it is its own goal. In either case, the goal or end has *worth* for the agent as something to be reflectively chosen, aimed at, and achieved. And this worth is not merely instrumental; it characterises at least some of the agent's ends themselves as he conceives and pursues them.[14]

This grounding of human rights in the necessary conditions of human agency, it is submitted, serves to emphasise that the ultimate purpose of these human rights is to preserve for each person a certain moral status and to underscore the fact that these rights are, conceptually, not the determinations of political will, but are rather rights grounded in a 'higher law' of reason.[15] Thus, for example, the existence of human rights may be construed as consisting in certain positive institutional conditions.[16] However, this positivist interpretation of human rights is posterior to a normative moral interpretation, given that human rights are, first and foremost, justified moral entitlements. In other words, the existence of human rights is independent of whether they are guaranteed or enforced by legal codes or are socially recognised. For if the existence of human rights depended on such recognition or enforcement, it would follow that there were no human rights prior to or independent of these positive enactments.[17]

This view of human rights is critical, because their specification in a political constitution as the basic human, civil and political rights of the citizen gives an unmistakable moral content to that constitution. They give expression to the central moral values embedded in the constitution's text, summed up in an understanding of ourselves as rational agents who can direct and control our individual lives; these rights demarcate for each of us some *moral space* or *zone* of personal sovereignty within which we may pursue our life-plans without fear of encroachment from others or from the state. Their legitimizing force is therefore incontrovertible, for they are 'the rights secured by justice and are not subject to political bargaining or to the calculus of social interests.'[18] They are the constitutive and regulative institutional norms of debate in democratic societies and cannot be transformed or abrogated by simple or special majority decisions.[19] In a word, they constitute the substantive constraints on majoritarian politics. For, in a constitutional democracy, we expect that certain aspects of the 'higher law' would be entrenched against revision, even by the people themselves.

These core moral values embedded in the constitution's text are in fact expressed and embodied in the political and legal procedures of constitutional democracy. Professor George Kateb of Princeton University makes this point admirably in his essay, 'Procedures of Constitutional Democracy.' He writes that 'constitutional democracy is a way of life; its distinctive features constitute its claim to moral superiority; and these features are accommodated, embodied, and expressed in its political and legal procedures'[20] – most notably, the right to vote and due process of law. Indeed, 'the unelaborated intuition is that the political and legal procedures of constitutional democracy are the most intrinsically valuable of all political and legal procedures.' These two great procedures have intrinsic moral value and constitute the soul of constitutional democracy.[21] According to Kateb, the filling of political offices through contested elections held at suitably frequent intervals, decided by the majority, on the basis of universal adult suffrage, and the legal procedure of due process of law are the most important procedures of constitutional democracy.[22] For example, the electoral system of constitutional democracy accommodates values by giving citizens the opportunity to the morally valuable and enriching experience of choosing their political leaders. It therefore establishes formal relationships between the government and all citizens, and among all citizens themselves. The first relationship is a crystallization of the idea that political officials, who make and enforce the law and policies, in fact, hold their offices temporarily since the grant of authority to them is indeed revocable. And the second relationship is a crystallization of the idea that the right to vote rests on the more fundamental idea of equal citizenship. These two senses of the intrinsic value and importance of the right to vote are captured in Jurgen Habermas' statement that

> The right to vote ... [is] ... the paradigm of rights ... not only because it is constitutive for political self-determination, but because it shows how inclusion in a community of equals is connected with the individual right to make autonomous contributions and take personal positions on issues.[23]

The constitutional right of due process of law is the greatest legal procedure of constitutional democracy. It is based on the fundamental moral and universal right of every person not to be disparaged or debased, or to be arbitrarily and unjustly treated. But from the perspective of constitutional right, the government is the principal agent or actor in due process. Thus, the due process requirement is designed, first and foremost, to protect all citizens against arbitrary government decision making. In a word, it is a bulwark against arbitrary and capricious government. It is therefore one of the conditions that must be met for the morally acceptable exercise of power.[24] It 'aims to provide some assurance of non-arbitrariness by requiring those who exercise authority to justify their intended actions in a public proceeding by adducing reasons of the appropriate sort and defending these against critical attack.'[25] Constitutional due process, in other words, condemns governmental denials of life, liberty, or property based on mere opinions or beliefs having no factual support.

In sum, then, due process of law, whether it asserts itself in the form of a basic and indispensable injunction against arbitrary and capricious legislative deprivation of life, liberty, or property; or as the criminal defendant's right to a fair trial; or as the citizen's right to notice and a hearing before an administrative agency, it embodies the intrinsic value of human dignity or 'respect for persons.' Indeed, both of these two major procedures of constitutional democracy are committed to the principle of dignity or 'respect for persons.' Together, they have in common a devotion to the idea that the individual is the moral center of the society.[26] The electoral right pays homage to the person as a free and moral agent. And the values embodied and expressed in due process comprise one of the ultimate refinements of secular morality – of *morality*, not supererogation;[27] that which is the citizen's due as a matter of *right*, and not a matter of *grace*. Without the electoral system as the modern basis of governance, governance lacks legitimacy and respect for persons has been denied. Without due process as the basis of criminal justice, legal justice cannot be done or, at best, legal justice can only be attained at the expense of certain individual rights, and hence of justice.[28] To repeat: 'The fundamental reason for this unyielding position is that the values contained in these two procedures are necessary to establish the principle of respect for persons in society as a whole, in all its relations and institutions.'[29]

One of the basic substantive human rights specified in virtually every democratic constitution, and also in every international human rights instrument, is the right against torture and cruel, inhuman or degrading punishment or treatment. The fundamental moral value that this 'right' unmistakably embraces is the value of human dignity. Indeed, dignity is considered by some to be the fundamental value underlying the whole catalogue of constitutional rights secured by the typical Western democratic constitution. The late Justice William Brennan, for example, has proclaimed 'the US Constitution a sublime oration on the dignity of man, a bold commitment by a people to the ideal of libertarian dignity protected through law.'[30] And for Gewirth, human dignity is the *antecedent* and justificatory ground of all human civil and political rights.[31]

This relation between dignity and human rights has in fact been defended by the distinguished moral philosopher Immanuel Kant, who wrote that man 'is obligated to acknowledge, in a practical way, the dignity of humanity in every other man. Hence he is subject to a duty based on the respect which he must show every other man.'[32] The relation has also been drawn explicitly in the preambles to the two international covenants adopted by the United Nations in 1966 - 'These [human] rights derive from the inherent dignity of the human person'[33] - and has been emphasised in the Universal Declaration itself, which states that 'everyone ... is entitled to the realisation ... of the economic, social and cultural rights indispensable for his dignity.'[34]

It bears reminding that dignity is here being used to signify a kind of intrinsic and indefeasible worth that belongs equally to all human beings. It is a distinctively moral status that secures us against arbitrary contempt and is not vulnerable to annulment or destruction.[35] It furnishes the ground or the defining limits regarding the ways the State may or may not treat its citizens. It therefore functions as a basic and indispensable constraint on the legislative process,[36] for example, constituting the basis for the specification of those rights the State must necessarily respect in establishing criminal offences and the forms of punishment it may legitimately enforce against the citizen.

The question then is that of the specification of the fundamental constitutional rights, deriving from the basic human rights, in the constitution's text. For the fundamental moral imperative of the just and well-ordered society is that it secures some of the most basic human rights of personhood, that is, instantiating (actualising, realising) those ultimate aspects of human flourishing as an essential part of its constitutional project. The US Constitution represents the first (and maybe classic) example in modern history of the articulation of fundamental rights and freedoms as part of the constitutional text; and of the comporting institutional arrangements for the interpretation and enforcement of these rights. What, therefore, needs to be remembered in the articulation, interpretation and enforcement of these fundamental rights, is that as rights constituting the moral core of the just constitution, they are not the product of any explicit conventional design, but are rather morally and epistemologically prior to the very determinate political structure that affords their protection.[37]

The specified list of fundamental rights and freedoms entrenched in a Commonwealth Caribbean Bill of Rights, rights and freedoms generally considered to be immune to political revision, includes rights that are indispensable to democratic legitimacy, such as freedom of conscience, thought and expression; religious liberty, the right to vote, due process of law; freedom from discrimination on grounds of race, religion, ethnicity, and sex; the basic right to a fair hearing, and the right against torture and cruel and inhuman punishment or treatment. These rights, it is sometimes said, establish a 'moral space' for each individual, free from unjustifiable encroachment by others and particularly by the State.[38] Indeed, our basic or fundamental constitutional rights are primarily conceived of as rights against the State. Hence the critical importance of the comporting constitutional structure of separated powers and the practice of judicial review and the basic democratic arrangements that give reality to these fundamental rights.

These fundamental rights referred to above, now generally considered the classic civil and political rights of democratic citizenship, in fact derive from conceptions of human rights based on the idea of moral agency. As was earlier noted, the ascription of these moral human rights to persons rests on an ideal conception of the *person* as a being capable of making critical choices about his or her own life, and should therefore be accorded the *moral space*, free from interference, within which to act on his or her 'higher-order' choices. So in order to exercise our distinctive powers of choice and self-determination, we are led to demand for ourselves, and to recognize in others, such categorical rights that define 'spheres of individual sovereignty' in which one is morally free to act on the basis of one's own choices.[39] The liberty rights stipulated in a bill of rights are in fact designed to promote and protect this *zone* of individual sovereignty.

But the idea of moral agency also entails arguments for certain derivative 'welfare rights' – rights to those opportunities and goods that are necessary for full membership in society.[40] For without access to certain basic resources, or the satisfaction of certain basic needs, it is impossible to exercise the powers of agency. Protection of a person's capacities for agency therefore requires that these resources be provided to individuals as a matter of right.[41] The question therefore arises whether the catalogue of fundamental rights, normally contained in a Bill of Rights, should be broadened to include certain socioeconomic, welfare or subsistence rights which, according to many distinguished philosophers, are comparable in fundamentality to the classic civil and political rights.[42]

Advocates of welfare rights often draw upon sources such as the Universal Declaration of Human Rights, which affirms that each person has a 'right to food, clothing, housing and education; rights to work, leisure, fair wages, decent working conditions, and social security; rights to physical and mental health; protection for the family and for mothers and children; a right to participate in cultural life.'[43] They argue that governments are obligated to assure for all citizens some minimum level of health care, education, or living standard, since these are generally understood to be a necessary component of any just society. Again, the root idea here is that some specified level of welfare goods would be, equally like basic liberties, essential conditions of human flourishing. As D.D. Raphael puts it:

One cannot exercise the initiative of a human being (which is what the rights of liberty are intended to protect), or indeed remain a human being at all, unless the basic needs of life are satisfied, and if a man is not in a position to do this for himself, it seems to me reasonable to say that he has a right, as a human being, to the assistance of others in meeting these needs.[44]

Again, one of the more positive and persuasive voices in favour of the legal recognition of social and economic rights is that of Alan Gewirth. Professor Gewirth grounds his case for social and economic rights as basic human rights in the moral principle of human agency. For him, as earlier noted, the concept of human agency is the ontological and justificatory context of the principle of human rights. Human agency, as a rationally justified moral principle, imports a conception of the human person as actual or prospective agent, capable of forming his or her own conception of the good life and of making critical choices about that life; and should therefore be enabled to live a life of dignity and self-fulfillment in mutual recognition of the same in others. On this view, human rights are considered morally necessary entitlements or justified claims, or the moral property of individuals in that they are the indispensable conditions of human agency and well-being. Put differently, the objects of human rights are certain essential interests of human beings as prospective and purposive agents.[45] To the extent, therefore, that social and economic rights may be seen as the proximate and necessary conditions of human agency and well-being, argues in their favour as moral claims or entitlements comparable to the classic liberal rights and, on this view, should be accorded the status of legal rights as well.

So Gewirth would make the principle of human rights a fundamental moral norm on which to mount the claim for welfare rights. Thus, for him, the existence of poverty is at least a *prima facie* violation of human rights. For all persons have moral claims to the necessary goods of human agency, and these claims entail correlative duties to provide them for persons who cannot obtain them by their own efforts. Thus, the State, as the central moral agent in society, should be the primary respondent of these claims. This is how the moral right to welfare is ultimately understood as a legal right.[46]

Gewirth's arguments for welfare as a basic right are admirably complemented by those of Professor Raymond Plant, who also bases the justification of the right to welfare on an account of the requirements of rational agency: an account of the agent to whom basic human rights are ascribed and the characteristics in virtue of which they are ascribed.[47] His is basically a Kantian approach that seeks a transcendental deduction of the grounds of rights by reflecting upon the necessary preconditions of morality.[48] For him, therefore, the question is whether there are any universal features of human life that may be regarded as necessary presuppositions or conditions for morality.[49] For Kant, such preconditions of morality were to be understood in terms of rational, autonomous agency and the ability to formulate rules of universal scope.[50] In other words, the capacity for rational agency might be regarded as both a universal and necessary condition for morality and therefore a possible foundation for a theory of rights, since there must be certain basic goods necessary to sustain a capacity for agency, irrespective of culture, religion, or ethnic origin.[51]

Now as was earlier intimated, agency and autonomy, as the basis of rights, presuppose a set of basic liberty rights that demand forbearances from coercion and interferences by others. But can agency and autonomy also ground a more positive view of rights as rights to resources? Professor Plant thinks that they can once we take account of the fact that there are basic goods of agency, autonomy, and liberty, irrespective of the particular culture within which an individual might live and the individual conceptions of the good life that individuals might be enabled to attain within that culture.[52] In other words, if there are such basic goods that are indispensable for agency, then they would define the set of basic rights that would reflect the need for such goods. As Plant puts it:

> The needs of agency will plausibly include, first of all, physical survival in the platitudinous sense that an agent is unable to exercise agency without physical integrity and survival. But there is more to the physical needs of agency than mere survival; agency must also include some element of a worthwhile life or physical well-being, because it is very difficult to imagine how a life of rational agency could ever be pursued if the whole effort of a person's life is devoted to securing the bare minimum to survive. In this sense, to secure the capacity for agency for individuals will require not just restrictions on coercion defined by negative rights but also positive rights to those resources that will contribute to both survival and well-being. Hence, food, shelter, and health care of a sort relevant to and effective in a particular society would constitute basic goods of agency. However, the capacity of agency will also require other kinds of basic goods such as education, which, in the terms relevant to a particular society, will be needed to sustain a capacity for agency, choice, and effective functioning.[53]

The basic needs of agency are said to have moral force in that they relate to the basic idea of dignity and worth: an indefeasible moral status of persons. On this view they are said to ground the basis for rights. Again, the root idea is that there are certain basic needs that must necessarily be fulfilled if *any* conception of the good is to be pursued.[54] 'These needs will be both negative and positive; that is, freedoms from intentional coercion and interference are necessary for agency, but so too are certain resources such as physical well-being and education.'[55] But the question still remains whether a human right to welfare should be accorded the status of a constitutional right. There is, after all, an important difference in the nature of the two sorts of rights in question. Basic liberty rights are deemed largely to be negative rights, while welfare rights, as claims to resources, are called positive rights. Put differently, basic liberty rights are said to be categorical whereas welfare rights are conditional and dialectical, in that recognition of a particular welfare claim as a legal right results from a political process through which competing claims are compromised.[56]

It is conceded that the notion of basic rights would embrace the idea of claims to recipience of certain goods acknowledged as well to be essentials of well-being. The fact that one has a need for a certain good must certainly figure within the moral calculus in that it is not a matter of moral indifference whether the need is satisfied.[57] After all, we cannot both respect a person's moral capacity and be indifferent as to whether he has the means on which the realization of that capacity depends.[57a] Still, it does not follow that another must do whatever will suffice to see that the need is satisfied. Against whom then would social and economic rights be claimed? It must be against society as a whole, or more specifically the government. Rights entail corresponding or correlative duties; welfare rights in particular entail positive duties on the part of government to provide for those rights. But as Professor Richard Epstein observes, 'no legal or political theory of rights is acceptable if it fails to generate rights and duties consistent with the limited resources that must be generated to satisfy them. As a necessary corollary, levels of production cannot be regarded as constant, independent of a scheme for distributing the goods produced.'[58] Any system of welfare rights demands elaborate and expensive pooling arrangements for allocating resources. If, therefore, a polity should determine that basic subsistence rights should be guaranteed to every person, then everyone has a duty to contribute to the cost of providing those rights.[59]

As Professor Loren Lomasky has observed, we can well imagine that individuals in, say, a Rawlsian original position, would *contract* amongst themselves to secure equal basic liberties for all, and at the same time to guarantee to each other some specified or minimum level of welfare goods. In other words, they may agree to arrange the basic institutions of their society in such a way that the basic liberties of each would be respected, and, at the same time, provide institutional channels of encouragement and support for individuals, on their own initiative and by their own industry, to provide these welfare goods for themselves. However, for those individuals who lack the capacity to provide these goods for themselves, the obligation falls to the State, as the proper repository of our collective commitments, to secure these goods for them.[60]

But to say that the obligation falls to the State is just a shorthand way of saying that everyone has a duty to contribute to the cost of providing these goods. What, therefore, is meant is that certain individuals, invested with state power, would institute the appropriate system of progressive taxation in order to provide welfare assistance to others. Any welfare scheme therefore entails some redistribution of wealth. As Professor Richard Epstein puts it: 'A system of welfare payments without taxation is the social equivalent of a perpetual motion machine.'[61]

This therefore puts in sharp relief the issue of the magnitude of sacrifice that must be exacted from others in order to provide welfare goods to some.[62] For example, if the transfer payments required to fund subsistence rights are so great, or the recipients so numerous, that the required taxes damage economic incentives, or reduce the accumulation of investment funds or otherwise significantly dampen economic output, then we may not be able to afford these rights.[63] Thus, in the circumstances where it is virtually impossible to supply these goods, notwithstanding the great need or demand for them, then it is no longer obvious, or even credible, that there is any right of recipience to these goods and thus a correlative duty to provide them.[64] In sum, then, it bears reminding that rights in general cannot be formulated and pursued in isolation; they require the commitment of resources to enforce them and a willingness on the part of most people to comply with them. Even so-called negative rights imply the commitment of resources, whether in the form of the institutional provision necessary to protect liberty rights in general or in the context of a specific allocation of resources to secure the right to a fair trial to the indigent criminal defendant. However, consideration of social or welfare rights particularly requires this kind of utilitarian calculation. For they can never be discharged by refraining from interference with a protected sphere of individual action, as can so many of our civil and political rights. They require the provision of specific goods and services. Therefore, this utilitarian calculation is an important expectation that must be satisfied in determining what interests should be accorded the status of constitutional rights; whether the government has the ability to provide for such rights;[65] and, therefore, whether we owe a correlative duty of affirmative support to those in need of welfare assistance.

Let us take the right to work as an example. Now, it is commonly understood that work is a critical social good. An impressive array of social psychological findings has confirmed that 'work roots a person in society.'[66] It encourages feelings of self-worth. Unemployment, conversely, threatens basic well-being. Indeed, there is widespread agreement that one of the most serious and debilitating contemporary social problems is the problem of enforced or involuntary unemployment. It can lead to severe under-nourishment, homelessness, lack of medical care, and inability to obtain other necessities of life. In addition, unemployment can undermine one's self-esteem and feeling of self-worth. In extreme cases, unemployment, coupled with the threat to livelihood, can lead not only to deep depression but to suicide. These factors, combined with considerations about productive agency, argue in favour of a right to employment, a right to be effectively able to earn a livelihood through one's own productive work in order to ward off such negative impacts.[67]

But can the right to work really be said to be a universal human right, in the common acceptation of that term, available at all times and in all places and, therefore, one which every society has an affirmative duty to secure? As presented in the Universal Declaration, for example, the right to work is understood to demand that a positive benefit – 'work' – actually be provided. Gewirth, in fact, sees the right to employment as both a negative and a positive right. It is a negative right in that all other persons and groups have the correlative duty, consistent with the moral requirements of the principle of human rights, to refrain from interfering with an agent's obtaining, performing, or retaining productive and remunerative work.[68] The duty to refrain includes the duty not to impose obstacles that prevent persons from working because of considerations of race, religion, gender, or other criteria that are irrelevant to the ability to perform the kind of work that is in question. It also includes the duty not to exclude persons from jobs, or fire them from jobs they already have, because they have objected to their work conditions on grounds of health or safety.[69] And even more stringently, this negative right entails the duty of corporate employers to refrain from policies that throw people out of work, in pursuit of profits that disregard the adverse impact on workers' continued employment.[70] It has even been suggested that

A government committed to [a] full employment objective might first establish and enforce standards of behaviour and decision-making on private capital – and particularly the large, concentrated, globally-oriented corporate and financial firms – focused on their job-creating, job-destroying decisions and choices. Public policy would apply incentives and rewards, penalties and obligations, analogous to those used in enforcing standards of environmental protection, consumer health and safety, and protection of investors' savings. Like the environmental impact statement now required before investment or land-use decisions may be implemented, employers would be required to develop "employment impact" statements wherever a decision about location or relocation, change of methods, scale, and process involved significant effects on jobs, skills, and earnings.[71]

From the standpoint of a positive right, the right to employment is advanced because of the crucial impact of unemployment on both freedom and well-being. Professor William A. Galston suggests that the category of 'welfare rights,' which includes the guarantee of employment, emerged in the European struggle to address some of the unwanted consequences of market economies.[72] Thus, insofar as the market, as represented by private employers, fails to provide work, its primary respondent must be the State as the central moral and political agent in society. That is to say, it is the State, acting through the government, which has the correlative duty to take the steps required to provide work for unemployed persons who are able and willing to work.[73] This claim for such a positive right and duty regarding employment, we have noted, has been given universal recognition in the Universal Declaration of Human Rights promulgated by the United Nations in 1948:

> Everyone has the right to work, to free choice of employment, to just and favourable conditions of work and to protection against unemployment.... Everyone who works has the right to just and favourable remuneration ensuring for himself and his family an existence worthy of human dignity.[74]

If one were to agree with the Harvard University philosopher, John Rawls, that self-esteem is the most important primary good – that without which nothing has much value – and if, in addition, one believes that work is one of the most important sources of self-esteem, then there would seem to be a strong case for a constitutional right to work.[75] But, alas, the very elaborate arguments advanced by Professor Gewirth for work as a legal, as opposed to a mere moral, entitlement reveal the infeasibility of its inclusion as a constitutional right. Take, for example, his argument that the right would entail the duty of corporate employers to refrain from policies that throw people out of work, in pursuit of profits that disregard the adverse impact on workers' continued employment. Now, as laudable as that may be, the question remains as to the appropriate formulation of the right in the constitution that would make possible its enforcement as any other constitutional right.

But, more importantly, the problem with the constitutionalization of the moral entitlement of the right to work means that the State, through the government, as the principal respondent of the right, would be in violation of the citizens' fundamental right whenever its economic policies fail to achieve the level of employment that would provide work for anyone willing and able to work. The simple fact is that the right to work, like virtually every other social and economic right, is so peculiarly dependent on social and economic contingencies that, as a constitutional right, it becomes virtually meaningless. In other words, the right to work, which includes the right of everyone to the opportunity to gain his living by work, can only be said to apply to a particular kind of settled and relatively developed economy and society, in which most work consists of employment in exchange for wages. But in other areas of the world, where vast numbers of people live in subsistence conditions, this understanding of the right to work just does not make sense.[76] As Professor Michel Rosenfeld has correctly observed, such rights are so dependent on social and economic circumstances of the particular society that, whereas in an industrially advanced society, the right to work, to food, shelter and clothing, and to a free education may amount to a legal guarantee, in an underdeveloped country with a very fragile economy, such rights can be nothing more than an aspirational hope.[77]

It is acknowledged that such things as food, shelter, clothing, education, work, health care etc. are socially necessary goods, the essential conditions of human well-being and our human flourishing; and, on this view, are the objects of our moral claims against each other and, therefore, against the State as the central moral agent in society, acting on our behalf. Who, for example, could question the pivotal importance of education for self-realisation and, ultimately, for democratic citizenship? But the inescapable fact is that these rights, as requiring some positive, affirmative act on the part of the government, are ever susceptible to social and economic contingencies. On this view, they should not be included in a bill of rights since they are hardly capable of judicial enforcement.

But a general presumption against their inclusion in a bill of rights does not signal an unwillingness to address them as important collective problems. Rather, given that they are moral entitlements, we may appropriately express our collective commitment to achieving them by the proper notation in a 'General Welfare Clause' of the constitution, to be supplemented wherever feasible by the appropriate legislation; in order to ensure that the distribution of welfare benefits would be orchestrated through rule-bound systems, so that those dispensing the benefits have minimal discretion to lay down conditions for receipt of benefits by those entitled to them.[78] In other words, our recognition of the moral claims to welfare is sufficiently strong that, though falling short of expression in the constitutional bill of rights, would nonetheless be realized within a system of rules, in order to ensure that those especially in need of welfare assistance – the elderly, the poor, the disabled – would be assured of that assistance at the least possible risk of insecurity or loss of dignity. It means, then, that the human and fundamental rights appropriately included in a bill of rights are the classical liberal rights, such as the right to personal dignity, to life, liberty, and bodily integrity; to freedom in the choice of one's vocation, to property, the inviolability of one's house; to freedom of opinion and information; the freedom of assembly and association; of belief, conscience and religion; to participate in political elections and voting processes, etc. This therefore brings us to the specific issue of the style of constitution writing and, more specifically, the 'language' of the fundamental rights provisions, which, in respect of our Independence Constitutions, seems rather to be a consequence of their statute-like quality.

Writing and Reading the Texts

As was earlier intimated, *West Indian Independence Constitutions* have come from the tradition of British draftsmanship and constitution writing. They have an unmistakable statute-like quality to them. The Grenada Independence Constitution is a classic example: its language is rather awkward and cumbersome, and too detailed in regulatory specifics; thus, the Constitution reads more like a poorly drafted statute or legal code rather than a constitution. It therefore lacks one of the essential qualities of a constitution: an elegant simplicity that makes it comprehensible to the citizen of moderate learning. In consequence, the understanding and interpretation of the Constitution remains the sole province of lawyers and judges. It is clearly not the citizens' document.

But as the document of fundamental law, articulating a vision of the people we are, or wish enduringly to be, the Constitution's literary felicity should be beyond question. To serve its constitutive and unifying function, and as the source to which the individual citizen may turn to engage his fellow citizens in meaningful dialogue on the nature of their polity, the Constitution's text must be cast in sufficiently general language about which virtually everyone can agree, and at the same time permit government to adapt its actions and institutions to changing circumstances and demands. This means that the substantive content of the Constitution should be limited to what all (or nearly all) would perceive to be constitutional essentials: the general structure of government and the political process, and the equal basic rights and liberties of the citizens.[79] For a constitutional document cluttered with regulatory specifics, as our Independence Constitutions are, would hardly command the respect of the citizens, since it would hardly be comprehensible to them. Indeed, it was from the pen of one of America's most eminent jurists, Chief Justice John Marshall, that we have had the most eloquent admonition as to the appropriate style of constitution writing:

> A constitution, to contain an accurate detail of all the subdivisions of which its great powers will admit, and of all the means by which they may be carried into execution, would partake of the prolixity of a legal code, and would scarcely be embraced by the human mind. It would never be understood by the public. Its nature, therefore, requires, that only its great outlines should be marked, its important objects designated, and the minor ingredients which compose those objects be deduced from the nature of the objects themselves.[80]

The choice as to what we say in our constitution is a matter of grave philosophical importance, for, in a constitution, a people inevitably aims to give expression to their best conception of themselves and, accordingly, to their idea of how they ought to treat one another, and to be treated by the State. In no section of the constitution is the truth of this more poignantly borne out than in the section on fundamental rights and freedoms. It bears repeating that the embodiment of fundamental rights in a written constitution bears witness to a people's acknowledgment of the dignity of the individual as being of the highest moral value, and as furnishing the ground or the defining limits regarding the ways the State may or may not treat its citizens. If, therefore, we were to accept as a standard definition of 'fundamental right', a right that protects such interests that are universally regarded as essentials of human well-being, then the understanding must be certain that the guarantees of fundamental rights and freedoms are to be everlasting, continuing, and sacred; that they are not to be abrogated at any time; that they are not susceptible of repeal.

It is impossible – and even unwise – to attempt to address every contingency in detail in the constitutional text. Therefore, an ambition for literary felicity should match our prudence in our choice of particulars. Unfortunately, the very area of the *West Indian Independence Constitution* which bears the greatest urgency for clarity and simplicity is the one most in breach of this ideal; that is, the fundamental rights provisions. This area of the *Constitution* suffers from all the excesses to which the British style of constitution – drafting is given. In consequence, the various provisions of fundamental rights and freedoms are so encumbered by detailed instructions as to how they are to be read and the qualifications and exceptions respecting their exercise, that one is left in doubt as to the substance of these rights and freedoms supposedly guaranteed. To borrow Professor Christopher Mojekwu's words regarding the 1963 Nigerian Republican Constitution:

'The numerous provisions for fundamental human rights [are] surrounded with so many provisos and exceptions that it looked as if what was guaranteed with one hand was taken away with the other.'[81] It is therefore submitted that, given the critical importance of these rights and freedoms in the lives of the citizens, the language most appropriate to their formulation must necessarily be a language of generality to be embraced by the ordinary mind, and that would allow the constitutional text to function as the evolving repository of our core political ideals, while, at the same time, permitting such interpretive possibilities to meet changing circumstances and demands. In a word, a language in which we all – judges, lawyers, citizens – may engage one another on the understanding of the moral principles about political decency and justice that these fundamental rights provisions invoke.[82]

Fundamental Rights and the Savings Clause

This problem regarding the understanding of the fundamental rights provisions in the *West Indian Independence Constitution* has been compounded with the inclusion of both a general and a special savings clause in the constitutional text. As Edward Fitzgerald puts it,

> savings clauses are the most dominant and distinctive features of Commonwealth Caribbean constitutions. They operate in all jurisdictions of the Commonwealth Caribbean except Belize to preserve the colonial status quo from constitutional challenge. They do this by one of two mechanisms: Either they rule out altogether any constitutional attack on the law in existence at the time of independence; or they at least prohibit any attack on the specific colonial penalties or punishments in existence at the time of independence, based on the alleged cruelty or inhumanity of those punishments, and therefore protect

penalties such as the death penalty or flogging from direct attack on grounds of constitutionality.[83]

On this view, then, a general savings clause is taken to be one that refers (in general) to the entire Bill of Rights; while a special savings clause is addressed to a specific section or provision of the Bill of Rights. For example, section 26(8) of the Jamaica Constitution states:

> Nothing contained in any law in force immediately before the appointed day shall be held to be inconsistent with *any of the provisions of this chapter*; and nothing done under the authority of any such law shall be held to be done in contravention of *these provisions*.[84]

And section 17(2) of the Jamaica Constitution reads:

> Nothing contained in or done under the authority of any law shall be held to be inconsistent with or in contravention of *this section* to the extent that the law in question authorises the infliction of any description of punishment which was lawful in Jamaica immediately before the [commencement of the Constitution].[85]

Notwithstanding the possibility that great analytic importance may attach to the distinction between the general and the special savings clause, they both serve to compound the problem of reading and understanding the fundamental rights provisions. Specifically, they are each in tension with the fundamental rights (or some of the fundamental rights) provisions of the *Constitution*. This problem was raised in high relief in the recent Privy Council ruling in the *Ophelia King* case;[86] and that decision has occasioned the Owen Arthur government's call for an amendment to section 26 – the Savings Clause provision of the Barbados Constitution.

Briefly, in the Privy Council's decision, it was determined that the Barbados Government's authority to cut the civil servants' salaries at will rested on a 1949 statute which was saved under the 'Savings Provision' (section 26) of the Constitution. The Savings Clause, in pertinent part, reads as follows:

> Nothing contained in or done under the authority of any written law shall be held to be inconsistent with or in contravention of any provision of sections 12 to 23 to the extent that the law in question –
>
> (a) is a law (in this section referred to as "an existing law") that was enacted or made before 30th November 1966 and has continued to be part of the law of Barbados at all times since that day;
>
> (b) repeals and re-enacts an existing law without alteration; or
>
> (c) alters an existing law and does not thereby render that law inconsistent with any provision of sections 12 to 23 in a manner in which, or to an extent to which, it was not previously so inconsistent.[87]

The Savings Clause, on a literal reading, preserves the validity of existing law at the time of independence and, more importantly, it is understood to bar constitutional review of any law saved. In the event, the constitutional validity of the 1949 statute was not itself in issue in the case. However, on the logic of the Privy Council's decision, which gave a very literal reading to section 26, the 1949 statute held primacy over the fundamental rights provisions of the Constitution. In order, therefore, to bar future governments from cutting the civil servants' salaries at will, the current government has proposed that section 26 be amended.

A 'savings law clause' serves a very valuable purpose in an independence constitution, which marks the movement of a society from colony to independent sovereign state. Political independence could never mean the repeal of all the ordinary laws of a society; for such would only result in chaos and anarchy. Therefore, all laws, except those of fundamental political importance, are saved according to their letter, either by an express provision of the new constitution; or are deemed to be saved, assuming no express provision. So, from a conceptual standpoint, every existing law is conceived *as if* reenacted by the *Independence Constitution*; and, on this view, would be read, subject to all constitutional prescriptions of the higher law. Therefore, cognizance must be taken of the substantive changes wrought by an independence constitution.

The addition of a Bill of Rights to an independence constitution is probably the most profound change made to a colonial constitution. The fundamental rights are substantive constraints on the powers of the central institutions of the State. They are therefore constraints on ordinary legislation. It means, then, that having regard to the content of the new constitution, some existing laws may be inconsistent with the constitution, and, therefore, could not now be read according to their original understanding. The 1949 statute is a classic case in point. The Privy Council may properly have read that statute so as not to allow its original legal consequences, without the need to pronounce it constitutionally invalid since, in the Court's view, that was a matter appropriately left to the legislature.

But, at bottom, the problem remains that of section 26 itself, and how it is understood according to its letter. From that standpoint, section 26 creates a serious contradiction in the constitutional text, and, for that reason alone, its amendment would be most appropriate. It would be well advised to 'rewrite' that provision so as to facilitate a more effective accomplishment of its essential purpose.

Assuming, then, the truth of the claim that section 26, as written, creates a serious contradiction within the constitutional text, the issue of its amendment may be used as a test case of what constitutional reform appropriately entails. Following Professor William Harris, it is precisely the need to maintain the nature of the constitutional order and thus to prevent the overthrow of its institutions of governance that animates amendability in the first place.[88] Thus, it must be understood that the powers constructed by the constitution are provided to preserve, fulfill, and improve the document's project of sustaining the political world it has purportedly established.[89] In other words, the regulative interpretive principle here is that of adapting the constitution's powers to its objects.[90] As Professor Harris notes:

> Textual provisions [of the Constitution] do not purport to debilitate the power they delineate; nor do they represent verbal warrants to unmake other commitments of the document in which they are situated or to undo the conditions for its political meaningfulness. [Thus], any interpretation of the text that works against the wholeness of the document's design or undermines the conditions of sovereign constitution-making is inherently unconstitutional. An interpretation that denies meaning to a constitutional provision – at least in the absence of an overriding theory of the Constitution's whole design and coherent ratification – refutes the authority of constitutional writtenness.[91]

In sum, then, the various clauses of the constitutional document are not to be read as free-standing, univocal commands. Rather, a constitutional provision is fundamental and meaningful in terms of some articulated political theory that gives coherence to the Constitution and to the constitutional order as a whole. It is this prescription of wholeness that drives the interpretive inclination to harmonize provisions of the constitution that may seem on the surface to conflict with each other; and that undergirds the assumption that the constitution itself may not be self-contradictory and therefore should be read by the interpretive principle that it is coherent in its meanings.[92] Put simply, the concept of 'wholeness' is an analytical, interpretive principle under which we search for meaning.

It is in terms of this interpretive standard of 'coherence' that the meaning of the 'Savings Clause' is properly understood. Therefore, to give literal effect to section 26 as written is to deny any special eminence to the Constitution and, in particular, to its fundamental rights provisions over all other law. The horror of this is brought home to the intelligent mind when one realizes that the literal consequence of section 26 is to give prominence to ordinary legislation over the Constitution. Section 26 may therefore appropriately be rewritten to say something to the effect that

> All laws existing at the time of Independence, unless otherwise expressly abrogated, are hereby saved; and to the extent that any existing law should prove inconsistent with the Constitution or any of the provisions thereof, the courts shall interpret such law in such a manner as to make it consistent with the Constitution.

The Special Savings Clause

The special savings clause raises a most egregious problem for Commonwealth Caribbean constitutional jurisprudence – particularly in the area regarding the enforcement of the death penalty statutes. This problem, to repeat, issues from the specific exception enjoined upon the proper interpretation of one of the most critical fundamental rights: the right against cruel, inhuman or degrading punishment or treatment. Take the Jamaica Constitution, for example. In section 17(1), the Constitution states that, 'No person shall be subjected to torture or to cruel, inhuman or degrading punishment or other treatment.' Section 17(2) immediately adds:

Nothing contained in or done under the authority of any law shall be held to be inconsistent with or in contravention of this section to the extent that the law in question authorises the infliction of any description of punishment which was lawful in Jamaica immediately before the [commencement of the Constitution].

This subsection, it bears emphasis, obviously derogates from the essence of the rights already guaranteed in subsection (1), and rather confirms the *lawfulness* of any practices and treatment of the citizens that would have obtained at the time of independence. The problem, specifically, arises most critically in respect of the way in which the special savings clause is understood to insulate the death penalty, and in particular hanging, from constitutional challenge. A recent Privy Council decision on this very issue is a case in point.

In the case of *Boodram v. Baptiste*[93] from Trinidad and Tobago, the Privy Council was asked to consider whether hanging constitutes cruel and unusual punishment, contrary to section 5(1) of the Constitution, which expressly prohibits the imposition of any punishment that is cruel and unusual. (This term 'unusual' is now generally taken to mean 'inhuman'). In a four-page, (oral) judgment, the Privy Council concluded that hanging was the lawful method of execution of a sentence of death in Trinidad and Tobago.

At the outset, the Council tacitly acknowledged that the issue before it was whether hanging is cruel and unusual, contrary to section 5(1) of the Constitution. But the Council also noted that the Constitution also in section 5(2) states that: '*Nothing in sections 4 and 5 shall invalidate – (a) an existing law....*'[94] An existing law is taken to mean a law that had effect as part of the law of Trinidad and Tobago immediately before the commencement of the Constitution.

In view of this foregoing section, it would seem, the Council has recast the issue to state whether hanging today in Trinidad and Tobago is a lawful method of execution. By a simple process of deduction, the Board was easily led to the conclusion that hanging is the lawful method of execution.

By way of a response to the issue as was first stated – whether hanging constitutes cruel and unusual punishment contrary to the provision in the Bill of Rights – the Board offered its interpretive approach to determining the issue. It stated:

> It is to be remembered, however, that the Bill of Rights does not stand alone and it is accepted that, even though the Bill is a constitutional document creating fundamental rights, *the Bill may be cut down by clear subsequent legislative provisions.* (emphasis added)[95]

Such subsequent – or even existing – legislation may be that which clearly states that 'Every person convicted of murder shall suffer death,' and also expressly recites that any person lawfully convicted of murder is to be 'hanged by the neck until he be dead.' Thus the Board concluded:

> It seems to their Lordships that these statutory provisions quite clearly must be read with the Bill of Rights, and that in Trinidad and Tobago they authorise hanging, not only as a method but as the only method of execution which may be ordered by the Court and the only method which may be carried out subsequent to the President's Order. That means that the Bill of Rights in itself is not a basis upon which the petitioners can put their case since it is to be read with subsequent legislation ...[96]

First, the issue of whether hanging is a lawful method of execution of the sentence of death in Trinidad and Tobago shall be dealt with. If the term 'lawful' is here taken to mean that which the law expressly prescribes, then the issue is rather uninteresting. Hanging is a description of punishment specially saved under the Trinidad and Tobago Constitution, therefore, hanging is *prima facie* lawful. What is more, opinion polls, taken in Trinidad and in other countries of the Commonwealth Caribbean, reveal that there is overwhelming popular support for hanging. But the fact that hanging is lawful in this sense, or is indeed highly popular, would not silence contending moral and constitutional objections to it, or to the death penalty as a whole. For, as Professor Bedau puts it: 'Popular attitudes and practices under law cannot by themselves *make* a severe punishment hitherto acceptable into one that is not, or preserve a widespread punishment from being judged excessively severe.'[97] Therefore, the more interesting and deeply profound issue is whether hanging, though specially saved, is nonetheless cruel and inhuman punishment, contrary to the Constitution. An adequate determination of this issue certainly requires a more sophisticated theory of adjudication and interpretation than that suggested in the Privy Council's judgment; a theory of adjudication and interpretation that takes account of the disabling contradiction within the constitutional text created by a special savings clause.

Capital punishment is an issue of transcendent importance; it is indeed the law's ultimate punishment. Along with the right to make war, the death penalty is the ultimate measure of sovereignty and the ultimate test of political power. The power to end a person's existence as a human being is unquestionably the most awesome power a state could lawfully exercise over a citizen.[98] The question, then, as to whether the method the state uses to carry out an execution is constitutionally valid, is bound to be one of the most profound issues of moral and political significance in constitutional jurisprudence.

As was noted, the Privy Council suggested that 'the Bill of Rights ... is to be read with subsequent legislation', since 'the Bill may be cut down by clear subsequent legislative provisions.' It can be taken that the Council meant to say that the Bill of Rights may also be read subject to existing law specially saved. If this assumption is correct, then the Council's interpretive premise is deeply flawed, since it would make the Constitution, the fundamental law, subordinate to ordinary legislation – be it existing or subsequent legislation – in which case the Constitution will no longer serve as an instrument for limiting government but instead becomes an ordinary law that can be modified by those who enact the laws.[99]

But, as was earlier intimated, the very idea of constitutionalism rests on a supposition of a body of supra-positivist, regulative standards, by which even pre-existing positive law may be rendered 'unconstitutional' and so invalid and inoperative because it is in conflict with imperative constitutional norms.[100] Let us therefore concede that what is needed is an adequate interpretive theory of constitutional adjudication that would reject the majoritarian premise of the British model, with its central principle of parliamentary sovereignty, and which would locate the normative essence of democracy in the right of the majority, acting through Parliament, to decide whether hanging, say, is cruel and inhuman, or whether the law mandating hanging for murder should be altered or repealed.[101]

Constitutional adjudication is unavoidably interpretive. It inevitably entails evaluative and moral judgments by a court in its account of what the constitution means in a particular case. This is especially so in cases concerning the interpretation and application of the fundamental rights provisions of the constitution. The constitutional question whether hanging is cruel and inhuman is a deeply profound moral question; it asks whether that punishment comports with the ultimate moral value of human dignity. It cannot therefore be answered without recourse to some element of moral reasoning. For, as we have noted, the fundamental rights stated in a Bill of Rights express moral principles about political decency and justice, which are the defining and regulative standards regarding the ways in which the government may or may not treat its citizens. Moreover, these rights, we have also noted, are the morally necessary requirements of personhood, and are often explained as grounded in a 'higher law' of transpolitical reason or revelation. As such, they are understood not to be subject to repeal or derogation. Their specification in the constitution introduces an unmistakable element of moral reasoning into constitutional law. Thus, in constitutional cases involving basic human rights issues, the real answer to the legal question entails the same answer to the corresponding moral question.[102] A special savings clause might therefore be one of the most disabling devices in the *West Indian Independence Constitution*. It indulges a very restrictive and crabbed reading of some of the more critical fundamental rights. It should therefore be removed.

Endnotes

1   *West Virginia Board of Education v. Barnette*, 319 U.S. 624, 638; quoted in Stephen Holmes, *Passions and Constraint: On the Theory of Liberal Democracy* 135 (1997).

2   See John Rawls, *Political Liberalism* (1993).

3   Ronald Dworkin, *Taking Rights Seriously* 177 (1977).

4   Stephen Holmes and Cass Sunstein, 'The Politics of Revision,' in *Responding to Imperfection: The Theory and Practice of Constitutional Amendment* 304 (Sanford Levinson ed. 1995).

5   John Finnis, *Natural Law and Natural Rights* (1981).

6   John Rawls, *A Theory of Justice* (1971).

7   Clark Wolf, 'Fundamental Rights, Reasonable Pluralism, and the Moral Commitments of Liberalism', in *The Idea of a Political Liberalism: Essays on Rawls* 111 (Victoria Davion and Clark Wolf eds. 1999).

8   Alan Gewirth, 'The Epistemology of Human Rights,' in *Lloyd's Introduction to Jurisprudence* 187 (M.D.A. Freeman ed. 1994). See also Bernard Cullen, 'The Right to Work,' in *Moral Philosophy and Contemporary Problems* 167 (J.D.G. Evans ed. 1988).

9   *Ibid.* 188.

10   *Ibid.*

11 *Ibid.*
12 *Ibid.*
13 *Ibid.*
14 *Ibid.* 201.
15 *Ibid.* 202.
16 *Ibid.* 189.
17 *Ibid.*
18 Rawls, *supra* note 2.
19 Seyla Benhabib, 'Toward a Deliberative Model of Democratic Legitimacy,' in *Democracy and Difference: Contesting the Boundaries of the Political* 79 (Seyla Benhabib ed. 1996).
20 George Kateb, 'Remarks on the Procedures of Constitutional Democracy,' in *Constitutionalism* 234 (J. Roland Pennock and John W. Chapman eds. 1979).
21 *Ibid.* 215.
22 *Ibid.* 218.
23 Jurgen Habermas, *The Inclusion of the Other : Studies in Political Theory* 242 (1998).
24 William A. Parent, 'Constitutional Values and Human Dignity,' in *The Constitution of Rights : Human Dignity and American Values* 65 (Michael J. Meyer and W.A. Parent eds. 1992).
25 *Ibid.*
26 Kateb, *supra* note 20, at 227.
27 *Ibid.* 228.
28 *Ibid.* 230.
29 *Ibid.* 231.
30 Remark made by Justice Brennan in a speech given at Georgetown University on October 12, 1985, and published under the title: '*The Constitution of the United States: Contemporary Ratification,*' in 8 *University of California Davis Law Review* 19 (1985). Quoted in William A. Parent, '*Constitutional Values and Human Dignity,*' in *The Constitution of Rights: Human Dignity and American Values* 47 (Michael J. Meyer and W.A. Parent eds. 1992).
31 Alan Gewirth, '*Human Dignity as the Basis of Rights,*' in *The Constitution of Rights: Human Dignity and American Values* 13 (Michael J. Meyer and W.A. Parent eds. 1992).
32 Immanuel Kant, *Doctrine of Virtue* (Part II of *The Metaphysic of Morals*), Part II, chap. 1, sec. 2, para. 38 (Akad. Ed., p. 461), trans. Mary J. Gregor (New York: Harper Torchbooks, 1964), 132. Quoted in Gewirth, *Id.* at 11.
33 *International Covenant on Economic, Social and Cultural Rights, 1966; International Covenant on Civil and Political Rights, 1966.* Quoted in Gewirth, *Id.* at 10.
34 *Universal Declaration of Human Rights,* arts. 22, 23. Quoted in Gewirth, *Id.*
35 Parent, *supra* note 24, at 63.
36 *Ibid.* 68.
37 Loren E. Lomasky, *Persons, Rights, and the Moral Community* 104 (1987).
38 *Ibid.* 111.
39 J. Donald Moon, 'Introduction,' in *Responsibility, Rights & Welfare : The Theory of the Welfare State* 4 (J. Donald Moon ed. 1988).
40 *Ibid.* 5.

41 J. Donald Moon, *Constructing Community: Moral Pluralism and Tragic Conflicts* 129 (1993).

42 See, for example, Stephen Holmes, expressing the idea that there is a 'fundamental continuity between liberal rights and welfare rights' in his essay, 'Liberal Guilt: Some Theoretical Origins of the Welfare State,' in *Responsibility, Rights & Welfare: The Theory of the Welfare State* Chp. 4 (J. Donald Moon ed. 1988). See also, Martin P. Golding, 'The Primacy of Welfare Rights' 1 *Social Philosophy and Policy* 119-36 (1984).

43 Gary C. Bryner, 'Constitutionalism and the Politics of Rights,' in *Constitutionalism and Rights* 18 (Gary C. Bryner and Noel B. Reynolds eds. 1987).

44 Quoted in Lomasky, *supra* note 37, at 85.

45 Alan Gewirth, *The Community of Rights* 9 (1996).

46 *Ibid.* 108.

47 Raymond Plant, 'Needs, Agency, and Welfare Rights,' in *Responsibility, Rights & Welfare: The Theory of the Welfare State* 55 (J. Donald Moon ed. 1988).

48 *Ibid.* 57.

49 *Ibid.*

50 *Ibid.*

51 *Ibid.*

52 *Ibid.* 60.

53 *Ibid.* 60-61.

54 *Ibid.* 66.

55 *Ibid.*

56 Moon, *supra* note 41, at 140.

57 Lomasky, *supra* note 37, at 84.

57[a] Plant, *supra* note 47, at 71

58 Richard A. Epstein, 'The Uncertain Quest for Welfare Rights,' in *Constitutionalism and Rights* 41 (Gary C. Bryner and Noel B. Reynolds eds. 1987).

59 Bryner, *supra* note 43, at 9.

60 Lomasky, *supra* note 37.

61 Epstein, *supra* note 59, at 43.

62 Lomasky, *supra* note 37, at 87.

63 Bryner, *supra* note 43, at 23.

64 Lomasky, *supra* note 37, at 87.

65 Bryner, *supra* note 43, at 24.

66 Robert E. Goodin, *Reasons for Welfare* 103 (1988).

67 Gewirth, *supra* note 45, at 215.

68 *Ibid.* 217.

69 *Ibid.*

70 *Ibid.* 218.

71 Sumner M. Rosen, 'The Right to Employment,' *Monthly Review* 45 (Nov. 1993: 5-6).

72 William A. Galston, 'Practical Philosophy,' in *A Culture of Rights: The Bill of Rights in Philosophy, Politics, and Law 1791 and 1991* 261 (Michael J. Lacey and Knud Haakonsen eds. 1992).

73 Gewirth, *supra*, note 45, at 219.

74 Quoted in *Ibid.* 220.

75 Jon Elster, 'Is There (or Should There Be) a Right to Work?' in *Democracy and the Welfare State* 74 (Amy Gutmann ed. 1988).

76 Cullen, *supra* note 8, at 169.

77 Michel Rosenfeld, 'The Identity of the Constitutional Subject,' 16 *Cardozo L. Rev.* 1049, 1064 (1995).

78 Goodin, *supra* note 67, at 19.

79 Rawls, *supra* note 2, at 228.

80 See *McCullock v. Maryland* 4 U.S. (Wheat.) 316 (1819).

81 Christopher C. Mojekwu, 'Nigerian Constitutionalism,' in *Constitutionalism* 169 (J. Roland Pennock and John W. Chapman eds. 1979).

82 Ronald Dworkin, *Freedom's Law: The Moral Reading of the American Constitution* 2 (1996).

83 Discussion paper presented at a Human Rights Workshop, June 2-3, 2001, at the Asta Beach Resort, Barbados.

84 See the Jamaica (Constitution) Order, 1962.

85 *Ibid.*

86 *King v. Attorney-General of Barbados* (1992) 44 W.I.R. 52; [1994] 1 W.L.R. 1560.

87 The Barbados Independence Order 1966.

88 See Simeon C.R. McIntosh, 'West Indian Constitutional Discourse: A Poetics of Reconstruction,' (1993) 3 *Carib. L. Rev.* 1

89 William F. Harris II, *The Interpretable Constitution* 167 (1993).

90 *Ibid.* 168.

91 *Ibid.*

92 *Ibid.*

93 *Ibid.* 189.

94 *Nankisson Boodram (Also called Dole Chadee) v. Cipriani Baptiste* [1999] 1 W.L.R. 1709.

95 *Ibid.* 2.

96 *Ibid.* 3.

97 *Ibid.*

98 Hugo Adam Bedau, 'The Eighth Amendment, Human Dignity and the Death Penalty', in *The Constitution of Rights* 164 (Michael J. Meyer and W.A. Parent eds. 1992).

99 Austin Sarat, 'Capital Punishment as a Legal, Political, and Cultural Fact : An Introduction,' in *The Killing State : Capital Punishment in Law, Politics, and Culture* 4 (Austin Sarat ed. 1999).

99 Carlos Santiago Nino, *The Constitution of Deliberative Democracy* 195 (1996).

100 Edward McWhinney, *Constitution-making: Principles, Process, Practice* 10 (1981).

101 Dworkin, *supra* note 83, at 18.

102 See Dworkin, *supra* note 83; and M.J. Detmold, *The Unity of Law and Morality : A Refutation of Legal Positivism* (1984).

Chapter 3

Reading Text and Polity: The Case for a Caribbean Supreme Court

> These Caribbean territories are not like those in Africa, with their own internal references that have been returned to themselves after a period of colonial rule. They are manufactured societies, labour camps and creations of empire and for long they are dependent on empire for law, language, institutions, culture, even officials. Nothing [is] generated locally, dependence [has become] a habit. – V.S. Naipaul

> Our Constitution came from Britain, but a dozen generations of Barbadians have made it their own. – Sir Hugh Springer

West Indian Independence Constitutions are among the central cultural artifacts of our *nation*. Unfortunately, they are largely of colonial origin, and are not the products of our own deliberative efforts. Rather, as the *Instruments* marking the 'birth' of the independent sovereign States of the Commonwealth Caribbean, they were made in pursuance of a legal authority residing in the British Imperial Parliament. In addition, they have never received ratification in popular referenda by the Commonwealth Caribbean populace. They are therefore not the authoritative expression of our collective will. As Ann Spackman has argued, there was no real involvement of the mass of the people in the process of constitution-making.[1] Yet, our Independence Constitutions remain forms of expression of Commonwealth Caribbean political culture and identity. This is one of the great paradoxes marking Commonwealth Caribbean Constitutions and political identity. And this is further compounded by the fact that we claim to have retained the (British) Crown as our own, and its Judicial Committee as our final court of appeal. The British monarchy has therefore remained a potent symbol of Commonwealth Caribbean political identity, a defining feature of the Commonwealth Caribbean constitutional order. And the Judicial Committee's location at the apex of the Commonwealth Caribbean judicial hierarchy holds important consequences for the development of an indigenous jurisprudence, and virtually seals the overriding influence of British constitutionalism on Commonwealth Caribbean postcolonial constitutional evolution. In the circumstances, there can be no gainsaying the shaping effects of these two English institutions on conceptions of the Commonwealth Caribbean constitutional *self*; their deep inscription in the Caribbean consciousness.

But the continuing *presence* of the Crown and its Judicial Committee in the post-independence Commonwealth Caribbean political order represents a vestigial incongruity, a contradiction in the constitutional symbolism of a politically independent sovereign order. The continuing *presence* of the Privy Council, in particular, has now become the occasion of great disquiet in some quarters. This situation is now considered to be an abdication of a fundamental aspect of our sovereignty; it is therefore deemed to be politically offensive. The domiciling of ultimate judicial power over our constitutions in London, it is reasoned, leaves our political independence incomplete. For the making of law in general, and adjudication in particular, have come to be seen as inseparable attributes of sovereignty.[2] As a very distinguished jurist, Mr. Justice Hyatali of Trinidad and Tobago has remarked: 'It is offensive to the sovereignty of independent nations, and therefore politically unacceptable, to have a foreign tribunal permanently entrenched in their constitutions as their final court.'[3] And to this a former Attorney General of Barbados, Sir David Simmons, adds:

The first reason for the abolition of appeals to the Privy Council must surely be the question of sovereignty and independence. The independence of the states of the region will not be complete, is not complete, when our constitutions entrench a foreign tribunal as our final court of appeal. It is inconsistent with independence: it is an affront to our sovereignty and the sovereignty of independent nations. You may say this is an emotional argument, but these psychological considerations are important and the symbolism is not to be discounted.[4]

The *validity* of these claims would seem unassailable. The establishment of a Regional Court of Appeal must therefore be seen as an essential aspect of the constitutional reform project. Indeed, the establishment of such an institution is indispensable to the overall nationalist project of reconstructing Commonwealth Caribbean political identity. But, sadly, the most urgent pleas in recent years for the establishment of a regional appellate court and for the abolition of appeals to the British Privy Council have come largely on the heels of certain Privy Council decisions, of which the most notable is the Jamaican case of *Pratt and Morgan*. Of all the invectives levelled against the Privy Council for some of its decisions, the most egregious, in my opinion, have come from the Barbados Government. In the 1999 Throne Speech, it was stated that

the rule of law which is the foundation upon which civil society is organised and regulated is being imperilled by judicial decisions in England. It cannot continue. [Therefore], having regard to the composition of this Parliament and with a view to giving fullest expression to the will of the Government and people of Barbados, my Government, without prejudice to the future enactment of constitutional amendments recommended by the

Constitution Review Commission, will shortly seek to amend the existing Constitution to reverse the effects of the *Pratt and Morgan* line of cases. [And], [f]or other reasons also, my Government will continue to support the regional effort for the establishment of a Caribbean Court of Justice as a matter of the greatest urgency.[5]

Political reaction to *Pratt and Morgan* and its progeny, whether in the form of withdrawal from the Optional Protocol to the International Covenant on Civil and Political Rights and other Human Rights Bodies,[6] the adoption of procedures to ensure swift executions after conviction and sentencing, or threats to amend the Constitution in order to ensure that hanging is carried out promptly, lends suspicion that, for some Commonwealth Caribbean governments, the sole and adequate ground for the establishment of a Caribbean Court of Appeal and for the abolition of appeals to the British Privy Council is their desire to carry out executions *at will*.

But as much as we have instanced urgent pleas for the abolition of appeals to the Privy Council and for the establishment of a Caribbean court of final appeal in its stead, we have instanced equally compelling claims against the idea of a regional supreme court and the removal of the Privy Council as our final court of appeal. These latter generally cite practical considerations such as the paucity of legal talent in the Caribbean to fill a qualified appellate court; the susceptibility of local judges to political control; and, generally, the socio-economic conditions of the Caribbean, which, they claim, militate against the possibility of our financing the establishment and maintenance of such a political institution so central to the basic structure of Commonwealth Caribbean society. These arguments cannot be taken lightly because their claims can never be denied.[7]

But these problems are not insurmountable. The Court, to be

styled The Caribbean Court of Justice, is to be a court of final appellate jurisdiction in all cases arising in law and equity and of original jurisdiction in all cases pertaining to the enforcement of the Treaty establishing the Single Market and Economy of CARICOM. With the requisite political will, a court can be permanently entrenched in all Commonwealth Caribbean Constitutions, following its establishment by treaty. Also, a process for the permanent financing of the Court can be devised, which would entail an initial Endowment Fund of approximately $25,000,000.00 (US), the investment of which on the world financial market can be managed by the Caribbean Development Bank. For the first two to three years of the Court's existence, financing would be undertaken by member governments, and following which, it is anticipated that the Court would become self-financing through returns on the investments.

The composition of the Court should also be consistent with our economic circumstances. In this regard, a court of possibly five, but certainly not more than seven, judges would suffice. Each judge should be afforded at least one law clerk or research assistant. Of the five or seven judges, one or two should have special competence in the interpretation of treaties, in order to facilitate the original jurisdiction of the Court in cases arising out of the implementation of the Treaty pertaining to the Single Market and Economy. The opinions of the Court in these cases may in fact be written by the 'specialist' judges. However, in all matters coming under the Court's appellate jurisdiction in law and equity, a judge is presumed to be highly competent.

Finally, regarding the appointment of judges to the Court, all could be appointed by a panel of Heads of State, assisted by a Regional Judicial Service Commission. Prime Ministers, in consultation with Leaders of Opposition, would make recommendations; and these recommendations would be acted upon by the Regional Judicial Service Commission, which would undertake a

thorough assessment of each nominee's work – whether as prac-
titioner or judge, or both – and present the Heads of State with a
written report on each nominee, giving an account of the breadth
and depth of the nominee's scholarship and the Commission's
view of his or her qualification to be a judge of a Commonwealth
Caribbean final court of appeal. The Heads of State would then
make the final decision. A competent court, free of political interference, could certainly be permanently established at the apex of
the Commonwealth Caribbean Judiciary. What would be especially unique about this institution, compared to our parliaments,
say, is the fact that, unlike the latter, it would not be an institution that developed from colonial times, but rather an institution
of our own deliberative efforts; an institution of our own making.

Assuming, then, that we were able to overcome these obstacles
and establish a regional supreme court worthy of its name, the
problem remains of advancing a philosophically compelling argument for establishing our own court and abolishing appeals to the
Privy Council. Such a philosophical defense of the idea of a
Caribbean court of final appeal, must ultimately rest on the most
profound argument from sovereignty: the idea of our taking into
our own hands the responsibility for defining our political and
constitutional identity and, ultimately, re-writing our *own*
jurisprudence.

The idea of a regional court replacing the British Privy Council
as our final appellate court is central to the development and
transformation of Commonwealth Caribbean constitutional
jurisprudence, and the achievement of what George Lamming has
called a *Caribbean philosophy of law*. The possibility of the latter is
predicated on the notion of our sovereignty as a people of a particular geographic region, sharing a similitude of circumstances
that, without doing violence to the idea of the rich cultural diversities of our peoples, still allows us to speak of our shared historical, social and political experiences, a common consciousness that

binds us together into a single whole; a common conviction, a kindred consciousness of an inward necessity.[8] In short, the idea is not to assume away our plurality, our rich diversities. Rather, it is to lay hold of certain commonalities such as geography, history, and cultural practices; a common background of political and legal institutions and our engagement in a common enterprise, bound together by widely held values, interests and goals. In this sense, we may speak of a common political identity essentially shaped by our colonial experience.

But this experience has had a devastating impact on the Commonwealth Caribbean consciousness. As the Barbadian writer, the late John Wickham, reminds us, we are given to mimicking those whom we may regard as our betters to the point that the places that we call home gain no acceptance as lodgings for the heart.[9] The Trinidadian writer V.S. Naipaul, is pessimistic about the possibility of escape from this situation, for he views mimicry as being endemic to the colonial experience and therefore implicit in the post-colonial condition; hence his refrain that nothing has been created in the Caribbean.[10] Without a doubt, we have laboured under the 'antagonistic weight of the past'; we have carried these past centuries a heavy psychological burden for slavery and colonialism. As Barbadian-born poet, Kamau Brathwaite, so poignantly notes,

> ... the land has lost the memory of the most secret places.
> We see the moon but cannot remember its meaning.
> A dark skin is a chain but it cannot recall the name of its tribe.
> There are no chiefs in the village.[11]

The fact remains that the 'dispossession' that followed upon the European discovery of these islands has had the effect of a massive brainwashing. Indeed, the Caribbean imagination has for centuries been imprisoned by the word 'discovery', a confinement which has its clear end-product in the desire to emigrate and to mimic those we may regard as our betters. And this desire, even the need, to emigrate is at the heart of the Commonwealth Caribbean sensibility - whether that migration is in fact or by metaphor. St. Lucian-born poet, Derek Walcott, has given expression to this tendency to reject that which is ours, and give ill-considered reverence to that which is foreign. He writes:

> Here there are no heroic palaces
> Netted in sea-green vines or built on magic savannahs,
> The cat-thighed, stony faces of Egypt's cradle, easily unriddled
> If art is where the greatest ruins are,
> Our art is in the ruins we became,
> You will not find in these green desert places
> One stone that found us worthy of its name,
> Nor how, lacking the skill to beat things over flame,
> We peopled archipelagoes by one star.[12]

It is submitted that this mimicking of our 'betters' is most dramatically borne out in the area of law and politics. Our legal and political institutions are not of our own creation, but are rather the legacies of our colonial past. Our constitutions came from Britain, but a dozen generations of West Indians have sought to make them their own, to paraphrase the late Sir Hugh Springer. Thus, given the history of the Caribbean and its colonial experience, it is entirely understandable that we would have the institutions of law and government of the colonial power, and that the Caribbean personality would carry a burden of self-deprecation and uncertainty of self. What, however, cannot be excused is our continuing reluctance, near forty years after independence, to fashion our own institutions to suit our particular circumstances. The retention of the British Privy Council as our final appellate court is a special case in point. As Professor Rex Nettleford rejoins: 'The restoration of trust to civil society is critical to the consensus we need for the establishment of a Caribbean Court of

Appeal ... It is thought that the House of Lords, however flawed, remains to many better than anything we can design for ourselves ... A West Indian Court of Appeal is therefore a necessary institutional manifestation of our will to self-respect and self-esteem'[13] - and of our will to self-definition.

It is given that the *Independence Constitution* marks the moment of founding of what are now the Independent Sovereign States of the Commonwealth Caribbean. But, notwithstanding the source of its *origin*, by our acceptance of it, our accession to its words, we have consented to be bound and to live within its sets of institutional structures that direct the exercise of power, and within its systems of meaning that define our collective identity. Thus, the *Independence Constitution*, like any constitution of a democratic society, is the act that founds the nation and the sign that marks it; the expression and annunciation of our collective identity.[14] It marks the coincidence of politics and semeiotics – the exercise of power and the inscription of meaning.[15]

The act of writing a nation's constitution is, more accurately, the act of constituting a people in writing. The constitution *makes* the people in its own image. A constitution is therefore a defining element of a people's political and civic identity. It is the act by which a democratic people choose to be known; the act by which the citizens' conceptions of their identities, individual as well as collective, become irrefragably altered.[16] For the constitution supplies the common set of categories for political thought, speech and action; it provides the grammar by which the people speak authoritatively about their public life. Put differently, 'the fundamental categories of political thought for the constitutional citizens are instructed by the principles of the constitution. These citizens learn to speak or write their political values through the language of the document. They explain themselves, to themselves and to the world, through its terms'.[17] As Professor Anne Norton puts it:

> The [constitution] speaks to those it constitutes, annunciating their identity and ends, instructing them in the means for ordering their common life, dictating the design of their governmental institutions. The constitution acts as author, creating a people, and a set of material circumstances, in its own image.[18]

But this *constitutional* identity would also find utterance and expression in authoritative constitutional interpretation. For collective identity is not simply an inheritance; it is not simply given in a single sublime moment. Rather, it is, in large measure, created by and perpetuated through a public discourse which consists of the vocabulary, ideologies, symbols, images, memories and myths that have come to form the ways a people think and talk about their political life.[19] And constitutional interpretation is a defining element of this public discourse. The constitutional text requires interpretation in order that the constitution be given reality in the lives of the people. The act of writing a constitution therefore initiates an unending dialectic in which the citizens continually seek expression of their collective identity.[20]

And one of the principal modalities of collective decision making in a democratic society, by which the constitution is given reality in the lives of the people and by which their collective identity is continually defined, is that of adjudication. For it is in adjudication that a court apprehends the basic terms of the image of the people's political identity in order to make it real. The instrument of the court's expression is the judicial opinion, itself an authoritative political text, which supplements the constitution. This therefore means that the 'Supreme Court' of a nation, as the ultimate interpreter of the constitution, is a defining agent of that people's collective identity. For the Commonwealth Caribbean, that institution is the British Privy Council. It means, then, not only did our constitutions come from Britain, but, by retaining the British Privy Council as the ultimate interpreter of our constitutions and author of some of our principal political texts, we have essentially made it a defining agent of our collective identity.

This must indeed give us pause for the interpreter of the law holds a power of no mean estate. Bishop Hoadly would have gleaned this when he intoned that: 'Whoever hath an *absolute authority* to *interpret* any written or spoken laws, it is he who is truly the *Law-giver* to all intents and purposes, and not the person who first wrote and spoke them.'[21] Thus, if we would take Sir Hugh Springer's words to heart, and *make* these constitutions our own, then we must undertake for ourselves this critical task of interpreting our fundamental laws. This is the single most compelling argument for the establishment of a Caribbean Court of Appeal; for it is an argument from sovereignty: the right of self-definition. For to understand the true import of Bishop Hoadly's aphorism is to understand the *power* that inheres in the *right* to interpret. Professor Anne Norton makes the point beautifully, in a way that bears signal importance for the Commonwealth Caribbean. She writes:

> It is interpretation that is the constitutive activity for those who inherit a Constitution, and [it is] from interpretation that they derive their authority. This authority is, as all authority must be, both political and semeiotic. In interpretation one acquires power not only over the present and future in the rendering of judgments or the design and workings of bureaucratic institutions, but over these and the past in the determination of meaning. In extending the meaning of nationality those who interpret alter the significance of the past: what it was, what was done, what came of it. They become authors, of themselves, their past and their posterity.[22]

So if we are to become our own authors, and in that event the authors of our past and our posterity, we are obliged to make the words of our constitutions our own. For, 'those who inherit rather than compose the words that rule them attain this authority in their accession to the words of the Constitution.'[23] But if we are to make the words of our constitutions our own, then, 'we must elect to exercise that authority in acts of interpretation and critical reflection.'[24] For it is from interpretation that we derive our authority to reforge the basic terms of our political order and to reaffirm and/or revise our constitutional commitments to a certain form of political life.

As was earlier intimated, a Caribbean court of final appeal would be central to the development and transformation of Commonwealth Caribbean constitutional jurisprudence. The focus here is primarily on constitutions and constitutional law because these are foundational and the most obviously defining features of our political and collective identity. Thus, the fundamental assumption on which my thesis rests is that a regional appellate court, sitting at the apex of our judicial system(s), would have the institutional incentives to serve as our premier educative institution on matters of constitutional principle; its judges being our teachers in a 'vital national seminar' on constitutional law.[25] In other words, the Court would teach a 'vital seminar' by propounding, through its written opinions, conceptions of Commonwealth Caribbean political and collective identity. This educative function would be central to the Court's interpretive supremacy in our constitutional jurisprudence and its obligation to make constitutional norms persuasive and understandable to the Caribbean people.

Following Professor Donald Lutz, we may speak of the *West Indian Independence Constitution* as the summary of our essential political commitments; a collective, public expression of particular importance; a definition for a form of life.[26] This view of the constitution suggests a certain picture of adjudication in which the constitution functions, at one and the same time, as *hard law* for the determination of cases, and as the expression of those political values that are constitutive of a national ethos; the principal vehicle by which a people defines itself as *a people*. On this view, constitutional adjudication – the giving of meaning to constitutional norms – is bound to assume central importance in the task of collective self-definition of a people. For constitutional adjudication necessarily entails the interpretation and application of those constitutional standards that define the national community.

In other words, constitutional adjudication, as one of the principal modalities of *collective* decision-making in a constitutional democracy, is necessarily one of the principal vehicles for giving expression to the national ethos of a people. In Hanna Pitkin's phrase, it gives expression to their 'fundamental nature as a people', and helps to sustain the 'general ends' constitutive of their 'fundamental frame-work' of governance.[27] On this view, constitutional adjudication functions as an ongoing process of national self-definition and self-interpretation, in which the courts become arbiters of the fundamental character and objectives of the nation; of those fundamental values that define a people as a particular kind of political community. Constitutional adjudication therefore becomes the locus of an overt struggle for the definition of a people's national identity – what they stand for – given that any one case may entail competing visions of that identity. That is to say, competing visions of a national ethos are at the core of our practice of constitutional adjudication.[28] For example, as Professor Robert Post observes, every time a court considers whether a governmental regulation is an unconstitutional 'taking' of private property, or whether a restriction of speech violates the free speech clause, or whether a certain punitive practice is cruel and inhumane, it must necessarily interpret and apply those standards that *constitutionally* define the national community. The challenge, therefore, is to determine which aspects of the national ethos may be regarded as *legitimate*, that is to say, as bearing on 'the essential content and spirit of the constitution.' [29]

But the 'classical' image of adjudication stresses the primacy of the intellect in constitutional interpretation; which is to say that the irrationality and emotionality of politics should be excluded from judicial decision-making.[30] Therefore, the thesis necessarily assumes the requisite theoretical competence that would facilitate the Court's role as the resident philosopher of Commonwealth Caribbean constitutional systems; for the accomplishment of the Court's educative responsibilities would depend very much upon the intellectual capacity of its judges to propound persuasive answers to difficult questions of constitutional interpretation.[31] Thus, assuming the appropriate reforms that would secure the Court's independence and its entrenchment in our respective constitutions, so as to allow its Judges to take a disinterested and principled approach in the decision of cases, and to imagine themselves writing for an audience concerned with the long-term import of a dispute, the Court, more so than Britain's Privy Council, would have the institutional incentive to tell 'the right story' about *us* by supplying educative descriptions of Commonwealth Caribbean political identity through their application of constitutional principles on our behalf. In this regard, the Court (through its Judges) would become one of *the titled authors* of our political identity. For it bears emphasis that the Court would truly be a central institution of our own creation; that is to say, it would, as others have already intimated, be truly symbolic of a genuinely constitutive act of our sovereign will.[32] In a word, the Court would be one of the principal agencies by which we affect to make our constitutions *our* own.

Put differently, a regional court, given its position in an amended constitutional order, would have the institutional incentives, through its judicial opinions, to teach the kind of civic or political lesson that would lead Caribbean peoples to a reformed understanding of their own identity. At its best, the Court might produce reasoned opinions that would school the nation to an exacting temper of justice and present us with a picture of our best conception of political identity. For example, in its interpretation of Commonwealth Caribbean law and, especially, the law of the Constitution(s), a regional supreme court can help mold the national mind and can play a major role in shaping and articulating fundamental principles of constitutional governance. This, as we have said, depends very much on the Court's theoretical competence and the excellence of its arguments in making constitutional norms persuasive to the citizenry. However, assuming the best, the Court might use the judicial opinion to persuade us to conform our behaviour to a certain conception of justice by convincing us that such a conception of justice is tacit to the very constitutional principles to which we have in fact committed ourselves. In other words, the Court, as 'Ideal Reader' of our constitutions, and 'Author' of some of our authoritative political texts (the Judicial Opinions), might move its audience to a higher (set of) moral standards implicit in the constitutions' meaning.

But above all, the judges' duty to interpret the constitutions will inevitably draw them into reflecting upon the question of our political identity. Constitutional adjudication, particularly of key constitutional cases, generally gives evidence of the character and content of a people's collective identity. This becomes evident if one were to take seriously the constitutions' role as the 'constituent agent' of our collective identity. For questions about constitutional meaning are, at bottom, questions about who and what we are as a community; about the character of our consti-

tutions and of our political society. Ideally, constitutional interpretation is a way of specifying the restraints which 'the People'
have imposed upon their exercise of political power. These
restraints are, however, in their turn, clues to the identity of 'the
People'; a people who apparently aspire to exercise power in a
certain way, within certain institutional constraints.[33]

This does not mean that every case will necessarily occasion
reflection on the constitutive features of our collective identity.
What it does say is that, inevitably, certain cases of profound constitutional importance would arise that would engage the Court
in complex theoretical and scholarly argument about the
Commonwealth Caribbean political character; about the character of our constitutions and the polities they mean to recommend. In fine, then, if we were to treat *descriptions* of our
collective identity as an important component of good constitutional interpretation, then the connection between judicial
opinion writing and descriptions of identity is drawn as one of the
principal educative tasks facing a Caribbean Court of Appeal.
The following section will therefore explore this issue, using a
few selective cases for illustration.

The Judicial Opinion in the Republic of Law and Letters

To write a constitution is to make a polity: 'a structured public
world, a second text, where people live and act together.'[34] A
regime of written constitutionalism is therefore a two-text polity:
the constitutional document itself and the polity or the constitutional order it narrates into existence. In other words, the constitutional document denotes by its own textual composition
another structure, an analogous referent, the polity that it purports to bring into being and define continuously.[35] 'On this
homology', reasons Professor William Harris, 'is based the very
plausibility of constitutional interpretation, as a form of discourse

articulating the connection between the written text and the political text-analogue whereby one gives meaning to the other.'[36] In other words, 'the resulting structure of constitutive signification ... compels reading both the document and the polity that it has signalled into existence – the republic that in turn gives the words their political meaning: both of which change over time, pushing, restraining, and adapting to each other in a profound illustration of the affinity of language and politics.'[37]

Authoritative constitutional interpretation is therefore a necessary correlate of written constitutionalism. That is to say, for a political order to be a constitutional polity and thus to be bound by a set of fundamental principles, there must be a systematic practice of constitutional review – a scrutiny of ongoing practices and policies to determine their compatibility with the constitutive values that define the character of the political order.[38] This authoritative constitutional interpretation, as the central feature of the adjudicative institutional practice of a nation's supreme court, constitutes an ongoing process of defining and refining the character of the constitution itself and of the political order that it recommends. Constitutional adjudication and interpretation therefore has the educative office of *explaining* the people to themselves; of reconnecting them to their *story*. This therefore means that a nation's supreme court's adjudicative office – the application of the law of the constitution in concrete cases – has profound implications for the definition of community and political identity. This work therefore assumes that the establishment of a regional appellate court would have the profound consequence of refashioning Commonwealth Caribbean political identity, consistent with certain attendant changes in constitutional form. It is on this premise that this work proposes to consider the appellate judicial opinion as a distinct literary genre within the larger republic of law and letters.[39]

Marbury v. Madison

It is submitted that the judicial opinion *par excellence* of this genre remains that of Chief Justice John Marshall in the 1803 decision in *Marbury v. Madison*.[40] In this opinion Marshall used his exemplary literary and rhetorical skills to construct an opinion that was nothing less than *a construction* of the *meaning* of the American Republic itself. Far beyond its doctrinal articulation of the principle of judicial review – for which the case is most famously known in American and Western jurisprudence – Marshall's opinion stands as one of the most outstanding examples of how the highest appellate court of a nation functions critically in the *construction* of the political community; how it functions as one of the defining agents of a people's political identity.

The success of the opinion rests largely on Marshall's insightfulness in apprehending the American Republic as a two-text polity: the Constitutional document established by the people of the United States, and the political order the Constitution brought into being.[41] To interpret one is to interpret the other. To give proper construction to one is to give proper construction to the other. In this regard, the opinion is made to seem *as if* it is the opinion of the American people; that is to say, an opinion uttered in their name. In the final analysis, *Marbury* stands as a judicial contestation of meaning of the American polity.

Marshall would therefore redact the story of constitutional *origin* as the sole and adequate ground for constitutional interpretation: the Constitution derives from the people as whole. In essence, he reaffirms the fundamental principle of republican government which admits of the original and supreme right of the people to frame their political constitution. 'That the people have an original right to establish, for their future government, such principles as, in their opinion, shall most conduce to their own happiness is the basis on which the whole American fabric has been erected.' These 'principles', in fact, are constitutive of the American political community; they establish the order of, and thus give shape to, the American polity.[42] In the Court's view, then, (the word) 'principles' here refers literally to the Constitution as a legal instrument to be given force and effect in judicial proceedings and, ultimately, in the people's collective *life*.[43]

In exercising their supreme and original right to establish the principles for their future government, the sovereign 'people' have chosen to organize their government into its various departments. One of these departments is the Judiciary – the Court itself. The Court therefore derives the authority to address the people *created* by the Constitution from that very instrument they themselves have uttered into existence in the exercise of their sovereign will. The Court is therefore a representative institution of the sovereign people – a necessary condition of political authority in a democratic polity.[44] The Congress' or the President's claim to represent the people may be more immediate – after all, they are elected institutions – but immediacy does not translate automatically into a stronger claim of representative authority.[45] The authority of the judicial opinion therefore rests on its appearance as a representation of the opinion of the American people. It means, then, that the Court's enunciation of the doctrine of judicial review – the power of the Court to pass on 'an exposition of the Constitution, deliberately established by legislative acts ...' – must be seen as the opinion of the people. This is the meaning of the American political order: a polity under the Rule of Law – a *law* established by the people of the United States. As Professor Paul Kahn remarks, at its most profound level, '*Marbury* is a self-conscious effort to constitute an American political order characterized by the rule of law.'[46] It is a particular construction of American political meaning, a competing vision of American political identity that clashed directly with that of then President Jefferson.

Marbury, therefore, is about the relation of courts to the rule of law and, more broadly, of courts to the political order.[47] And Marshall would claim interpretive supremacy over the Congress or the Presidency, in this regard. Because, for him, the possibility of judicial invalidation of legislative acts was contemplated by 'all those who have framed written constitutions.' Under the Constitution, 'The powers of the legislature are defined, and limited; and that those limits may not be mistaken, or forgotten, the constitution is written. To what purpose are powers limited and to what purpose is the limitation committed to writing, if these limits may, at any time, be passed by those intended to be restrained?' 'Certainly', he continued, 'all those who have framed written constitutions contemplated them as forming the fundamental and paramount law of the nation, and consequently, the theory of every such government must be, that an act of the legislature, repugnant to the Constitution, is void.' 'This theory is essentially attached to a written constitution, and is consequently, to be considered, by this court, as one of the fundamental principles of our society.'[48]

But why the Court as opposed to Congress or even the Presidency? For Marshall, written constitutionalism creates the possibility of delegating the interpretive power to a body of persons neither institutionally beholden to popular will nor vested with that very power that constitutional instruments exist chiefly to restrain.[49] 'It is too much to ask of anyone entrusted with immense power, or with control over a nation's treasure, to be the interpreter of principled institutional restraints on his power. To invest Congress with the interpretive power would be giving to the legislature a practical and real omnipotence with the same breath which professes to restrict their powers within narrow limits.'[50] On this view, then, constitutional adjudication cannot be done by popular vote – whether of the legislature or of the citizens themselves. Such a regime would collapse the distinction between enduring political commitment and momentary political will.[51] 'So, constitutional interpretation cannot be vested in organs of government beholden to or expressing popular will. Rather, interpretive power can only be vested in the judiciary, not simply because it is the "least dangerous branch", but because it is the only branch positioned to exercise the interpretive power in such a way as to avoid collapsing it into an exercise of present democratic will.'[52]

In essence, we have established so far that constitutionalism on the model of writing cannot exist without judicial review. This is so because constitutionalism, which begins with the memorialization of the foundational commitments, requires interpretation as an ongoing project in order that the constitution may achieve a deep inscription into the life of the nation.[53] This is accomplished significantly through the writing of the judicial opinion which is unavoidably rhetorical, in much the same way that literature is;[54] rhetoric here being considered not simply as a verbal art, but also as a normative principle that directs the systematic contemplation of any subject matter and contains the analytic tools necessary for the comprehension of diverse and often contradictory philosophic principles and systems.[55] In this sense, rhetoric is viewed as a central, critical method for the analysis of ideas. But rhetoric's central relevance to law is borne out in the fact that the field of rhetoric encompasses those areas in which decisions have to be made; that is, where judgment is required.[56] As Chaim Perelman reminds us, if judges were only docile instruments as Montesquieu described them: 'the mouth that pronounces the words of the law, mere passive beings, incapable of mediating either its force or its vigor', then judicial reasoning would be foreign to all concepts of rhetoric. But, to the contrary, rhetoric is eminently relevant where there is need to evaluate, to interpret or to judge; where judicial power must persuade as to the 'rightness' of its decisions rather than forcibly impose them.[57]

To repeat, then, law is at its heart an interpretive and compositional practice, and in this sense it is a radically literary and rhetorical activity. The activity of law is the interpretation and composition of authoritative texts – the judicial opinions.[58] And, from this perspective, law reveals itself as more than just 'a set of rules and incentives designed to produce results in the material social world, but as an imaginative and intellectual activity that has as its end the claim of meaning for human experience, individual and collective.'[59] Put differently, law 'receives its fullest definition not descriptively, but performatively, as the [Judge] finds a way of using language that transforms it, a way of defining himself and others in order to create a new community, a community of discourse, in the world.'[60] As Wittgenstein once remarked, 'To imagine a language means to imagine a form of life.'[61] This means that our acts of language are actions in the world, not just in our minds. Further, Professor James Boyd White observes that even when we think we are simply communicating information, or being rigorously or exclusively intellectual, or just talking, we are in fact engaged in performances, in relation to others, that are ethical and political in character and that can be judged as such.[62] This is true both in the private and the public worlds. It is especially true in the law (an area of the public world), which is above all the creation of a world of meaning: a world with its own actors, its own forms and occasions of speech, and its own language. Through its language we constitute a community of a certain kind.[63]

It is from this perspective that we consider language as that which is critical in shaping both who we are – our very selves – and the ways in which we observe and construe the world.[64] 'This is a way of imagining language not as a set of propositions, but as a repertoire of forms of action and of life.'[65] This is consistent with a view of law as a 'culture of argument' – 'as a language, as a set of ways of making sense of things and acting in the world.'[66]

On this view, the law is regarded as a set of ways of thinking and talking, which means a set of ways of acting in the world (and with each other) that has its own configurations and qualities, and its own consequences.[67]

Through its forms of language and of life the law constitutes a world of meaning and action: it creates a set of actors and speakers and offers them possibilities for meaningful speech and action that would not otherwise exist. In so doing it establishes and maintains a community defined by its practices of language.[68] Simply put, our community is defined by our language – our language being the set of shared expectations and common terms that enable us to think of ourselves as a 'we'.[69] Through a regional appellate court, therefore, we may at least contribute to the remaking of our shared resources of meaning, and thus of our public or communal lives.[70] This is obviously the case with (our) great writers and thinkers - (Lamming, Walcott, Brathwaite, to name a few) – whose works have changed the terms in which we think and talk, the ways in which we imagine and constitute ourselves.[71]

It bears emphasis that a constitution is notoriously not a self-interpreting document, but rather requires our repeated engagement with it, both as lawyers and as citizens.[72] The vast bulk of its authoritative readings are judicial, taking the form of opinions issued in the decision of particular cases: cases that often represent struggles between competing visions of the constitution and therefore of political society, rather than merely arguments about principle and doctrine. Consider, then, that the decision of the highest court becomes part of the political culture; that it affects the ways in which people conceive of themselves and their possibilities for life; the ways in which they view themselves as a community. It therefore follows that the more significant decisions of the highest court would help shape our 'prejudices', our attitudes and feelings, the ways of imagining our world and affiliating ourselves with it, and that make us what we are. As Professor Robert

Ferguson puts it, when judges 'deliver the opinion of the Court,' they impose a cumulative history along with the decision of an immediate institution. They are, in every sense of the word, the keepers of the past and, through this role, holders who safeguard the present.[73] And a critical aspect of this past is the Founders' achievement in the constitutional settlement under which current and future generations must live. The courts' understanding of the Founders' achievement therefore functions critically in the composition of the judicial decision. On this issue, Justice Felix Frankfurter of the US Supreme Court, a master craftsman of the judicial opinion, waxed poetic when he intoned that the Founders operate in the judicial opinion as one of 'those agencies of mind and spirit which may serve to gather up the traditions of a people, transmit them from generation to generation, and thereby create that continuity of a treasured common life which constitutes a civilization.'[74]

Given these possibilities, the question of the adequacy of the constitutional language in which judicial inquiry must proceed, and of the categories of our constitutional discourse, must necessarily be addressed. For Commonwealth Caribbean jurisprudence, this issue entails a profound struggle with the 'imperial' tradition out of which our constitutions have emerged, very much analogous to the struggle in which our great writers are inevitably engaged with the authority of 'established' poetic conventions. This is fundamentally a struggle with 'their' language, with its historical contingency and cultural particularity. Our constitutional language, for example, has set the terms within which we must move to a transformed understanding of our political commitments. What a (constitutional) text offers is a whole way of thinking and talking and being, a way of acting in relation to one another as members of a collectivity.[75] The struggle with the language we have inherited is therefore inevitable, because it is the language in which we must define and speak of our constitutional identity; the language in which judges, lawyers, scholars, or political officials conduct their discourse; the language that phrases the issues they count as relevant, valid, and legitimate.[76]

The organizing of a political order according to a written design, the authoritative modelling of a polity in words, anticipates the complementary, literary pole of reading. The writing of a constitution is an inscription of meaning. Constitutional adjudication, as was earlier noted, is therefore a profoundly literary activity. It involves the way or ways of reading and criticizing our fundamental political texts, and also of composing other authoritative texts: the judicial opinions.

> In every opinion a court not only resolves a particular dispute one way or another, but validates or authorizes one kind of reasoning, one kind of response to argument, one way of looking at the world and its own authority ... Whether the process is conscious or not, the judge seeks to persuade the reader not only of the rightness of the result reached and the propriety of the analysis used, but of his or her understanding of what the judge, the law, the lawyer and the citizen are and should be – in short, of his or her conception of the kind of conversation that does and should constitute us.[77]

In every opinion, the court constructs (or reconstructs) a narrative or conversational composition about the constitution – how the court understands and defines the constitution it is interpreting, and, therefore, the nature of the political order narrated by the text. 'The reading of the constitution is a stage in the making of the constitution, and everything that is present in that activity is present in this one: the definition of a civilized polity operating under the rule of law and protecting the deepest values of the culture.'[78] It is in the act of reading that the subject matter of the text would come to light. Constitutional adjudication therefore requires that the judge be ever cognisant of the 'language' he or she inherits and must use; the language in which the text is constituted, and, therefore, the social, ethical, and political relations the text establishes.[79]

To repeat, constitutional adjudication is a profoundly literary and rhetorical activity, considering rhetoric as the theory of rational argumentation, which relies on an appeal to reason and is addressed to an ideal audience of reasonable and competent men and women.[80] And the ultimate purpose of argumentation in law, as of all argumentation, is to obtain or intensify the adherence of the audience – the parties, lawyers and judges, and enlightened public opinion – to the correctness of the decision reached.[81] The critical importance of a regional appellate court to the public life of the Commonwealth Caribbean might be gleaned if we were to consider the broader 'cultural' task of adjudication in drawing and defining the proper relation between the constitution as our central political text and Commonwealth Caribbean society; in defining the social role of the constitution – how it shapes society as it is made to respond to the interests and claims of a Caribbean people; how it shapes their constitutional identity. Thus, to repeat, the establishment of a regional appellate court might yet be our most conscious use of constitutional reform since independence, to refashion our political identity.

The central role of adjudication is the realisation of the constitution in the life of the community, thus making the constitution the citizens' rather than a government's or a lawyer's document, by defining the rights of citizens and their collective identity. Through adjudication and interpretation, the constitution is indeed made to function as the principal text of our political culture – the common ground where readers meet to engage one another about the world they wish to represent, to criticise, and even to change.

From the standpoint of adjudication we consider the ways constitutional texts are and can be read, and the implications of those readings. As Dena Goodman observes: 'Texts can be understood as active forces in the world, forces that shape the thinking and acting of particular individuals who are engaged with them in the act of reading and who form a community of discourse within the greater social, political and intellectual contexts by which history is defined.'[82] This further speaks to the semiotic and rhetorical function of discourse in determining a particular community. In other words, if we were to consider our Independence Constitutions as our central political texts that define the relationship between citizen and state and the political or power relationships constitutive of community, then the judicial opinion, as an interpretive statement of the meaning of the constitutional text, exploits the semiotic and rhetorical function of language in order to constitute a form of action meant to have an effect on the world.

A distinctive challenge for Commonwealth Caribbean judges is therefore how to represent our political identity in the absence of monarchy; how to move beyond that sort of cultural particularity and the historical contingency of its language to constructing universals by which our society might rightly be governed. It is the problem of establishing the ideals and principles of our independent political order, and whether these ideals and principles may be adequately expressed through the language and the cultural symbols borrowed from Britain – a language in which there is a clear absence of any determinate relationship between certain words and things West Indian, between signs and signifiers. For example, the word 'crown', so central to Commonwealth Caribbean constitutional and legal discourse and practice, does not signify any indigenous Caribbean institution. Thus, since the *Independence Constitution* is the central political text in the 'new' legal order – the text defining the rights of the citizen and the arrangement of political power in the society – then to interpret the Caribbean text in terms of English jurisprudence is to continue English colonialism under the disguise of independence. In addition, the retention of the Privy Council as our final court of appeal would ensure that the central terms of English jurisprudence would continue to dominate Commonwealth Caribbean constitutional discourse. A brief consideration of the Privy Council's decision in the famous Jamaican case of *Hinds & Ors. v. The Queen*[83] would bear out this claim.

Here, it was duly noted that the appeals in the case had come to Her Majesty in Council under section 110(1)(c) of the Jamaica Constitution on the question of the constitutional validity of the Gun Court Act, 1974. In addition Lord Diplock noted that (in briefs and arguments) they were properly referred to a number of

> previous authorities dealing with the exercise of judicial power under other written constitutions, established either by Act of the Imperial Parliament or by Order in Council, made by Her Majesty in Right of the Imperial Crown, whereby internal sovereignty or full independence has been granted to what were formerly colonial or protected territories of the Crown. [84]

All these constitutions were in fact negotiated as well as drafted by persons nurtured in the tradition of that branch of the common law of England that is concerned with public law and familiar in particular with the basic concept of separation of legislative, executive and judicial power as it had been developed in the unwritten constitution of the United Kingdom. In all those constitutions which have their origin in an Act of the Imperial Parliament at Westminster or in an Order in Council, there is a common pattern and style of draftsmanship which may conveniently be described as 'the Westminster Model.'[85] He further noted that the more recent constitutions on the Westminster

Model, unlike their earlier prototypes, include a Chapter dealing with Fundamental Rights and Freedoms. The provisions of this Chapter form part of the substantive law of the state and until amended by whatever special procedure is laid down in the constitution for this purpose, impose a fetter upon the exercise by the Legislature, the Executive and the Judiciary of the plenitude of their respective powers.[86]

No text achieves final conceptual clarity of expression and thus no independence from the circumstances in which it was expressed. Every text remains inextricably bound to its context.[87] Therefore, no text can be understood in and of itself apart from tradition; that is to say, the larger historical context of its composition. Lord Diplock was therefore well on target when he intoned that 'a written constitution, like any other written instrument affecting legal rights and obligations, falls to be construed in the light of its subject-matter and of the surrounding circumstances with reference to which it was made.'[88]

But this, interestingly, is the very nub of the issue regarding continuing appeals to the British Privy Council. For, the very fact that *West Indian Independence Constitutions* belong to the British monarchical/common law tradition means that their interpretation by a 'Supreme Court' (the Privy Council) which is one of the central agencies of that tradition would only serve to reinforce the authority of that tradition upon our political and constitutional identity. It therefore bears reminding that as our constitutional practice now stands, we locate all authority in the reading of our central political texts externally to ourselves, in the authoritative declarations of a foreign court. For there is authority in our constitutional texts and in the cases explicating them and in the tradition out of which our current 'Supreme Court' purports to speak. The judicial opinion of a nation's highest appellate court, we have noted, is the model *par excellence* of constitutive rhetoric whereby community is established and defined. We have left this authority to define the Commonwealth Caribbean political community with the British Privy Council. Therefore, no matter how positivistically correct *in law* its decisions might be, the British Privy Council would have neither the competence of mind nor the inclination of heart to render the kind of critical re-construction of the monarchical/common law tradition out of which it speaks that would reveal the inappropriateness of that tradition for a proper construction of the Commonwealth Caribbean political identity. In any event, as already observed, the most profound argument from sovereignty militating in favour of a Caribbean Court of Appeal – and against the 'retention' of the Privy Council as our final appellate court – is the argument for the right of a sovereign people to define for themselves the foundational terms of their political order. In a word, this is the right of self-definition.

Therefore, on this view, our detachment from the British Monarchy and its attendant institutions would not only be a symbolic act of supreme importance, in that it would make possible the re-presentation of our political identity in terms of the ideals and principles of modern and contemporary constitutionalism rather than as 'subjects' of the British Crown; it would also make possible a 'new' constitutional conversation in the Commonwealth Caribbean. That is to say, it would open up the possibility for the construction of a 'new grammar' in terms of which the citizens might think and talk of themselves. It therefore bears reminding that constitutional reform has consequences for conceptions of community and citizens' identity. For, to an indeterminate, but non-trivial extent, the self-conceptions of citizens are derivative of constitutional arrangements.

Our (current) constitutional Britishness naturally privileges the language of monarchy and parliamentary sovereignty. The Judicial Committee's location at the apex of the judicial system of the Commonwealth Caribbean therefore has consequences for the way we define our constitutional identity. Cognizance of this offers the distinct possibility that a regional appellate court might be the fillip for the emergence of a (true) Caribbean jurisprudence, which has too long remained subordinate to English jurisprudence. For as long as we remain the 'subjects' of the British Crown, with its Judicial Committee at the apex in the hierarchy of our legal system, it is to be expected that our constitutional discourse would reflect a cluster of values, intellectual orientations, and practices that carry a distinctly British cast.

It bears repeating that *West Indian Independence Constitutions* are not expressions of our popular sovereignty. The citizens were never really privy to the 'agreements' reached on these constitutional instruments of political independence and, therefore, on the form of constitutional order and the world of everyday politics thereby constituted. In consequence, our constitutions and our constitutional politics are in reality the imposition, or at least the export, of an imperial order and, as such, they do not establish an 'authentic' form of constitutional conversation in which each speaker is given a 'voice'. Rather, our constitutional conversation is carried on in a 'foreign' voice. We are either silenced or are constrained to speak within the institutions and traditions of interpretation of the colonial constitutions that have been imposed. Needless to say, the language of West Indian constitutional thought and practice must be amended and reconceived if the courts are to do *justice* to the claims of the citizens, who, like Sophocles's Antigone, demand a hearing as to the justness of their cause. Therefore, in order that the courts may respond justly to their cause, it is necessary to inquire as to the appropriateness of the language in which enquiry now proceeds; to call into question and amend a number of unexamined conventions, inherited from the imperial age, that continue to inform the language of Commonwealth Caribbean constitutionalism in which the demands of the citizens are taken up and adjudicated.[89]

It bears reminding, however, that *who* and *what* we are is a contingent achievement, the product of a particular history and geography and specific constitutional arrangements and policies – in short, specific constitutional choices. Constitutional identity is therefore likely to be immersed in complex and ambiguous relations with other identities, such as national, ethnic, religious, or cultural identity. In addition, in written constitutions, the question of constitutional identity remains problematic, given that the constitutional text is inevitably incomplete and subject to multiple plausible interpretations. It is incomplete not only because it does not cover all subjects that it ought ideally to address, but also because it cannot exhaustively address all conceivable issues arising under the subjects that it does encompass. Moreover, precisely because of the incompleteness of the constitutional text, constitutions must remain open to interpretation and re-interpretation. Thus, an adequate picture of constitutional identity would entail supplementing the constitutional text with the interpretations and elaborations given to it over time. This underscores the central role of a supreme court in shaping a country's constitutional identity. In a word, the constitutional identity of a community over time is articulated and preserved in the ascription of constitutional meaning in interpretation. Secondly, constitutional identity is in constant need of reconstruction; however, no such reconstruction could ever become definitive or complete.

In sum, then, a people's constitutional identity is in large measure forged through the medium of constitutional discourse, embedded in a common and 'universal' language of modern constitutionalism; a language that is capable of binding together the plurality of interests (and selves) in society, given that constitutionalism implies pluralism and heterogeneity. This constitutional discourse must build upon a constitutional text which must be placed in its proper cultural and societal context, taking into account relevant normative and factual constraints.[90] And given that the context is open-ended and subject to transformation over time, the Ideal Reader (the court) must resort to constitutional discourse to invent and reinvent the constitutional identity.[91] That is to say, the Ideal Reader must use the tools of constitutional discourse to construct a coherent narrative in which it can locate a plausible 'self-identity' of the *constitutional people*.[92]

As Professor Michel Rosenfeld further elaborates, constitutional self-identity revolves around the antinomies between real and ideal.

> The antinomy between fact and norm manifests itself through the juxtaposition of constitutional norms, and sociopolitical and historical facts, as well as through the conflict between an actual existing constitution and the normative requirements of constitutionalism. In terms of the relationship between constitutional norm and historical fact, application of the same constitutional norm may lead to different outcomes, depending on the relevant historical facts.[93]

For different factual conditions may in certain circumstances change the meaning of the same constitutional norm.[94] For example, a constitutional right to subsistence may well amount to a legal guarantee in an industrially advanced society, but can be no more than an aspiration of hope in an underdeveloped country with widespread starvation.[95]

The likely conflict, therefore, between actual constitutions and constitutionalism as embodying certain normative prescriptions, is in a sense a clash between the fact of a particular constitution and the norms that prescribe what constitutional democracy ought to be; or, as a clash between those norms promoted by an actual constitution and inconsistent norms inherent in constitutionalism – norms such as adherence to the rule of law, and protection of fundamental rights. Such clashes are resolved in interpretation through a construction and reconstruction of constitutional self-identity. This means that in order to establish a viable constitutional self-identity the constitution must be interpreted against the normative constraints inherent in constitutionalism, and which entails evaluating the legitimacy of actual constitutional norms and practices.

It bears reminding that constitutional decision-making involves settling the constitutional issues in terms of choices between two or more plausible alternative readings; and the choice made has fundamental implications for the particular conception of constitutional self-identity that is promoted and fostered. 'What will we *be* if we were to read the text this way as opposed to that?'[96] Take as an example the American Supreme Court's decision in the case of *Dred Scott v. Sanford*.[97] The case dealt with the constitutionality of a federal law that provided for the emancipation of slaves upon being brought into federal territory by their owners. Dred Scott was thus emancipated, but upon his subsequent return to the state where he had formerly been a slave, his former owner reclaimed ownership over him. Dred Scott sought a declaration that he was a free man. The question before the Supreme Court was whether the federal statute providing for emancipation was unconstitutional as a violation of the slave owner's constitutionally protected property rights.

The Court held that the federal statute providing for emancipation was unconstitutional as violative of the legitimate property rights of the (former) slave owner. This holding obviously rested on the premise that members of the Negro race were less than human. But had the Supreme Court treated Dred Scott as a full human being, then considering him property would have been a contradiction in terms, and his liberty due process rights had to prevail over any property rights that his former owner may have had in him. Put differently, the alternative ruling would have revealed the moral absurdity of the claim that one's alleged 'property' rights in another human being could logically be protected by the fundamental right to due process of law. A decision in favour of Dred Scott would therefore have revealed a glaring contradiction between the Constitution and constitutionalism, for the Constitution itself had sanctioned slavery. So the decision was in fact consistent with actual constitutional norms, but told an unflattering story of American self-identity that was in fact inconsistent with the fundamental notion of the moral equality of all human beings. The Court's decision had indeed accelerated the country's plunge into a bloody civil war.

Later in this chapter the case of *Ophelia King* is discussed to show that, as a significant constitutional decision, it too has had an unmistakable and significant impact on the constitutional self-identity of Barbados. It is submitted that recognition of the 'Crown's constitutional authority to cut the civil (the Crown's) servants' salaries at will projects a noticeably different image of Barbadian constitutional self-identity than that which would have emerged had the Privy Council refused to recognize such authority in the Crown, and instead had allowed that the salary was property protected against unlawful governmental taking by the fundamental rights provisions of the Barbados Constitution. It is hardly an exaggeration, therefore, to claim that the decision has provoked a crisis in the constitutional self-identity of Barbadians, hence the current government's move to secure civil servants' salaries against any such governmental action in the future.

The theme of this work is that the Commonwealth Caribbean constitutional subject would locate a more plausible self-identity within the broader constitutional language and tradition of modern republican constitutionalism, given that Commonwealth Caribbean constitutions already share in that rich republican tradition from Plato to Madison. It bears reminding that the language of modern and contemporary constitutionalism is the language in which the constitutional claims of citizens of modern societies are taken up and adjudicated. 'It is the terms and the uses of those terms that have come to be accepted as the authoritative vocabulary for the description, reflection, criticism, amendment and overthrow of constitutions and their characteristic institutions over the last three hundred years of building modern constitutional societies.'[98] This language consists in the uses of the term *'constitution'*, its cognates, and the other terms associated with it, such as popular sovereignty, people, self-government, citizen, agreement, rule of law, rights, equality, recognition and nation.[99] And, notwithstanding the complexity of this language, what has happened is that a relatively narrow range of familiar uses of these terms has come to be accepted as the authoritative political traditions of interpretation of modern constitutional societies.[100] Thus, given that a constitutional self-identity is not forged *in abstracto*, but rather in the resonant context of the sociocultural heritage of a particular society, it means that the universal terms of modern constitutionalism establish the critical perspective in terms of which the sociocultural practices and beliefs of a society are rendered to critical assessment. After all, politics can be defined in terms of a finite range of distinct universal or 'basic' issues, encapsulated by such terms as *power, justice, sovereignty, obligation, state*, or by such expressions as *the public good* or *the limits of government*, upon which legal and political theory focuses.[101] This issue-orthodoxy expresses a belief that beneath the diversity of language and institutional forms lies a substratum of ideas which is only inadequately expressed in the language of any people, and toward the common understanding of which the great political theorists (together with their modern legatees) have struggled.[102]

As was earlier intimated, political independence has not resolved the question of Commonwealth Caribbean political and constitutional identity. Retention of the (colonial) infrastructure - particularly *the* 'monarchy' and the Privy Council - has ensured that post-independence constitutional discourse reads as a subset of English constitutional jurisprudence. There therefore remains the task of reinterpreting and reconstructing a viable Commonwealth Caribbean constitutional identity.

But a post-independence Caribbean jurisprudence does not necessarily mean a total rejection of the received English constitutional tradition and a radical rupture in our political continuity in order to give meaning to the reality of the 'Caribbean situation'. In the area of law, in particular, we could not possibly expect any radical departure from the 'colonial' tradition. What a Commonwealth Caribbean jurisprudence therefore demands is a critical re-examination of that tradition in order to challenge its totalizing gestures and its pretended claims of 'universality'; and also to test its relevance to the Caribbean situation in order to expose the real discontinuity beneath the apparent continuity of our legal systems and institutions. The validity of the basic concepts of modern and contemporary constitutionalism are not rejected; rather, what is to be rejected is our continued valorisation of certain inherited categories that are peculiarly British, or the peculiarly British cast given to certain fundamental terms of modern constitutional and political theory. In other words, Caribbean jurisprudence must deconstruct the fundamental terms of English jurisprudential thought as a necessary step toward fashioning the grounds for its own modes of representation of our constitutional self-identity.

Again, this is not to say that we would be able to construct an 'original' model of thought, free from all influence of English discourse. Rather, the claim is that Caribbean jurisprudence must be conceived as a small but significant part of a broader quest 'to inscribe Caribbean selves and voices within an economy of representation whose institutional and symbolic structures have

been established since the "discovery".'[103] So, in order that
Caribbean jurisprudence should not remain enslaved to a canonical English tradition that burdens us with its 'sacred' claims, it
must confront this colonial tradition and seek to establish its own
identity within the broader discourse of modern constitutionalism.

A most powerful analogy is found in the area of the more genuinely literary endeavour. For example, George Lamming's
provocative and insightful re-reading of Shakespeare's *The
Tempest* is an eloquent reminder of how Caliban must expropri-
ate the master's language in order to redefine and transform the
colonized cultural space.[104] Thus, Caliban's new identity is not
defined by his absolute rejection of his colonial education and its
cultural traditions, but by his violent claims to an authority of
language previously denied him.[105] For, as Lamming reminds us:

> Caliban received not just words, but language as sym-
> bolic interpretation, an instrument for exploring con-
> sciousness. Once he had accepted language as such, the
> future of his development, however independent it was,
> would always be in some way inextricably tied up with
> that pioneering aspect of Prospero. Caliban at some stage
> would have to find a way of breaking that contract, which
> got sealed *by language,* in order to structure some alterna-
> tive reality for himself.[106]

It means, then, there must inevitably be an engagement with the
colonial language and its ideological terrain. It means that this
language must be appropriated and modernized, wherever possible, to represent a new consciousness; it must be redefined to
contain 'elements of universality that would go beyond the
bounds of the originating nation.'[107]

In summary, then, it would not be an overstatement to say that
post-independence Commonwealth Caribbean jurisprudence

has remained entrapped in a colonial hermeneutics, with the English common law and its constitution constituting the canonical text. The mythology of empire has fostered the belief that the coloniser and the colonised share a common identity. The supposed 'retention' in post-independence Commonwealth Caribbean of the English monarchical constitution, with a single British monarch continuing to serve as monarch to its remnants of empire, only serves to underscore this point. It means, then, that the colonial *contract* has to be re-read and rewritten. Therefore, a post-independence hermeneutics that would no longer remain subject to the authority of English jurisprudence must assert its claims to an authority of language that transcends the cultural particularity of that jurisprudence, in order to structure some alternative reality for itself. From the standpoint of political and legal hermeneutics, the Caribbean *self* and community have to 'reinvent' themselves using this more universal language, for its concepts are seen as adequate for constructing an alternative reality and for synthesizing the pluralistic, ethnic, cultural and class differences that define the new nation. In the sections to follow I discuss a sample of cases to illustrate how this 'language' might indeed render alternative decisions that paint a more plausible picture of Commonwealth Caribbean constitutional self-identity.

The Cases
Jaundoo and *King*

The cases bear out the truth of the claim that the story a people tell themselves about their constitution's origin is a profoundly significant act of collective self-identity, and that its continual re-telling plays a critical role in the ongoing construction of their political and constitutional identity.[108] This story is in fact constructed and re-constructed in virtually every important constitutional law case. That is to say, constitutional adjudication is part of the hermeneutic enterprise in which deeper interpretive issues regarding the character of the constitution and of the political society are necessarily engaged; issues about our collective identity and the form of our politics.

Constitutional adjudication is therefore at the core of a constitutional discourse, in which collective identity is articulated and constructed. As was earlier intimated, the critical role a country's supreme court decisions play in shaping and defining collective and constitutional identity could not possibly be overemphasized. For, a people's constitutional identity is in large measure forged through the medium of a constitutional discourse which builds upon a constitutional text, placed in its proper cultural and societal context, taking particular account of the relevant normative constraints and the functional imperatives of the society. Two cases in particular: *Jaundoo v. A.G. (Guyana)*[109] and *Gladwyn Ophelia King v. A.G. (Barbados)*,[110] are highly illustrative of this point.

Jaundoo v. A.G. (Guyana)

Jaundoo's case, before the Privy Council, involved the question of a private citizen's claim for injunctive relief against the Guyana Government over the compulsory acquisition of the citizen's land. What is of the utmost importance was the operative premise on which the Privy Council determined the issue before it.

The Privy Council, through Lord Justice Diplock, intoned that Guyana (at that time) was a constitutional monarchy, in virtue of which the court, an agent of the Crown, could not issue a coercive order against the Crown. In their words, the Privy Council invoked the relevant 'constitutional theory that the court exercises its judicial authority on behalf of the Crown.'[111] It means, therefore, that Guyana's entire judicial system, with the British Privy Council at its apex, was then in the service of the British

Crown. This bears careful analysis.

Above all else, the *Jaundoo* decision establishes the truth of the proposition that the story of the constitution's origin establishes the authoritative ground for the interpretation of the constitutional text and the construction of collective identity. Guyana, at that time, had recently emerged from being a British colony to the status of an independent state. Its constitution therefore came from Britain. What is more, Guyana, like so many countries throughout the Commonwealth, had supposedly 'retained the monarchy'. Therefore, Guyana was a constitutional monarchy.

But Lord Diplock afforded no explanation of his characterisation of Guyana as a constitutional monarchy. There was no need to, for, on the authoritative understanding of the circumstances under which Guyana had gained its independence and had supposedly 'retained the monarchy,' the issue of the country's true constitutional status was closed. But precisely whose 'authoritative understanding' was at play here? The British of course, for Britain had indeed settled the question as far back as 1931, when, in an act of self-interpretation of its 'masterly' position *vis-à-vis* its colonies, it had devised the means whereby they may be granted political independence, while yet remaining in allegiance to the British Crown. The situation in respect of Guyana, and the rest of the Commonwealth Caribbean, was only compounded by the fact that, out of expediency, the request was made of the British Crown that its Judicial Committee (the Privy Council) would continue to serve as the final court of appeal. Therefore, as Guyana's then 'Supreme Court', the Privy Council rendered the authoritative readings of Guyana's constitutional text and tradition, and, in consequence, held a defining role in the construction of the country's political and constitutional identity.

It means, then, that this interpretive characterisation of our constitutions - which, to this day, remains unchallenged in the Commonwealth Caribbean - is determinative of many a constitu-

tional issue. In *Jaundoo's* case it had the consequence of eliding
the substantive merits of the plaintiff/appellant's case for injunctive relief. An adequate interpretation of the (written) constitution
of the sovereign state of Guyana would have determined whether
the circumstances, or the specific statutory provisions, under
which the Government affected to take the citizen's land were
indeed constitutionally valid, that is, being consistent with the
citizen's fundamental right to property and the adequate protection thereof; and whether, in the circumstances, injunctive relief,
as opposed to damages, say, was the appropriate remedy. Barring
Britain's own peculiar constitutional tradition which denies coercive remedies against the Crown, the fact remains that in constitutional democracies wherein the practice of judicial review is
entrenched, injunctive relief against the government is a permissi-
ble constitutional remedy in the appropriate circumstances.

It therefore bears repeating that our signal failure to grasp the
republican nature of the *West Indian Independence Constitution*
and the consequent dissolution of the colonial monarchical connections, holds dire consequences for Commonwealth Caribbean
constitutional discourse. Our view of ourselves as monarchical
states commits our discourse to the political idiom of British constitutional jurisprudence, with its principal assumptions and
attendant practices. Put differently, our assumption of the image
of constitutional monarchy imposes its constraints on our discourse and makes it virtually impossible for Commonwealth
Caribbean constitutional law to function as a tool of radical
transformation of our constitutional politics. Thus the possibility
of a *genuine* Commonwealth Caribbean constitutional jurisprudence remains distant unless we are sensitive to the fact that the
'language' in which we are forced to conduct our discourse, and
the categories in terms of which we formulate our central constitutional questions, are themselves the symbols and categories
peculiar to a society quite unlike our own. Thus the intimate link

between the 'language' of our discourse and our constitutional Britishness forces Commonwealth Caribbean constitutional discourse into a stilted affectation. In no other case is this more dramatically borne out than in the recent Barbadian case of *Gladwyn Ophelia King v. A.G. (Barbados)*.

Gladwyn Ophelia King v. A.G. (Barbados).

The recent Barbados case of 'Mrs. Gladwyn Ophelia King and the Attorney General'[112] would suffice to substantiate the above claims. In this case, Mrs. King, a civil servant, challenged the constitutionality of the 1991 Public Service Reduction of Emoluments Act, by which the Government of Barbados effected a unilateral reduction in the emoluments (annual salaries) of public officers and other employees in the public service and related bodies by eight per cent, on the ground that it (the Act) constituted an unlawful taking of property without just compensation, contrary to sections 11 and 16(1) of the Barbados Constitution.[113]

In her complaint, the plaintiff, through her counsel, claimed that she was deprived of emoluments properly earned under her employment contract by the defendant who represents *the Crown*. And in her supporting affidavit, the plaintiff deposed that she had performed those services 'as are required by me under the terms of my appointment and contract of service with the Crown in right of the Government of Barbados.'

The defendant, the Attorney General, rejoined that, 'The legal position of the plaintiff *in relation to the Crown*[114] depends more on status than on contract.' 'The hall-mark of status is the attachment to a legal relationship of rights and duties imposed by the public law and not by mere agreement of the parties.' The plaintiff's emoluments and her terms of service are governed by statute or statutory rules which may be unilaterally altered by the Crown without her consent. The Attorney General further noted that, 'Even if her legal relationship with the Crown is contractual, it is a contract which the Crown could alter unilaterally.'

In summarizing the basic principles that would guide [him] in reaching a decision, the Chief Justice, Sir Denys Williams, began with a passage from Professor de Smith's *The New Commonwealth and Its Constitutions*:

> Among the characteristic features of modern Commonwealth Constitutions are the limitation of parliamentary sovereignty, guarantees of fundamental human rights, judicial review of the constitutionality of legislation ... The aim of many of these provisions is to capture the spirit and practice of British institutions; the methods of approach involve the rejection of British devices and the imposition of the un-British fetters on legislative and executive discretion.[115]

The Chief Justice observed that Barbados has such a constitution (as described by Professor de Smith). Therefore, the 'plenitude of sovereign legislative power' of the Barbados Parliament is denoted by the constitutional provision that, 'Any laws could be made for "the peace, welfare and good government of the colony."'[116] The Chief Justice also noted as one of the principles 'that must guide [him] in reaching a decision', 'the common law power of the Crown to dismiss its servants at will'.[117] Of course, he noted that 'the question whether the Crown, in light of the constitutional provisions relating to the Public Service Commission, still has the right to dismiss at will an officer who is subject to the Commission's authority', was not to be decided in the instant proceedings.[118]

The question of 'Parliament's sovereignty' bears further examination. If the Chief Justice had reflected deeply on the language used by Professor de Smith, he would have discerned the disabling contradictions in his (Professor de Smith's) thought, and, in consequence, its inappropriateness as an operative premise for a decision under the Barbados Constitution.

In contemporary political theory, the term 'sovereign' expresses the idea that there is a final and absolute political authority in the community. It is a theory or assumption about political power: a way of thinking and speaking about political power in a defined community.[119] In the Hegelian sense, it is the state conceptualized as an organic unity that is sovereign.[120] And the concept of the state typically refers to a particular society characterized, among other things, by the presence of institutions having the authority to coerce.[121] On this view, the sovereignty of the state may actively manifest itself in one or another of its members; hence we can say that decisions came directly from this or that institution.[122] But to say that the legislature or the monarch is sovereign over against the rest of the state is to ignore the state's fundamental unity.[123]

A critical flaw in our constitutional theorizing is our failure to consider the extent to which the premises and categories of British constitutional jurisprudence are historically and culturally particular, so that we in the Commonwealth Caribbean could not adopt them without significant emendation. We have earlier drawn attention to the fact that in the absence of a written constitutional text in Britain, and, therefore, no written constitutional provisions establishing Parliament and defining its powers, it was correlatively conceived that there was no positive legal and political authority above Parliament. But, in contrast, our adoption of written constitutions, which contain certain specified exceptions to legislative (and executive) authority, already represent a 'radical' departure from British constitutional practice. Expressed authorial intentions of the framers and drafters of West Indian Independence Constitutions to the contrary notwithstanding, it would be a fundamental contradiction in terms to think that it were possible to imitate or re-enact, without significant emendations, English constitutional traditions and practices in our constitutional texts.

If it is correct to hold that sovereignty is a peculiar kind of authority that only the state in its entirety (*summa potestas*) can possess, and that this sovereignty is written into the constitutional text which creates and bounds governmental power, then Professor de Smith's language becomes radically nonsensical. For it must be a fundamental contradiction in terms to speak of the sovereignty of parliament – an institution of the state – being circumscribed by positive legal authority: the constitution. It would rather seem that Professor de Smith has egregiously misread these written modern Commonwealth Caribbean constitutions which, he claims, have imposed limitations on 'parliamentary sovereignty', through guarantees of fundamental human rights and the consequent practice of judicial review, and at the same time imports that 'the aim of many of these [constitutional] provisions is to capture the spirit and practice of British institutions ...'.[124] It would suffice simply to repeat that the language of 'sovereignty' is so obviously inappropriate with respect to a governmental institution whose powers are expressly cabined by specific provisions of the constitutional text.

In the same view, the 'language of monarchy' similarly 'corrupts' our constitutional discourse. Mrs. King was a civil servant in the Government's employ; yet her counsel framed her complaint in terms of her 'appointment and contract with the Crown.' The Attorney General, sharing the common misconception of the (British) monarch's constitutional presence in the political order of independent Barbados, appropriately responded that the citizen's relation to the Crown is one of status. The very idea of the citizen having the legal capacity to enter into a contractual relationship with the Crown (the Monarch) is *infra dig*. The court, sharing a common constitutional image, was to decide whether or not Mrs. King's employment was properly cast in terms of a contractual relationship with the Crown. And assuming that it was so affirmatively cast, whether any legal consequences attached to such a contract, in contradistinction to a contract, say, between two private citizens.

If this is a fair representation of the case, then one immediately perceives the confusion that is wrought by this shared constitutional image. For the constitutional issue raised by Mrs. King's case – whether the 1991 Act is unconstitutional in that it constitutes an arbitrary and unlawful taking of property in contravention of Mrs. King's fundamental right to the due process of law and just compensation – itself engages more critical questions of constitutional discourse, *viz.*, the nature of the constitutional polity and of the citizen's relation to the state. That is to say, they are questions about the nature of the constitutive principles at the 'heart' of our constitutional order in terms of which we have 'agreed' to chart our collective life and to share the benefits and burdens of our living together.

To put the argument another way, it is to say that the dominant constitutional image, and the constraints it imposes on those who would work within its prism, did not lend itself to the proper reconstructing of the narrative of Mrs. King's case, in order that it may be decided 'according to law', which is a necessary part of the judicial process. Instead, Mrs. King's case was addressed in a 'constitutional language' that judges and lawyers alike understand to be the appropriate language in which they must conduct their business; and the 'organizing abstractions' of this language have led to the formulation of the problems of the case in terms of the sovereignty of parliament, the citizen's relation to the Crown, and, of course, the power of the Crown to deal with the citizen at its pleasure. Now, as Professor Peter Goodrich reminds us, it is indeed the case that the categories of sovereign and subject are intrinsic to legal discourse and have long been recognized within jurisprudence as essential features of legal semantics.[125] In fact, theories of law, from Hobbes to Austin and, to a lesser degree,

Kelsen, have, at bottom, been theories of sovereignty (defined either literally or metaphorically) and have tended to view the specificity of the legal in terms of a sovereign power to command the subjects of a legal system.[126] Still, in modern constitutional thought, the description and analysis of legal relations, which evidence the continuity of concepts of sovereign and subject, are often cast in terms of the normative and underlying ethical connotations of the constitutionalist state, and not simply in terms of an architectonic of command and subjection.[127]

The Chief Justice's ruling was affirmed by the Barbados Court of Appeal in a two-to-one decision. The case was then heard by the Privy Council which settled the issue of the Crown's authority to vary the emoluments of its 'servants' at will on the authority of a 1949 statute, which was saved as valid law under the Savings Clause provision of the Barbados Constitution. In the Board's view, the 1949 statute had already reposed the authority to vary the salaries of civil servants at will in the Minister of the Crown; and given that civil servants were themselves 'servants' of the Crown, it was not really necessary that the Government of Barbados should have effected the taking by new legislation. The 1991 Public Service Reduction of Emoluments Act was therefore constitutionally valid. The Board's decision is telling of its *view* of the Barbados Constitution that such an important constitutional case should be made to rest on the continuing *validity* of a 1949 law, which is in direct contradiction with the fundamental rights provisions of the Constitution. But that was to be expected given the Board's understanding that Barbados shares the very constitutional tradition of Britain, with its 'language' of monarchy and its central principle of 'parliamentary sovereignty.'

Justice Husbands' Dissent

The dissenting opinion of Mr. Justice Clifford Husbands merits special attention, not simply because it had raised the lone dissenting voice, in the entire case, in concluding that the Public Service Reduction of Emoluments Act, 1991 was unconstitutional, but because it helps make the crucial point under discussion: that our 'constitutional language' has forced us into a stilted affectation in the adjudication of momentous constitutional cases. As Mr. Ezra Alleyne has remarked, Mr. Justice Husbands' finding re the power of the Crown in post-Independence Barbados is 'of the greatest and deepest constitutional significance, and from a jurisprudential perspective is without doubt the most significant statement made in the entire case by anyone – the Privy Council included.'[128] It is therefore hoped to be shown that, notwithstanding his dissent, Justice Husbands, given his tacit acceptance of certain received premises, was forced to articulate his dissent within the very structure of argument appropriate to the discourse for a constitutional monarchy. That is to say, he too was entrapped within a 'colonial' hermeneutics – an understanding of our constitutional world through the prism of British jurisprudence. It means, then, that the possibility of our developing a distinctly Caribbean hermeneutics – 'our own way of interpreting our constitutional and political world'- must indeed turn on a rethinking and rejection of the authoritativeness of the English canonical tradition and its 'sacred' claims to truth. A Caribbean hermeneutics would come into its own only when it has freed itself from bondage to English constitutional 'dogma' and emerges as an authentic voice within a universal organon of interpretation.

For Justice Husbands, this was a case 'not without complexity and fundamental constitutional significance.' He opened his opinion by pointing to the fact that 'Mrs. Gladwyn Ophelia King was appointed to her position as a clerical officer in the public service of Barbados by the Governor-General acting in accordance with the advice of the Public Service Commission, established by section 90 of the Constitution of Barbados.' This means that Mrs. King was 'appointed' by the Crown since the

Governor-General is the Queen's local representative in Barbados. The specific nature of the relationship between the Crown and its employees is thus herein defined. Indeed, this has been the subject of prior Privy Council rulings, most prominently, the case of *Endell Thomas* v. *Attorney-General of Trinidad and Tobago*,[129] on which Chief Justice Sir Denys Williams had placed great store in his High Court ruling in *Ophelia King*. In *Thomas*, the Board opined that 'the constitutional doctrine of dismissibility of Crown servants at pleasure is, as a matter of legal theory, based upon an implied term in their contracts of employment.' It was further noted that this

> implied term has the unique feature that it is treated as overriding even an express term to the contrary, unless incorporation of such a term by the executive acting on behalf of the Crown, in entering into the contract, has been authorised by the legislature, *i.e.* the Queen in Parliament. Nevertheless, when the Crown summarily dismisses a Crown servant without needing to show any cause, it does so in the exercise of a right conferred upon it as employer under the contract of employment which it has entered into with the servant.[130]

For the Chief Justice, the above language gave 'a clear indication of the legal relationship that exists between the Crown and Mrs King: She is a public officer under a contract of employment, and if dismissibility of the Crown's servants at pleasure is based upon an implied term in their contacts of employment, it would seem logically to follow that this too is the legal basis supporting the Crown's power to vary her emoluments at will. In my view, the plaintiff is employed by the Crown under a contract of employment subject to an implied term which enables her emoluments to be varied by the Crown unilaterally.' So then, the critical question for the Chief Justice was whether the 1991 Act validly effected such a variation.

Justice Husbands, in response, conceded that, prior to independence, 'appointments to public offices were to be at pleasure.' However, on his reading of the constitutional developments of Barbados from its status defined in Letters Patent dated June 4, 1914 to the Barbados Independence Order, 1966 (the Independence Constitution of Barbados) which revoked the Barbados (Letters Patent Consolidation) Order 1964, 'and by so doing revoked any power remaining in the Governor to terminate at pleasure appointment in the public service,' Justice Husbands came to the view that 'No such power was re-enacted and given to the Governor-General, or transferred to the Services Commissions by the Constitution.' On this view, therefore, he held that when Barbados attained Independence in 1966, the concept of 'dismissibility at pleasure of public officers and any concomitant disability such as the Crown's power to reduce emoluments at will, which may be said to be attendant on that state, ceased to have any validity in Barbados.'[131] From this starting point, Justice Husbands was able to reason quite persuasively to the conclusion that the 1991 Act effected an unlawful taking of the plaintiff's property in contravention of the constitutional 'protection from deprivation of property' without provision for reasonable compensation.

As was earlier intimated, the objective here is not to defend Justice Husbands' holding against those of his brethren. Rather, it is to show that he shares with his brethren a common, 'received' language and, therefore, his willingness to work within the 'terms' of that language denied any attempts at broader conceptualisations appropriate to a case of such 'fundamental constitutional significance.' That is to say, his too was the 'lawyer's' narrow quest to determine the specific question whether the Crown had retained the power under the Independence Constitution to reduce the emoluments of its servants at will. Put simply, the question for Justice Husbands was to determine what powers the Crown retained, subject to the constitutional injunctions of the fundamental rights provisions.

But casting a judicial judgment in such narrow 'lawyerly' terms hardly makes possible the kinds of rhetorical moves that might free Commonwealth Caribbean jurisprudence from an uncritical dependence on the canons of English constitutional thought. Put differently, the operative premise that Barbados is a constitutional monarchy, that 'our Constitution came from Britain,' means only that, to the extent that we have made it our own, we have merely accepted it as our fundamental rule of governance, but have not, in our interpretive readings, succeeded in giving to it a 'local habitation and a name.'

The *Ophelia King* case implicates deeper issues of constitutional fundamentals particularly appropriate to a Caribbean jurisprudence. For example, the question of Barbados' status as a 'monarchy' is itself a question of constitutional fundamentals, for it is on this authoritative premise that much of constitutional interpretation proceeds. This issue, therefore, cannot be assumed away; it must be explained. But no judge would likely assume the competence to challenge that premise, since he or she understands his or her office as a 'servant' of the Crown. So Justice Husbands, like his brethren, showed no inclination to conduct his inquiry within the terms of the broader normative theory of contemporary republican constitutionalism. That is to say, there was a failure to grasp the salient fact that the case had put in high relief the fundamental issue of the nature of constitutional adjudication in a republican democratic polity.

It is submitted that the fundamental aim of constitutional adjudication, in seeking to render justice in each case, is to the ultimate good of the society. Constitutional adjudication is therefore a critical moment in the realisation of the constitution in the life of the community. It is an interpretive, theoretic procedure by which the character of the constitution, and of the political society it means to recommend or cast forward into the world, is continually defined. For, our written constitution denotes by its own textual composition another structure, an analogous referent, the polity that it purports to bring into being and define continuously. And one issue that is central to this definition of the character of our political community is that of the relationship between the citizen and the state. The issue, therefore, of the relationship between the citizen and the (British) Crown is obfuscating and misdirects the inquiry away from matters of fundamentals: the character of our constitution and of the political order.

It also bears repeating that constitutional adjudication is a rhetorical institutional practice by which a society gives meaning to its central terms of value; to its criteria for judgment; to what it considers just and unjust. In a word, constitutional adjudication is an institution by which community is defined. It gives credence to rhetoric's claim to be the central art by which community is established and maintained. For Gorgias, in Plato's dialogue, rhetoric, as the art of persuasion, is primarily concerned with persuasion about matters of justice and injustice in the public places of the state. It is in this sense that it is argued that the most central question of constitutive rhetoric engaged in constitutional adjudication is the question of what kind of community we should wish enduringly to be; and around what values our community should be organised; and what ambitions we hold for ourselves and our posterity.

It has been established thus far that we have appropriated the language of monarchy as our way of imagining our world and for the determination of constitutional issues involving the citizen and the state. It bears emphasis that the discourse of constitutional monarchy establishes the conventional ways of characterizing facts, stating values, and articulating criteria of judgment. It is the language that our judges understand they must use and they will demand of it that it speak to each situation, each case, in a way they can respect: it is the language in which the representatives of both the citizen and the state can carry on intelligible argument about the transaction that they share, and in which, so far as is possible, justice is done to the legitimate claims and expectations of both sides. In fine, then, the making of such a language of adjudication, setting the terms in which conversation will proceed, is one way in which constitutional adjudication contributes to the definition and to the education of a national community.[132]

Put differently, both sides to the dispute must find in that language an expression or recognition of what they regard as their important and legitimate concerns. And to the extent that this is so, constitutional discourse functions as an important force of social definition and cohesion, placing the individual citizen and the official in a comprehensible public world in ways that each can respect. But to the extent that the individual citizen faces a public world defined by a language he cannot speak, in which he cannot locate himself because he finds it alienating, and which does not deal in intelligible ways with claims he regards as important, then constitutional discourse becomes exclusive and authoritarian in character, denying the significance of his experience and silencing his attempts to express its meaning.[133]

Sadly, our 'monarchical' language has revealed itself to be woefully inadequate for grasping the deeper philosophic issues at the heart of the *Ophelia King* case; issues which, in their proper resolution, would lead us to a more adequate conception of our political community. Therefore, one of the reasons this case is so attractive for a disquisition on Commonwealth Caribbean constitutional discourse is that it raises one of the central challenges for Commonwealth Caribbean constitutional theory: namely, the possibility of articulating a coherent understanding of constitutional problems in terms of some overarching conception of a just community, or giving universal principles a local application. Otherwise put, the case raises special problems of distributive justice, problems concerning the specification of those moral principles that can provide the foundation for a just society, and also mediate the allocation or distribution of benefits and burdens among members of the society. For example, a particular distribution informed by a Kantian, non-instrumental notion of personhood achieves its immanent intelligibility in the fact that political authority has given due regard to the moral equality of those who must share in the distribution.[134] As Professor Ernest Weinrib reminds us,

> legislative and administrative action can legitimately be made to respect the conceptual contours of personhood and equality that underlie the ordering of distributions ... Personhood and equality are the presuppositions that make distributive justice conceivable ... Bereft of the principles that give them order from within, distributions would be internally indistinguishable from haphazard dispersions.[135]

Distributive justice is primarily a political, not an individual moral issue.[136] But distributive justice can never be without moral concerns since it requires some normative, adjudicative criterion or principle in terms of which the state makes distributions in society. This is the powerful insight of Rawls' work that *prima facie* cases of distributive justice may be seen in principle as problems of fairness in the distribution of costs and benefits of collective action.[137] It means, then, that the instrumentalism of extrinsic purpose entailed in every distribution, or in every governmental assessment of the legislative mandate to make laws for the peace, order and good governance of the society, must be constrained by substantive principles of justice, fairness, and equality.[138]

The *Ophelia King* case addresses a crucial constitutional question regarding the extent to which the legislature is permitted to impair private property rights. The issue was compounded by the fact that the people directly affected by the legislation in question were civil servants – government employees. Questions such as whether the plaintiff, Mrs. King, enjoyed by her employment a contractual relationship with the 'Crown', or whether she had a vested property right in her employment, are really the surface issues that mask deeper philosophical issues, *viz.*, the substantive moral principles in terms of which the constitution may be defined and the conception of person entailed and, therefore, the appropriate interpretive theory for reading the constitutional text. For example, it would seem inevitable that some utilitarian thinking - the maximization of the net social welfare - would have informed legislative deliberations on the matter in question, given that the Barbados Government was in fact responding to certain IMF (International Monetary Fund) demands to take corrective measures to address the prevailing economic crisis. But this fact only forces the critical question: whether, notwithstanding the alleged economic crisis, the Government may legitimately force some citizens alone to bear burdens which in all fairness and justice, should be borne by the public as a whole.[139] For economic crisis notwithstanding, government and policy makers are still morally enjoined in a constitutional democracy by the Kantian categorical imperative not to 'conceive of their fellow citizens as merely means to the larger end of maximizing social utility, but are instead to treat them as ends in themselves.'[140]

Thus the fundamental question of how citizens are treated in the distribution of benefits and burdens is engaged; and in constitutional adjudication, judges may reinforce the citizens' claims of personhood and equality by raising a 'sobering second thought' about legislative action and give due regard, say, to the importance of certain forms of property to the individuals' self-hood and human flourishing.[141] For, in life we form individual and communal attachments; and one instantiation of such attachments is the 'crystallization of one's expectations around certain "things", the loss of which causes more disruption and disorientation than does a simple decrease in aggregate wealth.'[142] In this regard, a unilateral governmental taking of a property interest, so indispensable to someone's well-being, could not possibly be effected without resultant 'psychological shock, emotional protest, and symbolic threat to all property and security.'[143] A right-claim to income entails a right-claim to security – that is, to immunity from its expropriation.[144] This is not to say that the right is absolute; rather, that the government is morally enjoined to offer a justification whenever it acts in a manner that adversely affects such property.[145] It is hoped that the foregoing discussion suffices to underscore the claim made throughout this work: that the constitution functions in large measure as the rhetorical framework in terms of which we fashion our collective identity as a moral and political community; that the political authority of the constitution reinforces its rhetorical force in the realisation of community. This view is especially borne out in adjudication on fundamental and human rights.

In sum, then, in a case so obviously instinct with invocations of political identity, a regional supreme court, as the 'resident philosopher of our constitution,' and conscious of its defining role in specifying and protecting the fundamental rights of the citizen in a constitutional democracy, would indeed address the government's – not the Crown's – authority to cut the salaries of its employees at will, without provisions for reasonable compensation, within the broader normative terms of contemporary constitutional theory, rather than within the terms of the canonical tradition of English jurisprudence; and, in so doing, render a decision consistent with our best conception of political identity. For the constitution is presumed to have normative authority for everyone, particularly judges, given their central office of interpretation and application. Therefore, the task of a hermeneutic understanding of the constitution is simply to help transmit the content of its normative claims. In this view, hermeneutics has a largely pedagogical task: it is supposed to exhibit the truth that inheres in a given claim so that its audience can understand and learn from it.[146] Moreover, constitutional adjudication is itself a normative or justificatory enterprise that articulates the fundamental moral and political values embedded in the constitutional text and practice.

But the fact that the Barbados High Court and Court of Appeal judgments in *Ophelia King* are judgments of local judges, and not those of members of the British Privy Council, should give us pause. It does raise in a very serious way the question as to any possible changes that might be wrought by a regional supreme court. Put simply, the argument is that a regional supreme court, in place of the Privy Council, would hardly affect the direction of Commonwealth Caribbean jurisprudence since, as the (local) judgments in *Ophelia King* show, Caribbean judges would, more likely than not, decide cases very much the way the Privy Council would. As a reading of local judgments would show, there is the disposition to follow closely the authoritative declarations of the Privy Council; to act under an obligation of fidelity to those pronouncements. After all, the Privy Council is the highest appellate court for the entire Commonwealth Caribbean (Guyana excepted), therefore, we are legally and conceptually bound by its pronouncements - even those that do not directly pertain to us. It could be said then, that the Barbados judges in *Ophelia King's* case were legally and conceptually constrained to render judgments within the structure of thought available to the Privy Council, to which they are subordinate.

The problem here, then, is one of any possible continuing hold of prior Privy Council decisions on the mind of a regional supreme court. Given the need for consistency in judicial decision making, and the important values of stability and certainty in law, what sort of respect should a regional supreme court pay to prior decisions of the Privy Council? In other words, given that Privy Council decisions explicating Commonwealth Caribbean constitutions are now part of our constitutional law, how, henceforth, are we to read the precedents established by the Privy Council?

Reading Precedent

Simply put, the doctrine of precedent, or *stare decisis*, requires courts to follow earlier judicial decisions on matters of law.[147] That is to say, the doctrine makes a court's determinations of law in one lawsuit binding on all other courts of equal or inferior rank within the first court's jurisdiction, even if the lawsuits and the parties in the subsequent cases are completely distinct from the lawsuit and the parties in the precedent case.[148] The doctrine of precedent, or principle of *stare decisis*, as Professor Larry Alexander puts it, is one of several doctrines of repose – that is, doctrines for settling issues with finality.[149] On this view, the doctrine of precedent serves as a critical component of the rule of law.[150] It ensures that courts will decide cases on the basis of public and predictable rules, applied in an evenhanded manner, and upon which people can rely in the conduct of their lives.[151] This means that the doctrine of precedent serves the important values of stability, consistency, and fairness in the law. In the area of constitutional adjudication this is of overriding importance since the constitution or constitutional law is foundational of all other law. As Professor Henry Paul Monaghan puts it, in constitutional adjudication, 'adherence to precedent can contribute to the important notion that the law is impersonal in character, that the Court believes itself to be following a "law which binds [it] as well as the litigants."'[152] The principle of *stare decisis* thus helps to ensure that our constitutional order retains the kind of stability and continuity that are prerequisite for institutional legitimacy.[153] Put differently, interpretation of the constitution must be constrained by the values of the rule of law, which means to say that courts must construe it through a process of reasoning that is replicable, that remains fairly stable, and that is consistently applied.[154] Without such consistency and stability, it would be difficult to understand the constitution as having any existence as law.[155]

In Commonwealth Caribbean adjudicative practice, the principle of *stare decisis* has always been an essential aspect of the rule of law. In constitutional adjudication, Caribbean courts look to the judicial precedents of the Privy Council at least as much as to the language of the constitutions; for the Privy Council cases interpreting Commonwealth Caribbean constitutions are themselves entitled to virtually conclusive authority on the question of their meaning. One might assume that, over the years, the Privy Council has decided a chain of cases elaborating in a consistent way a particular reading of our constitutional texts. It means, then, that a critical question for a regional supreme court is not what the constitutions mean, standing alone, but rather what they should be taken to mean given their interpretive history.[156] Thus, in addition to the specific question of the continuing authoritativeness of prior Privy Council decisions on the mind of a regional supreme court, the question of the way these decisions should be read; how they should be interpreted as single texts; and, even more importantly, how a set of opinions, decided over time by a foreign tribunal, should be interpreted, becomes critical. When, for example, should they be overruled or, better yet, disregarded? Such a critical question could only be adequately answered within a broader hermeneutic theory of adjudication.

As was earlier intimated, a regional supreme court, conscious of its defining role in the framing of our constitutional identity, in the absence of monarchy, must, of necessity, re-make a language of adjudication that would lend rhetorical coherence to our public life. And the language in which this is to be done must be much more than a technical or professional language, to be evaluated by its clarity, precision and efficiency. No, it is to be a social and intellectual force of enormous significance, an expression of value and attitude that would in some ways be far more important to the quality of the community it defines than the particular decisions taken under it.[157] For, a *constitutional* language is itself a way of constituting and thinking about the world, a way of defining relations among citizens and between the citizen and the state; in a word, a way of defining community. If, therefore, we were to consider the reading of constitutional texts as an exemplification of constitutive rhetoric, then the task of a regional supreme court is not simply to declare results: to decide particular cases and to publish the decisions in forms that will translate into rules that can be followed.[158] Rather, it is to decide constitutional cases in a way that would bring to the fore the normative values embedded in our constitutional texts and practices; in short, the values that would define our political society as a community of principle: one of justice and fairness.

It is submitted that the central excellence of the judicial mind is an excellence in the art of composition by which the construction of community is achieved. Law, we have said, is at its heart an interpretive and compositional, and in this sense radically literary, activity.[159] The adjudicative task of a regional supreme court must necessarily encompass an interpretive understanding of our constitutional texts, the history of their enactment, prior decisions of the Privy Council interpreting them, and the longstanding traditions of our political culture.[160] Or, we might rather say, a regional supreme court would now affect to read our constitutional texts in a fresh light, on the basis of a rational reconstruction of the historical and political circumstances and tradition out of which they have emerged. For this tradition must be read and we bear ethical responsibility for the way we choose to read it, and hence construct it.[161] Thus, as one author has surmised:

> The task of the judge is to engage with the traditions of the law and of our country in a responsive and responsible way; to defer in all reasonable ways to the judgments of others; to educate, and thus transform, his own mind by full consideration of what others have said and done; and, in a case which calls for it, to make his judgment whether the State has interfered with a liberty defined by that tradition.[162]

It is submitted that the typical *West Indian Independence Constitution*, with its entrenched Bill of Rights, is a normative text; in Jeffrie Murphy's elegant phrase: 'a document of moral principle.'[163] It must therefore be read in a manner consistent with its nature as such, in order to transmit the content of its normative claims. In other words, the *West Indian Independence Constitution* must be subjected to the kind of *moral* reading, such as that advanced by Professor Ronald Dworkin of the US Constitution;[164] a reading that gives expression to the fundamental moral and political values embedded in the constitutional text and practice. As Professor Dworkin reasons, the Bill of Rights must be understood as setting out general moral principles about liberty and equality and dignity, and that private citizens, lawyers, and finally judges must interpret and apply those general principles by posing and trying to answer more concrete moral questions: for example, whether capital punishment by hanging is cruel and inhuman and degrading punishment and other treatment, contrary to certain constitutional prescriptions; whether a delay of five years or more in the execution of a condemned person is unconstitutional; whether it comports with the fundamental rights of due process and the equal protection of the law to cut the salaries of government employees at will, without provisions for reasonable compensation.

According to a moral reading, the clauses of a constitutional Bill of Rights must be understood in the way their language most naturally suggests: they refer to abstract moral principles and incorporate these by reference, as limits on governmental power.[165] Judges are therefore required to make fresh moral judgments when they decide important constitutional cases that turn on deep issues of political morality. But such a reading, Professor Dworkin insists, is constrained by the requirement of constitutional integrity. That is to say, judges must read the abstract moral clauses consistent in principle with the structural design of the constitution as a whole, and also with the dominant lines of past constitutional interpretation.[166] In other words, they must regard themselves as partners with other officials, past and future, who together elaborate a coherent constitutional morality, and they must take care to see that what they contribute fits with the rest.[167] In a word, judges must decide cases in a way that fits constitutional language, precedent, and practice.

Another way of putting the above argument is to say that constitutional adjudication is a system of meaning, which has at its heart a way of telling a complex story about our world. Each judge must therefore tell the story in a way that expresses the most appealing conception of our constitution and of the character of our political society. This critical hermeneutical procedure Dworkin describes as 'constructive interpretation', one that makes the rationality of the interpretive process explicit by referring to a paradigm of 'purpose.'[168]

> Constructive interpretation is a matter of imposing purpose on an object or practice in order to make it the best possible example of the form or genre to which it is

taken to belong .... We would say that all interpretation strives to make an object the best it can be, as an instance of some assumed enterprise, and that interpretation takes different forms in different contexts only because different enterprises engage different standards of value or success.[169]

But an adequate theory of adjudication must simultaneously satisfy the principle of legal certainty and consistency and the legitimacy claim of law, in face of the possibility that past practices or decisions may sometimes reveal a misunderstanding of the moral principle underlying a particular constitutional provision. This is an especially critical issue facing a regional supreme court for, indeed, much of the past decisions of the Privy Council may have to be rewritten. That is to say, the story to be told in adjudication may now be offered as a corrective to certain past decisions of the Privy Council.

In a word, then, we are back to the critical question of construing precedent. Clearly, it is not enough to follow precedent on the claims of a requirement of articulate consistency and legal certainty, for precedent must be validated or justified by a scheme of moral principle, in terms of which the legal system as a whole is ultimately justified.[170] In other words, in the 'hard case', a court's decision is not justified if it cannot be shown to be consistent with the demands of moral principle. Fortunately, in a constitutional democracy, this does not require the court's stepping outside of law for, here, the moral content of constitutional rights and principles is explained by the fact that the basic norms of both law and morality substantively intersect.[171] On this view, law as integrity insists that judges enforce the constitution through interpretation, meaning that their decisions must fit constitutional practice, not ignore it.[172] This idea, to repeat, emerges from a normative self-understanding of constitutional orders and penetrates the political reality of constitutionally structured processes.[173] 'The judge's obligation to decide the individual case in the light of a theory that justifies law as a whole on a principled basis reflects a *prior* obligation of citizens, one attested to by the act of founding the constitution: an obligation to maintain the integrity of a life in common by following principles of justice and respecting one another as members of an association of free and equal persons.'[174]

But integrity does not require consistency in principle over all historical stages of a community's law; rather, it requires that quality of argument for a decision that might explain why past decisions may have been misconceived. This, to repeat, could only be done in terms of some set of fundamental principles of political morality – principles that must justify the standing as well as the content of these past decisions.[175] In other words, law as integrity aims to justify past decisions in an overall story about our constitutional world – a story worth telling because it shows that our constitutional order and present practice can be organized by and justified in terms of principles of moral measure.

So, judicial judgments must satisfy simultaneously the conditions of *consistent decision making* and *rational acceptability*:

> On the one hand, the principle of legal certainty demands decisions that can be consistently rendered within the framework of the existing legal order. An existing legal order is the product of an opaque web of past decisions by the legislature and the judiciary and it can include traditions of customary law as well. This institutional history of law forms the background of every present-day practice of decision making.[176]

And,

> On the other hand, the claim to legitimacy requires decisions that are not only consistent with the treatment of

similar cases in the past and in accord with the existing legal system. They are also supposed to be rationally grounded in the matter at issue so that all participants can accept them as rational decisions. That is to say, these decisions claim validity in the light of rules and principles that are accepted as legitimate....As in the case with laws, court decisions, too, are "creatures of both history and morality": what an individual is entitled to have, in civil society, depends on both the practice and the justice of its political institutions.[177]

An interpretive judgment is, at bottom, a discriminating judgment that does not merely repeat past judgments in the name of consistency. Rather, it is a judgment that reads the constitutional text, practice, and the nations's political culture and traditions in terms of an articulated public conception of justice that the citizens of a democratic society, as free and equals, have in principle accepted. Such a judgment ultimately reconciles history with justice. It dissolves the tension between judicial originality and institutional history, for example, on the view that judges are required to make fresh judgments about the rights of the parties who come before them on the basis of a rational reconstruction of that institutional history, which may reveal some part of that history as mistaken.

Put differently, the fact that a particular way of reading an important constitutional provision has been followed in past cases will not necessarily provide a strong argument for its place in the best interpretation of the constitution.[178] For the argument from stability and certainty *in the law* is quite independent of any particular view about the justice or fairness of past decisions. In other words, the argument from stability, when taken as an argument of political morality, makes the claim that a political community with a written constitution will be better in the long run;

that it will be a fairer and more just and otherwise a more successful community, if it secures stability by making the correct interpretation of the constitution depend on following past decisions, no matter how wrong these might be, rather than on fresh, contemporary interpretive decisions that may contradict these.[179] But, certainly, this argument cannot be tenable in every area of constitutional law – certainly not in the area of fundamental rights adjudication. For, after all, fundamental rights are matters of principle: they are principles of political morality. Therefore, in taking account of a past line of cases interpreting the fundamental rights provisions of the constitution, a court must construct as attractive a political/moral theory as it possibly can that would justify these past decisions as correct – and, therefore, the decisions it has an institutional obligation to follow.[180] In so doing, contemporary interpretation may reveal the past interpretation to be incorrect. The principle of *stare decisis* therefore allows that, in the appropriate circumstances, courts may treat precedents as an amorphous mass of material to be rendered consistent through the virtue of 'integrity', rather than the source of specific and binding formal rules to be followed.[181]

The point of the foregoing argument may be illustrated by briefly recurring to the Privy Council judgment in the *Ophelia King* case. In that case, as earlier noted, the Privy Council decided that the Barbados Government's decision to cut the salaries of civil servants, without provision for reasonable compensation, was lawful on the authority of a 1949 statute, saved under section 26 of the Constitution. Now, the 1949 statute was enacted at a time when Barbados was still a colony of Britain and the 'Crown' was not yet subject to the injunctions of a constitutional Bill of Rights. It means, then, that the 'Crown,' unconstrained by an entrenched Bill of Rights, was free to determine the terms and conditions of the employment of its 'servants' at will. Indeed, the 1949 statute did just that: it reposed in the

Minister of the Crown the power to vary the emoluments of civil servants at will. In a word, the power of the Crown in pre-independence Barbados was virtually arbitrary.

In *Ophelia King*, the constitutional validity of the 1949 statute was never in issue, for section 26 of the Barbados Constitution, referring to prior law, declares that 'Nothing contained in or done under the authority of any written law shall be held to be inconsistent with or in contravention of any provision of sections 12 to 23 (the fundamental rights provisions).' On this view, section 26 occasions a contradiction within the constitutional text. Thus, from the standpoint of integrity the Constitution contains two contradictory provisions, 'each of which is coherent in itself, but which cannot be defended together as expressing a coherent ranking of different principles of justice or fairness or procedural due process.'[182]

But this contradiction must be resolved in interpretation. On a hermeneutic understanding of the Constitution, the judge must take account of its normative authority and help transmit the content of its normative claims by interpreting it in a way that would make it as just as it might possibly be. In the instant case, ordinary law, saved by section 26, is in conflict with the Constitution. But in understanding a law that is still in force, the judge must be aware of the tension between past and present.[183] He must be aware of the change in circumstances and, conscious of this change, determine how the law is to be presently understood and applied.[184] In other words, in determining what the law now means, the judge must take account of its original meaning. If nothing has changed since the law's enactment, then to understand its present meaning is also to understand its historical meaning. But in the absence of an unaltered continuity, the judge, faithful to the normative authority of the Constitution, would determine how the law is to be presently understood and applied based on a rationally reconstructed history of existing law that coheres best with the normative claims of the Constitution. By reason of the very normative demands of the office, a judge cannot afford the luxury of relegating justice to history.[185] Rather, history and justice must be reconciled. A regional supreme court would therefore be ill advised to follow the Privy Council's ruling in *Ophelia King*; for that decision has revealed the absence of any critical reconstruction of the history of existing law that would have brought to light the dissonance between an ordinary law and the Constitution. Indeed, an adequate interpretation of the 1949 statute must be based on a background understanding of the critical importance of political independence, of a written constitution with an entrenched Bill of Rights, and of the deontological character of the fundamental rights stated therein.

The Neville Lewis Case

The point is further made by the very interesting debate between the majority and dissenting judgments of the Privy Council in the recent case of *Neville Lewis v. The Attorney General of Jamaica*.[186] In this case, the Board was asked to consider, among other things, (a) whether on a petition for mercy (after all domestic attempts to set aside the convictions or to prevent execution have been exhausted) the petitioners are entitled to know what material the Jamaican Privy Council had before it and to make representations as to why mercy should be granted and (b) whether they have a right not to be executed before the Inter-American Commission on Human Rights or the United Nations Human Rights Committee has finally reported on their petitions. At a more abstract level, the issue was whether the proceedings before the Jamaican (or local) Privy Council might be the subject for judicial review. The Board, through Lord Slynn of Hadley, answered the question in the affirmative, but Lord Hoffman dissented, largely on the view that the issue had already been decided in the negative in *Reckley v. Minister of Public Safety and Immigration No. 2*,[187] when the Board then decided not to depart from its earlier decision in *de Freitas v. Benny*.[188] Also, the Inter-American issue was decided in the negative in *Fisher v. Minister of Public Safety and Immigration No. 2*.[189] In essence, Lord Hoffman could see no justification for the Board's departing from its recent past decisions given that 'the concept of the rule of law underlying [the Jamaica] Constitution requires such continuity over time that a respect for precedent is, by definition, indispensable.'[190] In a word, with the Board's decision in the instant case, 'the rule of law itself will be damaged and there will be no stability in the administration of justice in the Caribbean.'[191] Issue is therefore joined on the question of the proper understanding of the role of the doctrine of precedent in fundamental rights adjudication.

The fundamental constitutional right entailed in the instant case is that of 'due process of law', otherwise referred to in Commonwealth Caribbean constitutional law as the right to 'the protection of the law'. This right was given an interpretation in the precedent cases of *de Freitas v. Benny* and *Reckley No. 2*, which presumed that the prerogative of mercy is an act of grace and clearly not a legal entitlement; therefore, the procedures by which the State affects to exercise this prerogative could not be the subject of judicial scrutiny.

It is indeed the case that, in the Christian tradition, for example, mercy is a free gift, an act of grace, something that cannot be merited. As the late Jean Hampton puts it, 'to be treated mercifully is to get a gift which we cannot merit, but which arises out of a regard for us that is not contingent on our displaying virtue.'[192] On this view, 'mercy is never owed to anyone as a right or a matter of desert or justice. It always therefore transcends the realm of strict moral obligation and is best viewed as a free gift – an act of grace, love, or compassion that is beyond the claims of right, duty, and obligation.'[193]

But this, notwithstanding, the State's moral and political obligation to treat its citizens with equal concern and respect enjoins it, whenever it dispenses mercy – particularly in the area of capital punishment – to honour its constitutional obligation in a manner comporting with standards of procedural fairness. Thus, whereas the condemned person may not be entitled to mercy as a matter of right, he is nonetheless entitled to be treated with the respect that is owed him as a responsible moral agent; in a word, to be treated with equal respect and concern in the distribution of the 'gift' of mercy. For as the philosopher Kant reminds us,

> The right to pardon a criminal, either by mitigating or by entirely remitting the punishment, is certainly the most slippery of all the rights [powers] of the sovereign. By exercising it he can demonstrate the splendor of his majesty and yet thereby wreak injustice to a high degree.[194]

It means, then, that when the constitutionalist State affects to dispense the 'gift' of mercy, through its Chief Executive Office – the Governor General or the President, say, – or any other office, for that matter, this cannot be viewed as a matter of personal grace to be dispensed willy-nilly at his or her discretion. Rather, that office is subject to the same constitutional and moral injunctions as any other institution of the State, regarding the distribution of benefits and burdens. And given that, in the instant case, the subject of the State's *largesse* is a matter of life and death, compliance with the constitutional injunctions becomes even more compelling. As Justice Holmes has remarked:

> A pardon in our days is not a private act of grace from an individual happening to possess power. It is a part of the constitutional scheme. When granted, it is the determination of the ultimate authority that the public welfare will be better served by inflicting less than what the judgment

fixed.[195]

So we are back to the issue of the correct interpretation of the constitutional right of due process in respect of the State's dispensation of the 'gift' of mercy. We regard the precedent interpretation to be in error because it denies the full moral import of the due process right. As the American philosopher T.M. Scanlon advises, claims to due process are grounded in principles of political morality.[196] Thus citizens always have moral claims against institutions to whose jurisdiction they are subject, and whose decisions are binding on them. An important political institution wielding significant power over the lives of citizens is enjoined to exercise that authority in a manner that respects the moral worth of every individual. Thus, the way in which the rights and powers which give some people a measure of control over the lives of others are constituted and established, and ultimately exercised, is one of the features of social institutions that is most subject to moral criticism and most in need of justification.[197] The authority of a judge or a head of state to decide whether a person lives or dies must always be exercised in accordance with the strictest moral requirements of due process. Failing this, suspicion would always remain that such power may be exercised in unjustifiable ways.[198]

On the strength of this argument, therefore, stability and consistency in the law, which in the instant case translates into the Commonwealth Caribbean states' reliance on the precedent cases, can never be the compelling moral warrant for continuing the 'mistake' and deny to condemned persons their constitutional and moral rights. And in any event, the crucial stability here is that the system of fundamental rights be interpreted, so far as possible, as expressing a coherent vision of justice[199] – which may sometimes mean correcting past mistakes. In the instant case, punctilious observance of the due process claims of the condemned person demands that the local Privy Council or Mercy Committee consider every conceivable bit of evidence, such as the reports of International Human Rights Bodies that may weigh in the petitioner's favour, and that the petitioner be afforded the opportunity to know what material the Mercy Committee had before it and to make representations as to why mercy should be granted.

The CCJ and the Future of Capital Punishment in the Commonwealth Caribbean

On no other issue would the strength of arguments for a Caribbean Court of Appeal be more tested than on the question of capital punishment - specifically, the issue of capital punishment by hanging. This is arguably the most controversial issue facing Commonwealth Caribbean society today and, as was earlier intimated, it is on this very issue that many of our political leaders, jurists *et al* have staked their claim for the abolition of appeals to the Privy Council and the establishment of a regional supreme court of final appeal.

The controversy over this issue, has been compounded by recent decisions of the Judicial Committee of the Privy Council in the Jamaica case of *Pratt and Morgan* v. *Attorney-General and Others*,[200] the Trinidad case of *Guerra* v. *Baptiste and Others*[201] and the Bahamian case of *Hensfield* and *Farrington* v. *Attorney General of the Bahamas and Others*,[202] all of which recognise that capital punishment is permitted by our Constitutions but hold that such punishment is cruel, inhuman and degrading punishment and treatment if there is unreasonable delay in carrying out executions after conviction. Indeed, the Privy Council's ruling in the landmark case of *Pratt and Morgan* has been recently applied in the High Court of Barbados in a case involving two condemned murderers, Lester Leroy Harewood and Vincent Murrell. Their death sentences were commuted to life imprisonment, and Mr. Justice Garvey Husbands, in his ruling, intoned that 'I have no doubt that to execute the applicants after such a lapse of time [4½ to 5 years] would constitute inhuman or degrading punishment in contravention of section 15 of the Barbados Constitution.'[203]

Specifically, the Privy Council rulings in the Jamaica and Trinidad and Tobago cases have occasioned urgent pleas from Prime Minister Patterson of Jamaica, and Prime Minister Manning of Trinidad and Tobago for the abolition of appeals to the English Privy Council and for the establishment of a Caribbean court of final appeal. So the strong opposition to the Privy Council decisions in *Pratt and Morgan* and its progeny seems to be virtually the sole predicate on which the advocates for a Caribbean Court of Appeal would rest their case. As a former Attorney General of Barbados, Mr. Maurice King, QC, puts it, the argument for the establishment of a Caribbean Supreme Court as our final Court of Appeal in place of the Privy Council is advanced in the context of a widely-held perception that a very high percentage of Barbadians and of other Caribbean people strongly support capital punishment for persons convicted of murder and severe corporal punishment for persons convicted of perpetrating other forms of violent crime.[204] 'The argument is premised on the assumption that a Caribbean Supreme Court would inevitably and of necessity reject and reverse the jurisprudence of the Privy Council in determining issues of what amounts to cruel and inhuman and degrading punishment and treatment. It is premised too on the assumption that the judges of a Caribbean Supreme Court would determine such issues by reference only to local views and without reference to international human rights norms and standards as agreed on by the international community.'[205] Unfortunately, these urgent pleas for a Caribbean court of final appeal, coming as they have in the wake of certain Privy Council rulings to which there is strong opposition, have in fact furnished the grounds for the critics' telling riposte that we wish to fashion a court to do our bidding.

Certainly, the most important, and the most controversial, of recent Privy Council decisions on capital punishment in the Commonwealth Caribbean is the Jamaican case of *Pratt and Morgan*, in which the Board has held that prolonged delay in carrying out a sentence of death could amount to 'inhuman and degrading punishment or other treatment' within the meaning of the prohibition against such punishment or treatment contained in the Jamaican Constitution.[206] By this decision the Privy Council has in fact overruled its previous majority decision in *Riley and Ors* v. *Attorney-General of Jamaica*,[207] in which it was held that delay (in and of itself) could never render execution by hanging unconstitutional. It should be noted that section 17(2) of the Jamaican Constitution preserves from challenge under the Constitution any description of punishment which was lawful in Jamaica before Independence; thus, the majority held that section 17(2) operated to save from challenge the carrying out of a death sentence, regardless of the extent of the delay that occurred between sentence and execution.

With the *Pratt and Morgan* decision, however, it means that a delay in the execution of a condemned prisoner of approximately five years and more is 'inhuman and degrading punishment and other treatment,' but hanging per se is immune from attack on the ground that it is 'inhuman and degrading punishment.' Put simply, the Constitutions of the region prescribe punishment by hanging for certain capital offences; therefore, execution by hanging is rendered immune from attack as being 'inhuman or degrading punishment.' However, a delay of approximately five years or more in carrying out a death sentence by hanging may constitute 'inhuman and degrading punishment or other treatment'.

Truth is, *Pratt and Morgan* may not have been that controversial, if the case were confined to its facts. Following a recitation of the facts, the Privy Council, in ruling that the appellants' sentences should be commuted to life imprisonment, observed that 'The statement of these bare facts is sufficient to bring home to the mind of any person of normal sensibility and compassion the agony of mind that these men must have suffered between hope and despair in the 14 years they have been in prison facing the gallows.'[208]

One may concede, without need of further argument, that the situation in *Pratt and Morgan* was particularly horrendous; therefore, the Board was justified in its conclusion. However, it is its further ruling that a mere delay of approximately five years between sentencing and hanging of the condemned that has brought Caribbean constitutional jurisprudence to a rather absurd 'turn in the road.' For what is entailed in hanging a human being can never be defended on moral principle. This confusion, however, could be adequately addressed by a Caribbean Court of Appeal advancing a theory of law and adjudication that defends a normative or moral reading of our Constitutions and laws. In other words, any possible reversal of the direction in which these Privy Council judgments have taken us must be based on a principled reading of our Constitutions, laws and institutional practice – whether by judicial decision making or the constitutional amendment process – and not on the intensity of local sentiment favouring the resumption of hanging.

It has been noted earlier that the typical *West Indian Independence Constitution*, with an entrenched Bill of Rights, is unquestionably a normative text, 'a document of moral principle.' The fundamental rights catalogued in the Bill of Rights are rights which, on a principled view of our Constitutions as higher law, legislative and national majorities are powerless to take away. In other words, considering the typical *West Indian Independence Constitution* as a principled expression in higher law of the political ideal of a people to govern itself in a certain way, we may rightfully assume that a national or legislative majority, in creating such a constitution, has in fact constrained its own quotidian legislative actions by a broader vision of justice, to be guarded by an independent judiciary.[209] For the very deontological character of these fundamental rights removes them from the contingency of arbitrary enactments or derogations and gives them a status in argumentation that allows a court to ground the premises for a moral justification of the individual decision and to challenge the correctness of the received arguments of prior decisions.[210]

Maybe no other sections of the fundamental rights provisions of West Indian constitutions are more deserving of a moral reading as those pertaining to the death penalty and to the matter of inhuman and degrading punishment and other treatment. Still, legal judgments in this area must satisfy the requirements of consistency with prior decisions and rational acceptability. But the claim to legitimacy, we have stated, requires that decisions are not only consistent with similar cases in the past; they must also be rationally grounded in the matter at issue in the light of rules and principles that are accepted as morally legitimate. This, as we have earlier intimated, makes for the possibility of 'single right' decisions being legitimated with respect to their content in light of recognised principles. On this view, a judge is never left wholly at the mercy of the historical authority of self-evident topoi.[211] Rather, in making what is inevitably a normative judgment in the ('hard') case at hand, the judge would cast a critical light on the historically proven topoi of a received ethos and justify and explain a choice whether to follow, revise and correct prior arguments in the light of moral principles already embedded in the constitutional text and in the legal system as a whole.[211a]

In fine, then, it is on a deontological conception of fundamental rights that judicial decision making may simultaneously satisfy the twin requirements of legal consistency and rational acceptability. If, therefore, future decisions on the issue of inhuman and degrading punishment are to satisfy the condition of rational acceptability, so that all participants can accept them as rationally correct decisions, then they must explain how the execution of the condemned by hanging comports with moral principles about human dignity, political decency and justice; and how the delay of approximately five years in the execution of the condemned by hanging is so obviously cruel that it amounts to inhuman and degrading treatment in violation of the same moral principles about human dignity, political decency and justice.

Conclusion

It has been earlier noted that a moral reading of the constitutions, laws, and institutional practice may reveal that past practices or decisions were based on a misunderstanding of the moral principle underlying a particular constitutional provision. The practice of capital punishment by hanging is a case in point;[212] and it has been shown that the Privy Council's decision in *Pratt and Morgan* regarding the five year delay in the hanging of the condemned is absurd. In this respect, company is joined with those who call for the abolition of appeals to the Privy Council and for the establishment of a Caribbean Court of Appeal; but there are different agendas. However faint, it is hoped that, left to stand on our own, we might rise to the occasion and render a higher quality of decisions than we have had (recently) from the Privy Council. This may sound ridiculous given the rather poor local decisions we have had recently in the *Muslimeen* case,[213] the *Ashby* case,[214] and the very *Pratt and Morgan* case, just to name a few.

These cases underscore a practical consideration militating against abolition of appeals to the Privy Council: the perceived paucity of legal talent in the region and therefore the difficulty of assembling a sufficiently qualified appellate court. Indeed, a very prominent local barrister, Mr. Angus Wilke, has wondered aloud why the Jamaican judges in *Pratt and Morgan* had so obviously failed to demonstrate the same sense of humanity and sensitivity to the agony and suspense which must have been experienced by the condemned men.[215] In a very thoughtful comment in the local press, he has ventured an opinion that we in these small Caribbean communities may be so much in the grip of fear over the dramatic rise in violent crimes that the extremity of our fear may affect our compassion and sense of common humanity. He therefore reasons that the fact that the English Privy Council is unaware of the social conditions in the region which may influence legal decisions, is not necessarily an argument in support of abolition of appeals to that body. For, 'on the contrary, the English Privy Council may, in the circumstances, be impartial and not swayed by current social and political considerations affecting the region.'[216]

Still, what is needed is not that our judges be removed from the social and political circumstances of our communal life but, rather, that they possess the quality of mind that would allow them to read local circumstances critically in coming to principled and reasoned decisions in individual cases. Remember, the case for a Caribbean Court of Appeal would ultimately come to rest on the most profound argument from sovereignty: our right of self-definition. And this could never come from the great imperial court of the British Empire but, rather, from an institution of our own making.

Endnotes

1 Ann Spackman, *Constitutional Development of the West Indies, 1922-1968* 37 (1975).

2 Richard S. Kay, 'Book Review' of *Imperial Appeal: The Debate on the Appeal to the Privy Council, 1833-1986*, in 4 *Connecticut J. of Int'l Law* 239, 248 (1988).

3 Quoted in Hugh Rawlins, 'The Privy Council or a Caribbean Final Court of Appeal?' (1996) 6 *Carib. L. Rev.* 235.

4 Quoted in Olutoye Waldron, 'No Reasons for Retaining Monarchy,' *Sunday*

Advocate, (February 23, 1997).

5 *The Throne Speech*, delivered by the Governor-General, Sir Clifford Husbands, (Tuesday February 16, 1999).

6 Note that in an attempt to bring Jamaica within the strict letter of *Pratt and Morgan*, the Jamaican Government has decided to withdraw Jamaica from the Optional Protocol to the International Convention on Civil and Political Rights. Trinidad and Tobago has threatened to follow suit in respect of those international human rights bodies of which it is a part.

7 For a very thoughtful essay addressing these issues, see Stephen Vascianne, 'The Caribbean Court of Justice: Further Reflections on the Debate,' 23 *West Indian Law Journal* 37 (1998).

8 Friedrich Carl von Savigny, *Of the Vocation of Our Age for Legislation and Jurisprudence* 28 (trans. A. Hayward, 1975).

9 John Wickham, 'People and Things,' *Daily Nation*, Wednesday, July 20, 1994.

10 Bill Ashcroft, Gabreth Griffiths, Helen Tiffin, *The Empire Writes Back: Theory and Practice in Post-Colonial Literatures* 88 (1989). For a very thoughtful comment on Naipaul's work see Ralph Jemmott, 'Naipaul's Work and the Region,' *The Barbados Advocate* (Thursday November 8, 2001). Jemmott notes that it is Naipaul's sense of our historical past of slavery, colonialism, dependency, poverty, exploitation and conflict that frames his exploratory frame of mind. However, he intones that the failure in Naipaul is the unwarranted assumption that a sense of history is a sense of irretrievable loss and that our history in the Caribbean is always to be penned in a tragic tone and expressed in a passive mood. True, societies may not fully escape their historical antecedents, but this is not to suggest that they are irrevocably tied to their organic roots in a way that Naipaul seems to suggest. 'In all history, creative forces are released that resuscitate, innovate and change direction, even in the absence of thorough-going creative revolution, as Naipaul would define it. The Caribbean, since Emancipation, has not been without its creative revolution or at least its creative evolution. Similarly, almost four decades after independence, it cannot be truly said that the post-colonial endeavour has been a failure.' In a word, then, this region, which was not established as a design for living, but rather as a commercial outpost of Empire, may yet be able to move beyond the Naipaulian vision of 'castrated hopelessness,' in order 'to control the burden of [its] history and incorporate it into our collective sense of the future.' *Ibid.*

11 Edward Kamau Brathwaite, *Islands* 5 (1969).

12 Derek Walcott, 'Royal Palms', *London Magazine*, 27 (February, 1962).

13 Professor Nettleford in a letter to me on the subject of this chapter.

14 Anne Norton, 'Transubstantiation : The Dialectic of Constitutional Authority,' 55 *Univ. of Chicago L. Rev.* 458, 459 (1988).

15 *Ibid.*

16 *Ibid.*

17 William F Harris II, *The Interpretable Constitution* 168 (1993).

18 Norton, *supra* note 14, at 470.

19 Sheldon Wolin, *The Presence of the Past* 9 (1989).

20 Norton, *supra* note 14, at 463.

21 Quoted in John Chipman Gray, 'A Realist Conception of Law,' in *Philosophy of Law* 50 (Joel Feinberg and Hyman Gross eds. 1975).

22 Norton, *supra* note 14, at 471.

23 Harris II, *supra* note 17, at 167.

24 *Ibid.*

25 Speaking about the American Supreme Court, Dean Rostow of Yale Law School has allowed that the 'Supreme Court is, among other things, an educational body, and the Justices are inevitably teachers in a vital national seminar.' See Eugene V. Rostow, 'The Democratic Character of Judicial Review,' 66 *Harv. L. Rev.* 193, 208 (1952). See also Richard Funston, *A Vital National Seminar: The Supreme Court in American Political Life* (1978); and for a recent insightful essay on this subject, see Christopher L. Eisgruber, 'Is the Supreme Court an Educative Institution?' 67 *N.Y.U. L. Rev.* 960 (1992).

26 Donald S. Lutz, *The Origins of American Constitutionalism* 3 (1988).

27 Cited in Robert C. Post, *Constitutional Domains: Democracy, Community, Management* 36 (1995).

28 Robert C. Post, 'Justice for Scalia' (a review of Justice Scalia's book, *A Matter of Interpretation : Federal Courts and the Law*, in *New York Review of Books* 46 (June 11, 1998).

29 Post, *supra* note 27, at 46.

30 Robert F. Nagel, *Judicial Power and American Character* 45 (1994).

31 Christopher L. Eisgruber, 'Is the Supreme Court an Educative Institution?' 67 *N.Y.U.L. Rev.* 960 (1992).

32 See in particular Michael A. de la Bastide, 'The Case for a Caribbean Court of Appeal,' (1995) 5 *Carib. L. Rev.* 401; and Hugh Rawlins, *supra* note 3.

33 Eisgruber, *supra* note 31, at 1010.

34 Harris II, *supra* note 17, at 4.

35 *Ibid.* 106.

36 *Ibid.* 3.

37 *Ibid.*

38 *Ibid.* 119.

39 Robert A. Ferguson, 'The Judicial Opinion as Literary Genre,' 2 *Yale J. of Law and the Humanities* 201, 202 (1990).

40 5 U.S. (1 Cranch) 137 (1803).

41 On this idea of a 'two-text polity,' see Harris, *supra* note 17.

42 Paul W. Kahn, *The Reign of Law: Marbury v. Madison and the Construction of America* 210 (1997).

43 *Ibid.*

44 *Ibid.* 207.

45 *Ibid.* 210.

46 *Ibid.* 211.

47 *Ibid.* 224.

48 *Marbury v. Madison*, 5 U.S. (1 Cranch) 137, 176-178.

49 Jed Rubenfeld, *Freedom and Time : A Theory of Constitutional Self-Government* 173 (2001).

50 *Marbury, op. cit.* at 178.

51 Rubenfeld, *op. cit.*

52 *Ibid.* 174.

53 *Ibid.* 176.

54 See Richard A. Posner, *Law and Literature: A Misunderstood Relation* 269

(1988).

55 See 'Introduction,' Richard McKeon, *Rhetoric: Essays in Invention and Discovery* (1987).

56 Chaim Perelman, *Justice, Law, and Argument: Essays on Moral and Legal Reasoning* 120 (1980).

57 *Ibid.*

58 James Boyd White, *Justice as Translation: An Essay in Cultural and Legal Criticism* 91 (1990).

59 James Boyd White, *From Expectation to Experience : Essays on Law & Legal Education ix* (1999); quoted in Gary Minda, 'Cool Jazz BUT NOT SO HOT Literary Text in *Lawyerland*: James Boyd White's Improvisations of Law as Literature', 13 *Cardozo Studies in Law and Literature* 157, 165 (2001).

60 James Boyd White, *Acts of Hope : Creating Authority in Literature, Law, and Politics* 306 (1994).

61 See Ludwig Wittgenstein, *Philosophical Investigations* (G. Anscombe trans. 3d ed. 1968).

62 Boyd White, *supra* note 59, at ix.

63 *Ibid.*

64 *Ibid.* xi.

65 *Ibid.* xiii.

66 *Ibid.*

67 *Ibid.*

68 *Ibid.* xiv.

69 *Ibid.* 23.

70 *Ibid.*

71 *Ibid.* 24.

72 Boyd White, *supra* note 61, at 154.

73 Ferguson, *supra* note 40, at 214.

74 Quoted in Ferguson, *ibid.* 215.

75 Boyd White, *supra* note 61, at 229.

76 William F. Conklin, *Images of a Constitution* 8 (1989).

77 James Boyd White, 'Judicial Criticism,' in *Interpreting Law and Literature* 394 (Sanford Levinson and Steven Mailloux eds. 1988).

78 *Ibid.* 408.

79 *Ibid.* 394.

80 Perelman, *supra* note 57, at 150.

81 *Ibid.* 151.

82 Dena Goodman, *Criticism in Action: Enlightenment Experiments in Political Writing* 3 (1989).

83 *Hinds & Ors* v. *The Queen* [1977] A.C. 195.

84 *Ibid.*

85 *Ibid.*

86 *Ibid.*

87 Joel C. Weinsheimer, *Gadamer's Hermeneutics: A Reading of Truth and Method* 136 (1985).

88 *Hinds & Ors.* v. *The Queen* [1977] A.C. 195.

89 James Tully, *Strange Multiplicity: Constitutionalism in an Age of Diversity* 34 (1995).

90 Michel Rosenfeld, 'The Identity of the Constitutional Subject,' 16 *Cardozo L. Rev.* 1049, 1062 (1995).
91 *Ibid.*
 92 *Ibid.* 1063.
 93 *Ibid.*
 94 *Ibid.*
 95 *Ibid.* 1064.
 96 Harris II, *supra* note 17, at 165.
 97 *Dred Scott* v. *Sanford* 60 U.S. (19 How.) 393 (1857).
 98 Tully, *supra* note 90, at 36.
 99 *Ibid.*
100 *Ibid.*
101 Conal Condren, *The Status and Appraisal of Classic Texts: An Essay on Political Theory, Its Inheritance and the History of Ideas* 44 (1984).
102 *Ibid.* 51.
103 Simon Gikandi, *Writing in Limbo: Modernism and Caribbean Literature* 10 (1992).
104 *Ibid.* 41.
105 *Ibid.*
106 Quoted in *ibid.* 27.
107 *Ibid.* 44.
108 Bruce Ackerman, *We The People: Foundations* 36 (1991).
109 *Jaundoo* v. *A. G. (Guyana)* [1971] A.C. 972.
110 *Gladwyn Ophelia King* v. *A. G. (Barbados)* (1992) 44 W.I.R. 52; [1994] 1 W.L.R. 1560.
111 See Margaret DeMerieux, *Fundamental Rights in Commonwealth Caribbean Constitutions* 468 (1992). It is significant to note that the Privy Council has now reversed itself on this issue. In the recent case of *Eric Matthew Gairy v. Attorney General of Grenada* (2001), the Privy Council has held that the court may issue a coercive order against the Crown, thereby reversing the OECS Court of Appeal decision which had followed *Jaundoo.* I am grateful to Nicole Sylvester for sharing this point with me.
112 *King v. A.G.* (Barbados), *supra* note 111.
113 Barbados Constitution, s.1 and 16(1): 'Section 11 of the Constitution recites that every person in Barbados is entitled to the fundamental rights and freedoms of the individual including the right, subject to respect for the rights and freedoms of others and for the public interest, to protection from deprivation of his property without compensation.' *Ibid.* 54.

'Section 16(1) enacts, *inter alia*, that no property of any description shall be compulsorily taken possession of, and no interest in or right over property of any description shall be compulsorily acquired, except by or under the authority of a written law, and where provision applying to that acquisition or taking of possession is made by written law (a) prescribing the principles on which and the manner in which compensation therefor is to be determined and given and (b) giving to any person claiming such compensation a right of access to the High Court, either directly or by way of appeal, for the determination of his or her interest in or right over, the property and the amount of compensation.' *Ibid.* at 54.

114 Emphasis added.
115 Quoted in *ibid.* 72-73.
116 *Ibid.* 73.
117 *Ibid.* 74.
118 *Ibid.*
119 F. Hinsley, *Sovereignty* 1 (2nd edn. 1986).
120 Peter J. Steinberger, *Logic and Politics : Hegel's Philosophy of Right* 214 (1988).
121 *Ibid.* 191.
122 *Ibid.*
123 *Ibid.* 214.
124 *Supra*, note 116.
125 Peter Goodrich, *Legal Discourse* 184 (1987).
126 *Ibid.*
127 *Ibid.* 185.
128 See Ezra Alleyne, 'Ophelia King's Case,' *Daily Nation*, (May 15, 1994).
129 *Endell Thomas* v. *A.G.* (*Trinidad and Tobago*) [1982] A.C. 113.
130 Quoted in Justice Husbands' dissent.
131 *Ibid.*
132 Boyd White, *supra* note 59, at 178.
133 *Ibid.*
134 See Ernest J. Weinrib, 'Legal Formalism: On the Immanent Rationality of Law,' 97 *Yale Law Journal* 949 (1988).
135 *Ibid.* 991.
136 Russell Hardin, *Morality Within the Limits of Reason* 126 (1988).
137 *Ibid.* 130.
138 Weinrib, *supra*, note 135, at 990.
139 See Scalia J.'s dissent in *Pennell v. City of San Jose*, 108 *Supreme Court Reports* 849 (1988).
140 Bruce Ackerman, *Private Property and the Constitution* 72 (1978).
141 See Margaret Radin, 'Property and Personhood', 34 *Stanford Law Review* 977 (1982).
142 *Ibid.* 987.
143 Frank Michelman, 'Property, Utility, and Fairness: Comments on the Ethical Foundations of 'Just Compensation' Law,' 80 *Harvard Law Review* 1165, 1214-15 (1967).
144 Lawrence C. Becker, 'The Moral Basis of Property Rights' in *Property* 191 (Nomos XXII, J. Roland Pennock and John W. Chapman eds. 1980)
145 See Hadley Arkes, *First Things : An Inquiry into the First Principles of Morals and Justice* 89 (1986).
146 Georgia Warnke, *Justice and Interpretation* 9 (1993).
147 Larry Alexander, *Legal Rules and Legal Reasoning* 167 (2000).
148 *Ibid.*
149 *Ibid.*
150 Post, *supra* note 27, at 30.
151 *Ibid.* 26.
152 Quoted in *ibid.*
153 *Ibid.* 26.
154 *Ibid.* 30.

155 *Ibid.*
156 Boyd White, *supra* note 59, at 160.
157 *Ibid.* 180.
158 *Ibid.* 164.
159 *Ibid.* 173.
160 Ronald Dworkin, *Law's Empire* 378 (1986).
161 Boyd White, *supra* note 59, at 172.
162 Boyd White, *supra* note 61, at 173.
163 Jeffrie Murphy, 'Cruel and Unusual Punishments,' in *Philosophical Problems in the Law* 500 (David M. Adams ed. 1992)..
164 See Ronald Dworkin, *Freedom's Law : The Moral Reading of the American Constitution* (1996).
165 *Ibid.* 7.
166 *Ibid.* 10.
167 *Ibid.*
168 Jurgen Habermas, *Between Facts and Norms : Contributions to a Discourse Theory of Law and Democracy* 210 (1996).
169 *Ibid.*
170 Dennis Patterson, *Law and Truth* 78 (1996).
171 Habermas, *supra* note 169, at 207.
172 Dworkin, *supra* note 161, at 378.
173 Habermas, *supra* note 169, at 216.
174 *Ibid.*
175 Dworkin, *supra* note 161, at 227.
176 Habermas, *supra* note 169, at 198.
177 *Ibid.* 199.
178 Dworkin, *supra* note 161, at 367.
179 *Ibid.*
180 Alexander, *supra* note 148, at 114.
181 Post, *supra* note 27, at 31.
182 Dworkin, *supra* note 161, at 184.
183 Weinsheimer, *supra* note 88, at 193.
184 *Ibid.*
185 *Ibid.*
186 [2001] 2 A.C. 50.
187 [1996] A.C. 527.
188 [1976] A.C. 239.
189 [2000] 1 A.C. 434.
190 Lord Hoffman citing with approval O'Connor, Kennedy and Souter J.J. in *Planned Parenthood of Southeastern Pennsylvania v. Casey*, at p. 88.
191 *Ibid.* 89.
192 Jeffrie C. Murphy and Jean Hampton, *Forgiveness and Mercy* 161 (1988).
193 *Ibid.* 166.
194 Quoted in *ibid.* 174.
195 Lord Slynn citing with approval Holmes J. in *Biddle v. Perovich* , at p. 70.
196 T.M. Scanlon, 'Due Process,' in *Due Process : Nomos XVIII* 93 (J. Roland Pennock and John W. Chapman eds. 1977).
197 *Ibid.* 94.

198 *Ibid.*
199 Dworkin, *supra* note 161, at 368.
200 *Pratt and Morgan* v. *Attorney-General and Others* (1993) 43 W.I.R. 340.
201 *Guerra* v. *Baptiste and Others* [1995] 3 W.L.R. 891.
202 *Hensfield and Farrington* v. *Attorney-General and Others* [1996] 3 W.L.R. 1079.
203 Quoted in *The Barbados Advocate*, Thursday, November 14, 1996.
204 Maurice King, 'Human Rights and Wrongs Worldwide,' *The Barbados Advocate*, Wednesday, December 25, 1996.
205 *Ibid.*
206 de la Bastide, *supra* note 32, at 404.
207 *Riley and Ors.* v. *Attorney-General of Jamaica* [1993] 1 A.C. 719.
208 Quoted in de la Bastide, *supra* note 32, at 405.
209 Margaret Jane Radin, 'Reconsidering the Rule of Law,' in *Wittgenstein and Legal Theory* 133 (Dennis M. Patterson ed. 1992).
210 Habermas, *supra* note 169, at 211.
211 *Ibid.* 203.
211ᵃ *Ibid.*
212 See Simeon C. R. McIntosh, 'Fundamental Rights and Democratic Governance in the Commonwealth Caribbean,' (1996) 6 *Carib. L. Rev.* 1; and 'Cruel, Inhuman and Degrading Punishment : A Re-Reading of *Pratt and Morgan*,' (1998) 8 *Carib. L. Rev.* 1.
213 See the Trinidad and Tobago High Court Judgment in *Lennox Phillip and Ors.* v. *The D.P.P.* (Unreported decision of The High Court of Justice, Trinidad and Tobago, No. 1337 of 1990, dated 30th June, 1992).
214 Consider Trinidad and Tobago's precipitous execution of Glen Ashby while his petition for a 'stay of execution' was being considered by the Court of Appeal.
215 Angus Wilke, 'Can Caribbean afford an Appeal Court,' *The Barbados Advocate*, (Wednesday November 27, 1996).
216 *Ibid.*

Select Bibliography

Ackerman, Bruce: *We the People.* Vol. 1: *Foundations.* Cambridge: Harvard University Press, Belknap Press, 1991.

_____. *Private Property and the Constitution.* New Haven: Yale University Press, 1978.

Adams, Henry: *The Great Secession Winter of 1860-61.* George Hochfield ed. New York: A.S. Bames, 1958.

Alexander, Larry: *Legal Rules and Legal Reasoning.* Dartmouth: Ashgate Publishing Company, 2000.

_____. ed. *Constitutionalism: Philosophical Foundations.* Cambridge: Cambridge University Press, 1998.

Allan, TR.S.: *Law, Liberty, and Justice: The Legal Foundations of British Constitutionalism.* Oxford: Oxford University Press, 1993.

Alston, William P.: *Illocutionary Acts and Sentence Meaning.* Ithaca: Cornell University Press, 2000.

Amar, Ahkil Reed: 'Philadelphia Revisited: Amending the Constitution Outside Article V.' 55 *U. Chi. L. Rev.* 1043 (1988).

_____. 'The Consent of the Governed: Constitutional Amendment Outside Article V.' 94 *Col. L. Rev.* 457 (1994).

Arato, Andrew: 'Dilemmas Arising from the Power to Create Constitutions in Eastern Europe.' In *Constitution, Identity, Difference and Legitimacy: Theoretical Perspectives* 179, Michel Rosenfeld ed. Durham: Duke University Press, 1994.

Arkes, Hadley: *First Things: An Inquiry into the First Principles of Morals and Justice.* Princeton: Princeton University Press, 1986.

Ashcroft, Bill, Gabreth Griffiths, and Helen Tiffin: 'The Empire Writes Back: Theory and Practice.' In *The Empire Writes Back. Theory and Practice in Post-Colonial Literatures* 88, Bill Ashcroft, Gabreth Griffiths and Helen Tiffin eds. London: Routledge, 1989.

Barker, Rodney: *Political Legitimacy and the State.* Oxford: Oxford University Press, 1990.

Baylis, Thomas A.: 'Presidents vs. Prime Ministers: Shaping Executive Authority in Eastern Europe.' 48 *World Politics* 297, 301 (1996).

Becker, Lawrence C.: 'The Moral Basis of Property Rights.' In *Property: Nomos XXII* 191, J. Roland Pennock and John W. Chapman eds. New York: New York University Press, 1980.

Bedau, Hugo Adam: 'The Eighth Amendment, Human Dignity and the Death Penalty.' In *The Constitution of Rights: Human Dignity and American Values* 164, Michael J. Meyer and W.A. Parent eds. Ithaca: Cornell University Press, 1992.

Beer, Samuel H.: *To Make A Nation: The Rediscovery of American Federalism*. Cambridge: Harvard University Press, 1992.

Benhabib, Seyla: 'Deliberative Rationality and Models of Constitutional Legitimacy.'1 *Constellations* 26, 31 (1994).

_____. 'Towards a Deliberative Model of Democratic Legitimacy.' In *Democracy and Difference: Contesting the Boundaries of the Political* 79, Seyla Benhabib ed. Princeton: Princeton University Press, 1996.

Bosworth, Stephen: *Hegel's Political Philosophy: The Test Case for Constitutional Monarchy*. New York: Garland, 1991.

Brathwaite, Edward Kamau: *Islands*. London: Oxford University Press, 1969.

Brennan, William: 'The Constitution of the United States: Contemporary Ratification.' 8 *U. C. Davis L. Rev.* 19 (1985).

Bryner, Gary C.: 'Constitutionalism and the Politics of Rights.' In *Constitutionalism and Rights* 18, Gary C. Bryner and Noel B. Reynolds eds. Albany, N.Y.: State University of New York, 1987.

Cairns, Alan C.: *Charter vs. Federalism: The Dilemma of Constitutional Reform*. Montreal: McGill-Queen's University Press, 1992.

Carey, George W.: *The Federalist Design for a Constitutional Republic*. Champaign: University of Illinois Press, 1989.

Carnegie, A.R.: 'The Importance of Constitutional Law in Jamaica's Development.' *West Indian Law Journal* 43 (October 1985).

_____. 'Floreat the Westminster Model? A Commonwealth Caribbean Perspective.' 6 *Carib. L. Rev. I* (1996).

Cheyfitz, Eric: *The Poetics of Imperialism: Translation and Colonization from the Tempest to Tarzan*. Philadelphia: University of Pennsylvania Press, 1997.

Cohen, Joshua: 'Deliberation and Democratic Legitimacy.' In *The Good Polity* 21, Alan Hamlin and Phillip Pettit eds. Oxford: Blackwell, 1989.

Condren, Conal: *The Status and Appraisal of Classic Texts: An Essay on Political Theory, Its Inheritance and the History of Ideas*. Princeton: Princeton University Press, 1984.

Conklin, William F.: *Images of a Constitution*. Toronto: University of Toronto Press, 1989.

Cook, David: 'Pluralism and the Death of Deference.' In *The Republican Ideal: Current Perspectives* 142, Norman Porter ed. Belfast: Blackstaff Press, 1998.

Cooter, Robert D.: *The Strategic Constitution*. Princeton: Princeton University Press, 2000.

Cullen, Bernard: 'The Right to Work.' In *Moral Philosophy and Contemporary Problems* 67, J.D.G. Evans ed. Cambridge: Cambridge University Press, 1988.

Dahl, Robert: *Democracy and Its Critics*. New Haven: Yale University Press, 1989.

Danto, Arthur C.: *Narration and Knowledge*. New York: Columbia University Press, 1985.

de la Bastide, Michael A.: 'The Case for a Caribbean Court of Appeal.' 5 *Carib. L. Rev.* 401 (1995).

DeMerieux, Margaret: *Fundamental Rights in Commonwealth Caribbean Constitutions*. Faculty of Law Library, University of the West Indies, West Indies, 1992.

Detmold, M.J.: *Unity of Law and Moralitly: A Refutation of Legal Positivism.* London: Routledge, 1984.

Diggins, John P.: *The Lost Soul of American Politics: Virtue, Self-Interest and the Foundations of Liberalism.* New York: Basic Books, 1984.

Dworkin, Ronald: *Taking Rights Seriously.* Cambridge: Harvard University Press, 1977.

_____. *Freedom's Law: The Moral Reading of the American Constitution.* Cambridge: Harvard University Press, 1996.

_____. *Law's Empire.* Cambridge: Harvard University Press, 1986.

Eisgruber, Christopher L.: 'Is the Supreme Court an Educative Institution?' 67 *N.Y.U.L. Rev.* 960 (1992).

Elster, Jon: 'Intertemporal Choice and Political Thought.' In *Choice Over Time* 41, George Loewenstein and Jon Elster eds. New York: Russell Sage Foundation, 1992.

_____. 'Is There (or Should There Be) A Right to Work?' In *Democracy and the Welfare State* 74, Amy Gutmann ed. Princeton: Princeton University Press, 1988.

Epstein, David F.: *The Political Theory of the Federalist.* Chicago: University of Chicago Press, 1986.

Epstein, Richard A.: 'The Uncertain Quest for Welfare Rights.' In *Constitutionalism and Rights* 41, Gary C. Bryner and Noel B. Reynolds eds. Albany, N.Y.: State University of New York Press, 1987,

Evans, E.W.: 'A Survey of the Present Constitutional Situation in the British West Indies.' In *Development Towards Self-Government in the Caribbean,* 23 (Symposium, The Netherlands Universities Foundation for International Cooperation at the Hague, 1954).

Ferguson, Robert A.: 'The Judicial Opinion as Literary Genre.' 2 *Yale J L. & Human* 201, 202 (1990).

Finnis, John: *Natural Law and Natural Rights.* Oxford: Clarendon Press, 1981.

Franco, Paul: *Hegel's Philosophy of Freedom.* New Haven: Yale University Press, 1999.

Funston, Richard: *A Vital National Seminar: The Supreme Court in American Political Life.* New York: New York University Press, 1978.

Galston, William A.: 'Practical Philosophy.' In *A Culture of Rights: The Bill of Rights in Philosophy, Politics and Law, 1791 and 1991* 261, Michael J. Lacey and Knud Haakonsen eds. Cambridge: Cambridge University Press, 1992.

Gewirth, Alan: 'The Epistemology of Human Rights.' In *Introduction to Jurisprudence* 187, M.D.A. Freeman ed. London: Sweet and Maxwell, 1994.

_____. 'Human Dignity as the Basis of Rights.' In *The Constitution of Rights: Human Dignity and American Values* 13, Michael J. Meyer and William A. Parent eds. Ithaca: Cornell University Press, 1992.

_____. *The Community of Rights.* Chicago: University of Chicago Press, 1996.

Gikandi, Simon: *Writing in Limbo: Modernism and Caribbean Literature.* Ithaca: Cornell University Press, 1992.

Golding, Martin P.: 'The Primacy of Welfare Rights.' 1 *Social Philosophy and Policy* 119-36 (1984).

Goldsworthy, Jeffrey: *The Sovereignty of Parliament: History and Philosophy.* Oxford: Oxford University Press, 1999.

Goodin, Robert E.: *Reasons for Welfare: The Political Theory of the Welfare State.* Princeton: Princeton University Press, 1988.

Goodman, Dena: *Criticism in Action: Enlightenment Experiments in Political Writing.* Ithaca: Cornell University Press, 1989.

Goodrich, Peter: *Legal Discourse: Studies in Linguistics, Rhetoric and Legal Discourse.* New York: St. Martin's Press, 1987.

Gordon, Scott: *Controlling the State: Constitutionalism from Ancient Athens to Today.* Cambridge: Harvard University Press, 1999.

Gray, John Chipman: 'A Realist Conception of Law.' In *Philosophy of Law* 50, Joel Feinberg and Hyman Gross eds. Belmont, Ca.: Wadsworth, 1975.

Habermas, Jurgen: *Between Facts and Norms: Contributors to a Discourse Theory of Law and Democracy.* Cambridge: MIT Press, 1996.

_____. *The Inclusion of the Other: Studies in Political Theory.* Cambridge: MIT Press, 1998.

Hardin, Russell: *Morality Within the Limits of Reason.* Chicago: University of Chicago Press, 1988.

Harris, William F., II: *The Interpretable Constitution.* Baltimore: Johns Hopkins University Press, 1993.

Hart, H.L.A.: *The Concept of Law.* Oxford: Oxford University Press, 1961.

Hinsley, F.: *Sovereignty 1.* 2d ed. Cambridge: Cambridge University Press, 1986.

Hogg, Peter: *Constitutional Law of Canada.* 3 d ed. Toronto: Carswell Publishing Company, 1992.

Holmes, Stephen: *Passives and Constraint: On the Theory of Liberal Democracy.* Chicago: University of Chicago Press, 1997.

_____. and Cass B. Sunstein: 'The Politics of Revision.' In *Responding to Imperfection: The Theory and Practice of the Constitutional Amendment* 285, Sanford Levinson ed. Princeton: Princeton University Press, 1995.

_____. 'Liberal Guilt: Some Theoretical Origins of the Welfare State.' In *Responsibility, Rights and Welfare: The Theory of the Welfare State* Chp. 4, J. Donald Moon ed. Boulder, Co.: Westview Press, 1988.

Huber, Evelyne: 'The Future of Democracy in the Caribbean.' In *Democracy in the Caribbean: Political, Economic and Social Perspectives* 68, Jorge Dominguez, Robert Pastor and DeLisle Worrell eds. Baltimore: Johns Hopkins University Press, 1993.

Hughes, Colin A.: 'Power and Responsibility: A Sociological Analysis of the Political Situation in the British West Indies.' In *Development Towards Self-Government in the Caribbean*, 95, (Symposium, The Netherlands Universities Foundation for International Cooperation at the Hague, 1954).

Judge, David: *The Parliamentary State.* London: Sage Publications, 1993.

Kahn, Paul W.: *The Reign of Law: Marbury v. Madison and the Construction of America.* New Haven: Yale University Press, 1997.

Kant, Immanuel: *The Metaphysics of Morals.* Mary J. Gregor trans. New York: Harper Torchbooks, 1964.

Kateb, George: 'Remarks on the Procedures of Constitutional Democracy.' In *Constitutionalism: Nomos XX* 234, J. Roland Pennock and John W. Chapman eds. New York: New York University Press, 1979.

Kay, Richard S.: 'Constitutional Chrononomy.' 13 *Ratio Juris* 30 (2000).

_____. 'Comparative Constitutional Fundamentals'. 6 *Conn. J of Int'l Law* 445, 449 (1991).

_____. 'Book Review' of 'Imperial Appeal: The Debate on the Appeal to the Privy Council, 1833-1986,' in 4 *Conn. J of Int'l Law* 239, 248 (1988).

Kelly, James B.: 'The Jamaican Independence Constitution of 1962.' 3 *Cbn Studies* 18, 36 (1963).

Kelsen, Hans: *General Theory of Law and State.* New York: Russell and Russell, 1961.

Kersting, Wolfgang: 'Kant's Conception of the State.' In *Essays on Kant's Political Philosophy* 154, Howard Lloyd Williams ed. Chicago: University of Chicago Press, 1994.

Lamming, George: 'In the Castle of My Skin: Thirty Years After.' In *Conversations with George Lamming. Essays, Addresses and Interviews, 1953-1990* 49, Richard Drayton and Andaiye eds. Ann Arbor: University of Michigan Press, 1994.

Laski, Harold J.: *Foundations of Sovereignty and Other Essays.* New Haven: Yale University Press, 1931.

Lijphart, Arend: 'Presidentialism and Majoritarian Democracy: Theoretical Observations.' In *The Failure of Presidential Democracy* 96, Juan J. Linz and Arturo Valenzuela eds. Baltimore: Johns Hopkins University Press, 1994.

_____. *Patterns of Democracy: Government Forms and Performance in Thirty-Six Countries.* New Haven: Yale University Press, 1999.

Linz, Juan J.: 'Presidential or Parliamentary Democracy: Does It Make a Difference?' In *The Failure of Presidential Democracy* Chp 1, Juan J. Linz and Arturo Valenzuela eds. Baltimore: Johns Hopkins University Press, 1994.

Lloyd, Dennis: *Introduction to Jurisprudence.* 3d ed. London: Sweet and Maxwell, 1972.

Lomasky, Loren E.: *Persons, Rights and the Moral Community.* Oxford: Oxford University Press, 1987.

Lutz, Donald S.: *The Origins of American Constitutionalism.* Baton Rouge: Louisiana State University Press, 1988.

MacInnes, C.M.: 'Constitutional Development of the British West Indies.' In *Development Towards Self-Government in the Caribbean,* 3 (Symposium, The Netherlands Universities Foundation for International Cooperation at the Hague, 1954).

Mansergh, Martin: 'The Republican Ideal Regained.' In *The Republican Ideal. Current Perspectives* 41, Norman Porter ed. Belfast: Blackstaff Press, 1998.

McIntosh, Simeon C.R.: 'Fundamental Rights and Democratic Governance in the Commonwealth Caribbean.' 6 *Carib. L. Rev.* 1 (1996).

_____. 'Cruel, Inhuman and Degrading Punishment: A Re-reading of Pratt and Morgan.' 8 *Carib. L. Rev.* 1(1998).

_____. 'Continuity and Discontinuity of Law: A Reply to John Finnis.' 21 *Conn. L. Rev.* 1 (1988).

_____. 'West Indian Constitutional Discourse: A Poetics of Reconstruction.' 3 *Carib. L. Rev.* 1 (1993).

_____. 'Reading Dred Scott, Plessy and Brown: Toward a Constitutional Hermeneutics.' *38 Howard L. J.* 53 (1994).

McKeon, Richard: *Rhetoric: Essays in Invention and Discovery*. Woodbridge, Ct.: Ox Bow Press, 1987.

McWhinney, Edward: *Constitution-making: Principles, Process, Practice*. Toronto: University of Toronto Press, 198 1.

Michelman, Frank I.: 'How Can the People Ever Make the Laws? A Critique of Deliberative Democracy.' In *Deliberative Democracy: Essays on Reason and Politics* 147, James Bohman and William Rehg eds. Cambridge: MIT Press, 1997.

_____. 'Property, Unity and Fairness: Comments on the Ethical Foundations of "Just Compensation" Law.' 80 *Harv. L. Rev.* 1165, 1214-15, (1967).

_____. 'Constitutional Authorship.' In *Constitutionalism: Philosophical Foundations* 64, Larry Alexander ed. Cambridge: Cambridge University Press, 1998.

Minda, Gary: 'Cool Jazz BUT NOT SO HOT Literary Text in Lawyerland: James Boyd White's Improvisations in Literature.' 13 *Cardozo Studies in Law and Literature* 157, 165, (2001).

Mojekwu, Christopher C.: 'Nigerian Constitutionalism.' In *Constitutionalism: Nomos XX 169* J. Roland Pennock and John W. Chapman eds. New York: New York University Press, 1979.

Moon, J. Donald, ed.: *Responsibility, Rights and Welfare: The Theory of the Welfare State*. Boulder, Co.: Westview Press, 1988.

_____. *Constructing Community: Moral Pluralism and Tragic Conflicts*. Princeton: Princeton University Press, 1993.

Morgan, Edmund S.: *Inventing the People: The Rise of Popular Sovereignty in England and America*. New York: W.W. Norton, 1987.

Munroe, Trevor: *The Politics of Constitutional Decolonization: Jamaica 1944-62*. I.S.E.R., The University of the West Indies, Mona, Jamaica, 1983.

Murphy, Jeffrie: 'Cruel and Unusual Punishments.' In *Philosophical Problems in the Law* 500, David M. Adams ed. Belmont, Ca.: Wadsworth, 1992.

_____. and Jean Hampton. *Forgiveness and Mercy*. Cambridge: Cambridge University Press, 1988.

Murphy, Walter F.: 'Merlin's Memory: The Past and the Future Imperfect of the One and Future Polity.' In *Responding to Imperfection: The Theory and Practice of Constitutional Amendment* 177, Sanford Levinson ed. Princeton: Princeton University Press, 1995.

Murray, D.J.: *The West Indies and the Development of Colonial Government, 1801-1834*. London: Oxford University Press, 1965.

Nagel, Robert F.: *Judicial Power and American Character*. Oxford: Oxford University Press, 1994.

Nettleford, Rex, ed.: *Norman Washington Manley and the New Jamaica: Selected Speeches & Writings, 1938-1968*. London: Longman Caribbean Publication, 1971.

Nino, Carlos Santiago: *The Constitution of Deliberative Democracy*. New Haven: Yale University Press, 1996.

Norris, Christopher: *Spinoza and the Origins of Modem Critical Theory*. Oxford: Blackwell, 1990.

Norton, Anne: *Reflections on Political Identity*. Baltimore: Johns Hopkins University Press, 1994

_____. 'Transubstantiation: The Dialectic of Constitutional Authority.' 55 U *Chi. L. Rev.* 458, 459 (1988).

Nwabueze, B. O.: *Constitutionalism in the Emergent State.* Madison, N.J.: Fairleigh Dickinson University Press, 1973.

Olafson, Frederick A.: *The Dialectic of Action: A Philosophical Interpretation of History and the Humanities.* Chicago: University of Chicago Press, 1979.

Parent, William A.: 'Constitutional Values and Human Dignity.' In *The Constitution of Rights: Human Dignity and American Values* 65, Michael J. Meyer and William A. Parent eds. Ithaca: Cornell University Press, 1992.

Patterson, Dennis: *Law and Truth.* Oxford: Oxford University Press, 1996.

Payne, Anthony: 'Westminster Adapted: The Political Order of the Commonwealth Caribbean.' In *Democracy in the Caribbean: Political, Economic and Social Perspectives* 60, Jorge Dominguez, Robert Pastor and DeLisle Worrell eds. Baltimore: Johns Hopkins University Press, 1993.

Perelman, Chaim: *Justice Law and Argument: Essays on Moral and Legal Reasoning.* Dordrecht: Kluwer Academic Publishers, 1980.

Pettit, Phillip: *Republicanism: A Theory of Freedom and Government.* Oxford: Oxford University Press, 1997.

_____. 'Reworking Sandal's Republicanism.' 45 *J. of Phil.* 73, 83 (1998).

Pitkin, Hanna: 'The Idea of a Constitution.' 37 *J. of Legal Education* 167 (1987).

Plant, Raymond: 'Needs, Agency and Welfare Rights.' In *Responsibility, Rights and Welfare: The Theory of the Welfare State* 55, J. Donald Moon ed. Boulder, Co.: Westview Press, 1988.

Porter, Norman. *The Republican Ideal: Current Perspectives.* Belfast: Blackstaff Press, 1998.

Posner, Richard A.: *Law and Literature: A Misunderstood Relation.* Cambridge: Harvard University Press, 1988.

Post, Robert C.: *Constitutional Domains: Democracy, Community, Management.* Cambridge: Harvard University Press, 1995.

_____. 'Justice for Scalia: Book Review of Justice Scalia's "A Matter of Interpretation: Federal Courts and the Law." ' *N. Y Rev. Books,* June 11, 1998: 46.

Preuss, Urich K.: 'Constitutional Powermaking of the New Polity: Some Deliberations on the Relations Between Constituent Power and the Constitution.' In *Constitution, Identity, Difference and the Legitimacy: Theoretical Perspectives* 143, Michel Rosenfeld ed. Durham: Duke University Press, 1994.

Radin, Margaret: 'Property and Personhood.' 34 *Stan. L. Rev.* 977 (1982). 'Reconsidering the Rule of Law.' In *Wittgenstein and Legal Theory* 133, Dennis M. Patterson ed. Boulder, Co.: Westview Press, 1992.

Rawlins, Hugh: 'The Privy Council or a Caribbean Final Court of Appeal?' 6 *Carib. L. Rev.* 235 (1996).

Rawls, John: *Political Liberalism.* New York: Columbia University Press, 1993.

_____. *A Theory of Justice.* Cambridge: Harvard University Press, 1971.

Redding, Paul: *Hegel's Hermeneutics.* Ithaca: Cornell University Press, 1996,

Richards, David A. J.: *Foundations of American Constitutionalism.* Oxford: Oxford University Press, 1989.

Robinson, Kenneth: 'Autochthony and the Translation of Power.' In *Essays in Imperial Government* 250, Kenneth Robinson and Frederick Madden eds. Oxford: Basil Blackwell, 1963.

Rosen, Sumner M: 'The Right to Employment,' *Monthly Review* 45, November 1993: 5-6.

Rosenfeld, Michel: 'The Identity of the Constitutional Subject.' *16 Cardozo L. Rev.* 1049, 1064 (1995).

Ross, Alf: *On Law and Justice.* Berkeley: University of California Press, 1958.

Rostow, Eugene V.: 'The Democratic Character of Judicial Review.' 66 *Harv. L. Rev.* 193, 208 (1952).

Rubenfeld, Jed. *Freedom & Time: A Theory of Constitutional Self'-Government.* New Haven: Yale University Press, 2001.

Russell, Peter: *Constitutional Odyssey: Can Canadians be a Sovereign People?* Toronto: University of Toronto Press, 1993.

Ryan, Selwyn: *Race and Nationalism in Trinidad and Tobago.* Toronto: University of Toronto Press, 1972.

_____. *Winner Takes All The Westminster Experience in the Caribbean.* I.S.E.R., The University of the West Indies, St. Augustine, Trinidad and Tobago, 1999.

Sarat, Austin: 'Capital Punishment as a Legal, Political and Cultural Fact: An Introduction.' In *The Killing State: Capital Punishment in Law, Politics and Culture* 4, Austin Sarat ed. Oxford: Oxford University Press, 1999.

Scalia, Laura J.: *America's Jeffersonian Experiment: Remaking State Constitution 1820- 1850.* DeKalb: Northern Illinois University Press, 1999.

Scanlon, T.M.: 'Due Process.' In *Due Process: Nomos XVIII* 93, J. Roland Pennock and John W. Chapman eds. New York: New York University Press, 1977.

Sellers, M.N. S.: *American Republicanism: Roman Ideology in the U.S. Constitution.* New York: New York University Press, 1994.

Spackman, Ann: *Constitutional Development of the West Indies, 1922-1968.* Barbados: Caribbean University Press, 1975.

_____. 'Constitutional Development in Trinidad and Tobago.' 4 *Social & Economic Studies* 283, 289 (1965).

_____. 'The Senate of Trinidad and Tobago.' 16 *Social and Economic Studies* 77 (1967).

Spurdle, Frederick G.: *Early West Indian Government. Showing the Progress of Government in Barbados, Jamaica and the Leeward Islands, 1660-1783.* Palmerston: New Zealand: The Author, 1963.

Steinberger, Peter J.: *Logic and Politics: Hegel's Philosophy of Right.* New Haven: Yale University Press, 1988.

Stepan, Alfred and Cindy Skach: 'Presidentialism and Partiamentarism in Comparative Perspective.' In *The Failure of Presidential Democracy* 128, Juan J. Linz and Arturo Valenzuela eds. Baltimore: Johns Hopkins University Press, 1994.

Stoljar, Natalie: 'Is Positivism Committed to Internationalism?' In *Judicial Power, Democracy and Legal Positivism* 175-179, Tom Campbell and Jeffrey Goldsworthy eds. Dartmouth: Ashgate Publishing Company, 2000.

Thompson, Norma: Herodotus and the Origins of the Political Community.' *Arion's Leap* 1 (1996).

Tully, James: *Strange Multiplicity: Constitutionalism in an Age of Diversity.* Cambridge: Cambridge University Press, 1995.

Vascianne, Stephen: 'The Caribbean Court of Justice: Further Reflections on the Debate.' 23 *West Indian L. J.* 3 7 (1998).

Von Savigny, Friedrich Carl: *Of the Vocation of Our Age for Legislation and Jurisprudence.* A. Hayward trans. New York: Arno Press reprint, 1975.

Wade, E.C.S. and A.W.Bradley: *Constitutional and Administrative Law.* 10h.ed. London and New York: Longman Press, 1985.

Waldron, Jeremy: 'Precommitment and Disagreement.' In *Constitutionalism: Philosophical Foundations* 275, Larry Alexander ed. Cambridge: Cambridge University Press, 1998.

Warnke, Georgia: *Justice and Interpretation.* Cambridge: MIT Press, 1993.

Weinrib, Ernest J: 'Legal Formalism: On the Immanent Rationality of the Law.' 97 *Yale L. J.* 949 (1988).

Weinsheimer, Joel C.: *Gadamer's Hermeneutics: A Reading of Truth and Method.* New Haven: Yale University Press, 1985.

White, James Boyd: *When Words Lose their Meaning.* Chicago: University of Chicago Press, 1984.

_____. *Justice as Translation: An Essay in Cultural and Legal Criticism.* Chicago: University of Chicago Press, 1990.

_____. *From Fxpectation to Experience: Essays on Law and Legal Education.* Ann Arbor: University of Michigan Press, 1999.

_____. *Acts of Hope: Creating, Authority in Literature, Law and Politics.* Chicago: University of Chicago, 1994.

_____. 'Judicial Criticism.' In *Interpreting Law and Literature: A Hermeneutic Reader* 394, Sanford Levinson and Steven Mailloux eds. Evanston: Northwestern University Press, 1988.

Will, H.A.: *Constitutional Change in the British West Indies, 1880-1903.* London: Oxford University Press, 1970.

Wittgenstein, Ludwig. *Philosophical Investigations.* G. E. M. Anscombe trans. 3d ed. Oxford: Basil Blackwell, 1968.

Wolin, Sheldon. 'Max Weber: Legitimation Method, and the Politics of Theory.' In *Legitimacy and the State* 63, William Connolly ed. New York: New York University Press, 1984.

_____. *The Presence of the Past.* Baltimore: Johns Hopkins University Press, 1989.

Wolf, Clark: 'Fundamental Rights, Reasonable Pluralism and the Moral Commitments of Liberalism.' In *The Idea of a Political Liberalism: Essays on Rawls* 111, Victoria Davion and Clark Wolf eds. Lanham, Md.: Rowman and Littlefield, 1999.

Wood, Gordon S.: *The Radicalism of the American Revolution I.* New York: Knopf, 1991.

Index